Women in Joyce

edited by SUZETTE HENKE

and ELAINE UNKELESS

WOMEN

IN

JOYCE

UNIVERSITY OF ILLINOIS PRESS

Urbana   Chicago   London

Library of Congress Cataloging in Publication Data

Main entry under title:

Women in Joyce.

Includes bibliographical references.
1. Joyce, James, 1882–1941—Characters—Women.
2. Women in literature. I. Henke, Suzette A.
II. Unkeless, Elaine, 1945–

Pr6019.09Z955   823′.912   81-4663
ISBN 0-252-00891-X   AACR2

To Elizabeth Henke, in memory of Jadwiga Wachowiak-Ward,
to the Rapps, and to Jay C. Unkeless, warmest friends.

Acknowledgments

Both editors have contributed equally to the publication of *Women in Joyce*. Our efforts have been mutual at all stages of writing, editing, and proofreading.

We wish to express appreciation to our contributors, who have been willing to share original and provocative ideas, and who have remained patient and enthusiastic over the years of production. We are grateful to Morris Beja and Michael Groden, who generously read portions of the manuscript and offered helpful suggestions. We would like to thank Cynthia Mitchell for her assistance in copyediting and proofreading, and Marie Grossi for her excellent typing.

Our families have given us constant encouragement. We want especially to thank Elizabeth Henke, Fred and Elsa Rapp, Madeline and Gerald Malovany, and Hedwig Nassauer. An enormous debt of gratitude goes to Jay Unkeless, who has offered continuing support, thoughtful criticism, and understanding.

Contents

Introduction

Carl Jung once commended Joyce for his remarkable insight into the female psyche. Jung described the "Penelope" episode of *Ulysses* as a string of "psychological peaches. I suppose the devil's grandmother knows so much about the real psychology of a woman. I didn't" (*Letters* III, 253). According to Richard Ellmann, however, Nora Barnacle Joyce used to protest that her husband knew "nothing at all about women" (*JJ* 642). Although a new understanding of woman's role in literature has recently begun to emerge, few critics have sought to provide fresh descriptions of Joyce's female characters. We have collected the following essays for precisely this purpose: to offer a contemporary perspective on the women that Joyce created and to present analyses that do not restrict the female personality to preconceived literary or social categories.

When we first commissioned these articles, we asked each of our contributors to focus on a particular dimension of Joyce's artistic treatment of women. Some of the essayists chose to interpret the canon from a feminist point of view; others emphasized social and historical patterns relevant to an understanding of Joyce's poetry, drama, or fiction. Gradually, the essays began to reveal a perspective divergent from that of traditional criticism. Although their approaches varied, all the contributors, whether or not they employed a feminist mode of analysis, attempted to place Joyce's writing within a "contextual" framework. In contrast to the advocate of stylistic formalism, the contextual critic refuses to abstract the work of art from its psychological, cultural, and economic environment. He or she tries to situate the aesthetic object within a larger frame of politics and history. Feminist analysis is, of course, a more specialized form of contextual interpretation. It attempts to examine the way in which a work of literature reflects, verifies, or criticizes prevalent beliefs about women, about gender identity and sex-role stereotyping, and about the relationships between the sexes in fiction.

In the early stages of Joyce criticism, women characters were con-
signed almost exclusively to archetypal or symbolic roles. Figures like
Gretta Conroy of "The Dead," Bertha Rowan of *Exiles*, and Molly
Bloom of *Ulysses* were seen as prototypes representing a pure sexual
abstraction. Stuart Gilbert set the stage for a mythic interpretation of
Molly when he described her as "Gaea-Tellus, the Great Mother,
Cybele." [1] William York Tindall observed that Bertha Rowan and
Gretta Conroy "are studies for Mrs. Bloom, whose image is the earth.
The relationship between proud Richard and earthy Bertha, anticipating the relationship between Stephen and Mrs. Bloom, is that between
intellect and reality." [2] Hugh Kenner, reading *Ulysses* in the Flauber-
tian tradition, saw Molly not only as an "earth-goddess" but as a
sensuous embodiment of material inertia, a deity that presides over an
"animal kingdom of the dead." [3] And S. L. Goldberg synthesized
these archetypal perspectives when he declared in *The Classical Temper*
that "Joyce's women are never really women." Molly, he tells us, "is
meant as a simple, shrewd, elemental figure, a spokesman and a
symbol of the processes of Nature. . . . Molly is less a woman than
Woman, a portrait decked with individual details. . . . She is the
Jungian Anima, the mystery of animate Flesh, the Earth, Nature." [4]

The tendency to interpret women characters symbolically, as universal images of woman, has dominated critical responses not only to
Ulysses but to the whole of Joyce's work. Thus Bertha Rowan becomes
a bovine earth-mother, a figure associated with nature—with flowers,
the moon, and the cow, suggestive of fertility. Gretta Conroy is perceived as a symbol of the emotional, intuitive life of woman, perpetu-
ally mysterious and enigmatic. And Emma Clery is a younger version
of the eternal temptress, nubile and seductive.

The sexual dimension of Joyce's women characters and, in particular, of Molly Bloom, has invited readers to construct further
stereotypes. Robert Martin Adams describes Molly as "woman in the
raw . . . designed to shock. . . . She is a slut, a sloven, and a voracious
sexual animal." [5] Darcy O'Brien presents her as a rapacious female
who "would devour any man" and claims that "for all of her fleshly
charms and engaging bravado, she is at heart a thirty-shilling
whore." [6]

Critics have generally accepted Richard Ellmann's assertion that
women in Joyce's fiction consistently reflect the virgin/whore dichotomy dominant in Western culture. Ellmann argues that Joyce

never transcended the Catholic urge to stereotype women as untouched virgins or defiled prostitutes: "For one thing, in the figure of the Virgin he had found a mother image which he cherished. He had gone to prostitutes and then prayed to the Virgin as later he would drum up old sins with which to demand Nora's forgiveness. . . . The novelty lay in his declining to confuse the two images and instead holding them remorsefully apart, opposing them to each other so that they became the poles in his mind. . . . In *Ulysses* and *Finnegans Wake* he apportioned womanhood in its sexual aspect to Molly Bloom, and in its maternal aspect to Anna Livia Plurabelle" (*JJ* 304-5).

Ellmann recognizes both the naturalistic and the symbolic dimensions of Joyce's female characters; but even when he analyzes them as realistic rather than archetypal figures, he sees them as representatives of all women. He speculates, for instance, that Molly's monologue in "Penelope" illustrates "Joyce's theory of [Nora Barnacle's] mind (and of the female mind in general) as a flow . . ." (*JJ* 387). Many critics have suggested that characters like Gabriel Conroy, Richard Rowan, and Stephen Dedalus are in some ways universal. Almost all describe Leopold Bloom as a prototype of the modern "Everyman." They portray him, however, as the "man on the street," reflecting various facets of the masculine psyche or the human psyche, not the "male mind in general." Readers tend to particularize Joyce's male characters but to treat his females as universal figures of womanhood.

Whereas traditional critics frequently praise Joyce for creating women who are at once symbolic and realistic, feminist readers often find Joyce's archetypal representations unconvincing. Kate Millett in *Sexual Politics* questions Joyce's assumptions concerning female passivity. She objects to his fondness for "presenting woman as 'nature,' 'unspoiled primeval understanding,' and the 'eternal feminine.' " [7] Florence Howe, in "Feminism and Literature," asserts that Joyce's view of women, and of the world in general, is tinged with a specifically male bias. According to Howe, the women in *A Portrait of the Artist* are "land-bound. The artist can fly and create, even in motion. We women are of the earth, we are the earth, we are the earth-mother." Howe argues that the "male artist, whether he is Stephen or Joyce or someone else, must conceive his power, or his difference from women, must take his measure against them, must finally define the two sexes as different species, active and passive, master and servant." [8]

Marilyn French contends in *The Book as World* that Molly Bloom is a female stereotype, a distorted "surrealistic" version of woman: "Molly is the mythic, the archetypal other. Not only for Bloom but for the rest of Dublin, she is woman as the object of desire." [9] Marcia Holly finds Joyce's Penelope "sensually inadequate because her sensuality exists not for herself but for the men to whom she reacts. . . . Because Molly represents only a male fantasy of sensuality and not what a truly sensual woman is or might be, it is an error to define her as a realistic portrayal." [10] It is possible, however, for Molly to be male-identified but nonetheless realistic. It might, in fact, be historically accurate to assume that a woman of Molly's era would probably interpret her sexuality in terms of male attraction. Her love affair with Boylan is perhaps motivated as much by a need for masculine approval as by a desire for sensuous pleasure.

The question of realism or, more accurately, of social and historical authenticity is crucial to feminist evaluation. Indeed, most of the essayists in this collection, whether or not they espouse feminist theory, discuss Joyce's women from a realistic perspective. Analysis from this point of view may be somewhat surprising since Joyce's portraits in the later works reach far beyond traditional notions of character. His probings into the unconscious, fragmentation of the individual figure, and emphasis on narrative style defy the boundaries of naturalistic fiction. Yet Joyce uses the nineteenth-century novel as a foundation for later experiments with character development and archetypal representation. He stretches the malleable integuments of historical fact and sociological detail to fracture and re-create a revolutionary aesthetic universe.

Critics have long recognized that Joyce's fiction presents a scathing critique of authority and an indictment of the paralyzing effects of Irish institutions on both male and female protagonists—from such willing victims as Eveline and Farrington to a more resilient character like Leopold Bloom. The contributors to this volume focus on the debilitating patterns of cultural oppression that restrict the lives of Joyce's women. They identify the specifically patriarchal nature of the authoritarian institutions under attack in Joyce's work. From *Chamber Music* to *Finnegans Wake*, Joyce deflates the male power drive that sanctions conquest as a form of mastery—whether in the political arena or in the theater of domestic conflict. His values are not only humanistic but traditionally female in their disdain for war, violence, and aggression.

Joyce disparages sex-role attributions that define manhood in terms of physical prowess or make all women into simpering figures of helplessness and passivity. He describes the intellectual, emotional, and political inhibitions that reduce the lives of men and women to a condition of despondency—a *malaise* frequently caused by pressures to conform to sex-stereotyped behavior.[11]

As realistic characters, Joyce's women have little power to assert themselves in the world of masculine activity. Often in his works, oppression of females becomes symptomatic of the tyranny and narrow provincialism of Irish patriarchy. Joyce acknowledges the social and historical constraints imposed on women, who are largely excluded from participation in decisions of the dominant society. Some essayists in this collection praise him for depicting the situation of Irish women accurately and, for the most part, sympathetically. Others object that despite his poignant satire of Dublin life, Joyce never envisions a female character who can transcend the limitations imposed by Irish culture.

All the essayists agree, however, that consciously or inadvertently, Joyce maintains a delicate balance of thought and feeling in all the women he creates. The time-honored dichotomy between "virgin and whore," "mother and temptress" may provide an oversimplified and radically deceptive schema. From Eveline and E—— C—— to Molly and Anna Livia, Joyce's women characters exhibit a paradoxical tension between the need for independence and the desire for fulfillment in traditional female roles. They are, by turn, nurtural and egocentric, sexually receptive and coldly aloof, altruistic, protective, and fiercely independent. None can be relegated to a single category: they all display far more psychological ambiguity and diversity of impulse than critics have traditionally recognized.

The woman of *Chamber Music* is a determined person, ready to follow her own inclinations when her lover wants to part. Robert Boyle believes that the poems in this collection resemble an Elizabethan sonnet sequence in which the woman, seen through the eyes of the male poet/lover, changes continually, reflecting either her own whims or the poet's evanescent moods. As in traditional patterns, the maiden at the beginning of the sequence delights in being wooed. But after she becomes the passionate "bride" who experiences sexual joy with her lover, she is transformed into the figure of a prostitute by society's scorn, her partner's indifference, and her own guilt. Joyce uses these images throughout his work, sometimes emphasizing the fickleness of the woman, sometimes deriding the male character's perceptions of the female—perceptions distorted by the lover's own frustrations. The woman in *Chamber Music* is an emanation of the poet's tortured consciousness: she reflects the agonies and the love-leaps of a troubled, visionary soul. When she becomes secretive and remains aloof, the poet is disturbed by her lack of responsiveness, though it was he who first demanded separation.

The women of *Dubliners* are almost always portrayed in relation to men—as mothers, wives, daughters, sisters, lovers, or would-be spouses. Florence Walzl discusses the ways in which these female characters are shaped by social and family relationships that mirror the cultural pressures of nineteenth-century Ireland. Using statistics on the family and information from *Thom's Directory*, Walzl describes the effect of economic deprivation on domestic and marital stability. Analyzing the stories, she concludes that the narrator exhibits a "masculine signature." In a society characterized by the camaraderie of pubs and political assemblies, women intrude as unwelcome reminders of church authority and family responsibility. Almost all of Joyce's Dubliners, both male and female, are tradition-bound and victimized by the nets of Irish patriarchy. Yet women are even more stultified by their acquiescence to paralyzing cultural and religious restrictions. Walzl shows that the daughters in *Dubliners* are destined to repeat the sometimes altruistic and always frustrated lives of their mothers.

Bringing together the conversations between Stephen Dedalus and Emma Clery in *Stephen Hero*, Bonnie Scott demonstrates the spontaneity and honesty of Emma's attempts to befriend the young artist. Emma, however, is insecure and ill-educated. As Scott shows from historical analyses, personal accounts, and present-day interviews, women's education at the end of the nineteenth century was deliberately restricted. Girls who did seek higher education were unusually motivated. Emma's difficulties and the contradictions in her behavior reflect the actual situation of female students at the turn of the century. It is not surprising that the young woman is at once proud and shy, sincerely inquisitive yet naive. Emma longs for a relationship that will offer both intellectual and romantic gratification. Denied one, she refuses the other and appears more Victorian than Elizabethan. Stephen's implausible proposition that they "live one night together," then part forever, would have shocked most girls of Emma's class and education. Unaware of Stephen's disdain for Irish Catholic puritanism, Emma remains oblivious of his bohemian program for spiritual liberation. She does not understand Ibsenian "free love" and cannot fulfill Stephen's sexual fantasies.

In *A Portrait of the Artist as a Young Man*, Joyce schematizes male/female sex-role divisions in order to illustrate Stephen's "flight from woman." As Suzette Henke suggests, the young artist unconsciously projects onto the mother responsibility for the loss of infant omnipotence. In an attempt to gain psychological mastery over the world, he rejects the threatening matriarchal figures who delineate the background of his childhood. For Stephen, women represent the fluid, chaotic dimensions of life; men offer a rational, logocentric model of mental and artistic control. Yet Stephen's fear of woman and his blatant misogyny are treated ironically by Joyce. Both appear to be adolescent traits that the young man must outgrow as he divests himself of the "spiritual-heroic refrigerating apparatus" cherished by the egocentric aesthete.

In *Exiles*, an Ibsenian drama, Joyce attempts to explore paradoxical ideals of free love and sexual non-possession. Bertha, the heroine, is a strong, fully developed protagonist who responds to an enigmatic situation with pride, dignity, and grace. Ruth Bauerle shows that Bertha is not just a supporting figure in the play but a central character in her own right. By revealing to Richard, Robert, and Beatrice the "secrets" of their lives, Bertha shares a close connection with her namesake, Perchta, a mythical figure associated with epiphany. Toward the end of the play, when Bertha encourages Beatrice to display her feelings, she offers one of the few examples in Joyce's work of one woman befriending another. Richard, for his part, learns from Bertha the luminosity of doubt, a negative capability from which art can at last be conceived. If Bertha sometimes appears weak, her "naturalness" redeems her ingenuous behavior. Despite her apparent aloofness, she is passionately dedicated to those she loves.

It is significant that the polarity of the intellect and the body—represented in the early works by Molly Ivors and Gretta Conroy or by Beatrice Justice and Bertha Rowan—no longer exists between the women in the later novels. What the reader learns about the two major female characters in *Ulysses*, Gerty MacDowell and Molly Bloom, is that each is excessively preoccupied with the concerns of physical life.

Gerty MacDowell is inordinately devoted to the cult of female beauty. Scents, tortoiseshell combs, pills, lotions, and elixirs are meant to cause miraculous changes in her appearance and physical well-being. As Suzette Henke points out, Joyce's Nausicaa is so influenced by popular advertisements that she continues to rely on cosmetic panaceas despite their ineffectiveness. Gerty longs for romantic love and masculine approval, but her fantasies exclude close physical contact with a man. She disdains her own bodily functions and fears sexual consummation. The narrative tone of "Nausicaa" is mockingly ambiguous. Did Joyce intend for the "marmalady drawersy" style of the chapter to convince us that his ingénue is the naive victim of popular romantic fiction? Or is he ridiculing Gerty in an attempt to exorcise what he perceives as the sentimental traits of his own personality?

Gerty MacDowell's veiled fascination with her body becomes an overt obsession in the case of Molly Bloom. Unlike the younger woman, Molly enjoys a love affair and finds sexual intercourse satisfying and "only natural." Elaine Unkeless illustrates the way in which Molly absorbs the prolific contradictions not only of her monologue but of the endless interpretations that profess to explain her character. Some readers who describe Molly as a realistic figure insist that she is exclusively a sexual object, a great "lust-lump" locked in the "bedsteadfastness" of lascivious desire.[12] Others assume that she represents woman as archetypal temptress, the Eve who causes man's destruction. But Molly can also be seen from a more positive perspective. Her sexual behavior is admirably uninhibited. And in some sense, her voluptuousness and symbolic fertility liberate both Stephen and Bloom. As sexual object or muse, however, Molly remains limited. Many of her characteristics are based on conventional, even stereotypical notions of female conduct. Readers who emphasize Molly's larger significance as temptress, wife, mother, goddess, or prostitute sometimes fail to acknowledge that in *Ulysses* the archetype emerges from the quotidian. Very much a product of her society, Molly is bound by the scripts available to women in turn-of-the-century Ireland. If Molly helps liberate Bloom and Stephen, she does so as a muse—a traditionally female figure who offers lyrical inspiration largely through erotic appeal. Insofar as she is confined to that role, her existence remains circumscribed.

In *Finnegans Wake*, Joyce constructs symbolic figures from an encyclopedic compilation of realistic, often trivial, detail. Like Molly Bloom, Issy has been derided as a prostitute and acclaimed for her natural enjoyment of sex. As temptress or redeemer, Issy has so many different features that her character apparently disintegrates into multiple personalities. Shari Benstock shows that Isabel's "split personality" reflects that of other *dramatis personae* in the novel. Earwicker, the dreamer of *Finnegans Wake*, envisions his daughter in a number of different aspects. Earwicker's own moods color and constantly alter his perceptions of the female, just as the emotions of the narrator in *Chamber Music* or of Stephen Dedalus in *Portrait* affect their responses to women. But here Humphrey Chimpden Earwicker is even more akin to Bloom, who, when he is content or sentimental, pictures an innocent, loving daughter, and when he feels guilty or disturbed, worries about Milly's seductiveness and confuses her with his wife. Despite their seeming independence, both Milly and Issy are portrayed in the context of their families: they are described fully as daughters and are seen as prospective mothers. Issy's "multiple personalities" reflect the various perspectives from which she is described, as well as the rebelliousness or "sauciness" of a child learning different roles. Her future may offer less potential for diversity.

To Issy, Anna Livia Plurabelle bequeaths the traditional functions of "womanhood," particularly the role of the mother who ministers to children and husband. Anna Livia's personality may seem more integrated than that of her daughter because the young Issy has numerous possibilities with which to experiment; ALP, the adult, is limited to performing wifely and maternal duties. But like Issy, Anna Livia seduces and reconciles, is hated and loved. Her contradictory qualities are due in part to the fact that we see her through her husband's eyes. Margot Norris links HCE's own feelings of pride or inadequacy with Freudian images associated with ALP. Earwicker dreams of Anna Liffey, river and mother, as a powerful force to her family. In his jealous and adoring eyes, she becomes a figure of spousal and maternal altruism: she is supportive, self-sacrificing, and continually protective. Yet, paradoxically, she remains independent and aloof. She retains an identity that is ever elusive and that dares to question a lifetime of self-effacing dedication. As Anna Livia flows to join her "mad feary father" in the final embrace of death, she realizes that her husband was not a lord or a king but "only a puny." She consigns him to the care of Issy, her daughter and successor. And she asserts her own primacy when, at the moment of annihilation, she returns to the egocentric memories of childhood.

Joyce has gone beyond "character" in *Finnegans Wake* to a description of Anna Livia as archetypal mother and lover, woman and river. As Margot Norris argues in *The Decentered Universe of "Finnegans Wake,"* Joyce's dream-work may be interpreted as a Freudian critique of patriarchal culture—a literary rebellion against the will to power operative in a father-dominated, repressive society.[13] A tyrannous male deity overshadows the *Wake,* and it is against this implacable authority that Joyce pits his verbal and linguistic "chaosmos." HCE is an omnipotent father-god who builds a masterful civilization that the anarchic sons, Shem and Shaun, try to usurp or destroy. The dialectical struggle of creation and destruction, of civilization threatened by radical discontent, is held together by the tension of female affiliation. ALP functions as an agent of reconciliation between father and sons, a bearer of love and of racial salvation.

As Joyce's final portrait of a woman, Anna Livia Plurabelle serves as a touchstone for a consideration of earlier female protagonists. Has Joyce, in depicting Anna Livia, presented us with a paradigm of woman's difference—a symbolic embodiment of what Simone de Beauvoir calls the "Other"? Does Anna Livia synthesize traditional feminine characteristics? And, from a feminist perspective, can we accept her as a representative mythic figure, a positive reflection of female potential? Joyce is laudatory in his description of ALP as mother and muse. And yet, there is a troubling ambivalence at the heart of his fictional tribute. In all Joyce's works, woman inspires art but does not create it. As Carolyn Heilbrun points out in her "Afterword," Joyce never gives us a literary portrait either of a female artist or of a woman with masculine characteristics.

Indeed, the fictional canon seems to ignore the significant role that women played in fostering Joyce's art. In 1922, when Joyce was having difficulty finding someone to publish *Ulysses,* an intelligent and courageous friend, Sylvia Beach, offered to undertake the project. Joyce admired and respected a number of other women whose support he cherished—people like Harriet Shaw Weaver, Margaret Anderson, Jane Heap, Adrienne Monnier, and Maria Jolas. Apparently, however, he did not consider them models for his characters. If these educated women inspired Joyce to think about their counterparts in Ireland— Lady Gregory, Speranza (Lady Wilde), the Sheehy sisters, or Mary

Colum—their influence was not reflected in the development of his art.

Joyce, it seems, tended to model his principal female characters on his own relationship with Nora Barnacle. From the recent publication of the long-censored 1909 correspondence, we can recognize the amorous fantasies that Joyce tried to enact through his wife. Nora was the "mistress" who could share his erotic and scatological obsessions. She was the Virgin Mother who patiently listened to Joyce's coprophiliac suggestions, endured his unfounded jealousy, and offered an absolution denied by the Catholic Church.

The essays in this volume attempt to explore the complexities of Joyce's ambivalent, even contradictory, attitudes toward women. Joyce apparently sympathized with the plight of women in Ireland and celebrated what he considered female spontaneity and intuitive wisdom. In Joyce's work, however, women rarely exchange the fluidity of life for the cerebral activities of art. They are excluded from both the political task of "world-making" and the artistic project of "word-making." Through the act of post-creation, the male artist gives birth to immortal brain-children. The female must remain content with the mortal functions of procreation and nurturance. Joyce believed that "a woman's love is always maternal and egoistic" (*Letters* II, 192). He could imagine woman as both goddess and muse, but not as an intellectual equal. Such were the dimensions of his accomplishment, and such were the limitations of his vision.

Elaine Unkeless
Suzette Henke

NOTES

1. Stuart Gilbert, *James Joyce's "Ulysses"* (1930; rpt. New York: Vintage-Knopf, 1952), p. 399.

2. William York Tindall, *A Reader's Guide to James Joyce* (New York: Farrar, Straus and Giroux, 1959), p. 121.

3. Hugh Kenner, *Dublin's Joyce* (1956; rpt. Boston: Beacon Press, 1962), p. 262.

4. S. L. Goldberg, *The Classical Temper* (New York: Barnes and Noble, 1961), pp. 293–95.

5. Robert Martin Adams, *James Joyce: Common Sense and Beyond* (New York: Random House, 1966), p. 166.

6. Darcy O'Brien, *The Conscience of James Joyce* (Princeton: Princeton University Press, 1968), pp. 207, 211.

7. Kate Millett, *Sexual Politics* (Garden City, N.Y.: Doubleday & Company, 1970), p. 285.

8. Florence Howe, "Feminism and Literature," in *Images of Women in Fiction: Feminist Perspectives*, ed. Susan Koppelman Cornillon (Bowling Green, Ohio: Bowling Green University Popular Press, 1972), pp. 263–64.

9. Marilyn French, *The Book as World: James Joyce's "Ulysses"* (Cambridge: Harvard University Press, 1976), p. 259.

10. Marcia Holly, "Consciousness and Authenticity: Toward a Feminist Aesthetic," in *Feminist Literary Criticism*, ed. Josephine Donovan (Lexington: University Press of Kentucky, 1975), p. 41.

11. According to recent theories of French semioticians, even Joyce's most radical experiments with language implicitly challenge the fundamental assumptions of patriarchal culture. Julia Kristeva, for instance, admires Joyce for his defiance of paternal authority "not only ideologically, but in the workings of language itself, by a return to semiotic rhythms connotatively maternal" (*Polylogue* [Paris: Editions du Seuil, 1977], p. 16).

12. In "Some Determinants of Molly Bloom," Darcy O'Brien describes Molly as "an eternally recurring version of Sheela-na-gig" (an Irish temptress), a "symbol of the immutable animality of womankind," and a "great lust-lump" (*Approaches to "Ulysses,"* ed. Thomas F. Staley and Bernard Benstock [Pittsburgh: University of Pittsburgh Press, 1970], pp. 140, 143, 148). See also Phillip F. Herring's "The Bedsteadfastness of Molly Bloom," *Modern Fiction Studies* 15 (1969), 49–61.

13. Margot Norris, *The Decentered Universe of "Finnegans Wake"* (Baltimore: Johns Hopkins University Press, 1976), chap. 3.

Women in Joyce

Abbreviations

Archive *The James Joyce Archive*, ed. Michael Groden. Associate editors, Hans Walter Gabler, David Hayman, A. Walton Litz, Danis Rose. 63 volumes. New York: The Garland Publishing Company, 1977–79.

CP Joyce, James. *Collected Poems*. New York: Viking Press, 1957.

CW Joyce, James. *The Critical Writings of James Joyce*, ed. Ellsworth Mason and Richard Ellmann. New York: Viking Press, 1959.

D Joyce, James. *Dubliners*, ed. Robert Scholes in consultation with Richard Ellmann. New York: Viking Press, 1967.
Joyce, James. *"Dubliners": Text, Criticism, and Notes*, ed. Robert Scholes and A. Walton Litz. New York: Viking Press, 1969.

E Joyce, James. *Exiles*. New York: Viking Press, 1951.

FW Joyce, James. *Finnegans Wake*. New York: Viking Press, 1939; London: Faber and Faber, 1939.

GJ Joyce, James. *Giacomo Joyce*, ed. Richard Ellmann. New York: Viking Press, 1968.

JJ Ellmann, Richard. *James Joyce*. New York: Oxford University Press, 1959.

Letters, Joyce, James. *Letters of James Joyce*. Vol. I, ed. Stuart Gilbert. New
I, II, York: Viking Press, 1957; reissued with corrections 1965. Vols. II
III and III, ed. Richard Ellmann. New York: Viking Press, 1966.

P Joyce, James. *A Portrait of the Artist as a Young Man*. The definitive text corrected from the Dublin Holograph by Chester G. Anderson and edited by Richard Ellmann. New York: Viking Press, 1964.
Joyce, James. *"A Portrait of the Artist as a Young Man": Text, Criticism, and Notes*, ed. Chester G. Anderson. New York: Viking Press, 1968.

SH Joyce, James. *Stephen Hero*, ed. John J. Slocum and Herbert Cahoon. New York: New Directions, 1944, 1963.

SL Joyce, James. *Selected Letters of James Joyce*, ed. Richard Ellmann. New York: Viking Press, 1975.

U Joyce, James. *Ulysses*. New York: Random House, 1934 ed., reset and corrected 1961.

ROBERT BOYLE, S.J.

The Woman Hidden in James Joyce's
Chamber Music

Joyce developed his suite of songs in an effort to create in words, like
Stephen Dedalus forming his Mercedes, the "unsubstantial image
which his soul so constantly beheld" (*P* 65). The youthful Joyce's
interest, like that of young Stephen, focused primarily on his own
soul, and only secondarily on that fragile and fragmented image which
that not-so-constant soul sought to bring into unity. Thus the woman
who emerges from Joyce's arrangement of his songs reveals in many
ways her varied sources and the adolescent narcissism, insecurity, and
ineptitude of her creator. Yet it is the young writer's artistic power that
reveals this evanescent but constantly intriguing woman who, like a
rainbow on the mist, shimmers with a mysterious radiance and power.

As with Stephen's "green rose," Joyce's ideal woman had not yet
found her embodiment outside his imagination. This ideal would be
fulfilled only in Nora Barnacle, to whom Joyce wrote in August, 1909:
"You were not in a sense the girl for whom I had dreamed and written
the verses you find now so enchanting. She was perhaps (as I saw her
in my imagination) a girl fashioned into a curious grave beauty by the
culture of generations before her . . . "(*Letters* II, 237). Joyce, in the
smithy of his soul, "fashioned" this woman in delicate Elizabethan
songs, and over some years evolved an arrangement of those songs in
a two-part sequence building to and falling from the consummation of
an ideal first love. Essential for retrieving the woman of *Chamber Music*
is to establish Joyce's ordering of the songs—a difficult task, for when
Chamber Music was published in 1907, the sequence which Joyce finally
adopted (not without reservation) was arranged not by Joyce but by his
brother Stanislaus.

In February, 1903, Joyce wrote to his brother about *Chamber Music*:
"Dear Stannie, I send you two poems. The first one is for the second
part . . ." (*Letters* II, 27). The poems were "I hear an army" (*CM* XXXVI)

and "When the shy star" (*CM* IV). Ellmann notes: ". . . Joyce planned to divide his poems into two parts, the first being relatively simple and innocent, the second more complicated and experienced. The second group would commemorate his departure from Dublin . . ." (*Letters* II, 27). Ellmann's adjectives may hint at some echo of Blake's songs of innocence and of experience, and perhaps at a foreshadowing of the early simplicity and later complications of a love affair, as in Elizabethan sonnet sequences like Sidney's and Shakespeare's. Ellmann's suggestion that the second "group" would, like the ending of *Portrait*, commemorate Joyce's departure from Dublin does seem to accord with an aspect of "I hear an army"; however, as a description of Joyce's plan for his sequence, the suggestion appears to be too restrictively autobiographical. As I see Joyce's own arrangement of his poems (different from the arrangement Stanislaus constructed for the long-delayed publication), it aims at building on Joyce's own experience a universal expression of youthful human love in all times and places. I suspect that from the beginning of his planning Joyce worked for a motion upward to the poem of consummation, "My dove, my beautiful one" (*CM* XIV), and downward gradually through the subsidence of passion, external difficulties, ultimate disillusion, and finally, as in the two poems he calls "tailpieces" in the published version, an Arnoldian listening to the noise of embattled waters.

The earliest manuscript of the suite, now owned by James Gilvarry, was sold by Sylvia Beach in 1935.[1] Twenty-seven of the thirty-three poems are, like those Gogarty saw in Joyce's hand in 1903, beautifully written in the center of large sheets, and Litz describes the arrangement: "In the Gilvarry sequence, I and III are the opening poems, XXXIV is the close, and XIV stands squarely in the middle, flanked by thirteen poems on either side. This perfect symmetry of musical and emotional effects was spoiled slightly as Joyce added later poems, until finally in the rearrangement for the 1907 edition it was almost entirely obscured" (*Archive*, xxxv).

Of the ordering of the poems in the 1905 Yale MS, "*Chamber Music* (a suite of thirty-four songs for lovers) by James Joyce, Via S. Nicolo, Trieste, 1905," Litz says, "This obviously represents a careful and long-considered plan." The climactic Poem XIV still stands as squarely as it can in the middle, No. 17 of the thirty-four poems.[2] And this is Joyce's final sequence before Stanislaus rearranged the poems for publication.

From the beginning Joyce took his ordering seriously. In 1902, he had shown the poems to Lady Gregory, and his concern for the form of the whole suite appears in her comment: "I think, from what you said, that you would not like to publish those poems till the sequence is complete . . ." (*Letters* II, 16). She was less frank than Yeats was a month or so later, when he commented on a poem Joyce had sent him. It was surely Joyce's original arrangement of his poems that Yeats had seen and that he found helpful to interpret the poem "in its place with the others": "Perhaps I will make you angry when I say that it is the poetry of a young man, of a young man who is practicing his instrument, taking pleasure in the mere handling of the stops. It went very nicely in its place with the others, getting a certain richness from the general impression of all taken together and from your own beautiful reading" (*Letters* II, 23). It is an interesting possibility that Yeats here by his pointed repetition laid in Joyce's imagination a foundation for the shift from *Stephen Hero* as a title to the final title of *A Portrait of the Artist as a Young Man*. Evidence that Joyce was impressed by Yeats's words seems to me apparent in a letter to Stanislaus written more than four years after he had read Yeats's judgment: "By the same post I received from Elkin Mathews the proofs of *Chamber Music*. It is a slim book and on the frontispiece is an open pianner! Shall I send you the proofs to correct. I don't know whether the order is correct. I don't like the book but wish it were published and be damned to it. However, it is a young man's book. I felt like that. It is not a book of love-verses at all, I perceive" (*Letters* II, 219). But the version that had gone to Mathews was not the arrangement Joyce had submitted to so many publishers for those exhausting years. On October 9, 1906, Joyce wrote to Stanislaus about Arthur Symons's advice to submit his poems to Mathews, and for some reason—I suspect a complex of reasons—agreed to change his own arrangement for one proposed by Stanislaus. Joyce sounds tired and discouraged—"Tell me what arrangement you propose for the verses. I will follow it perfunctorily as I take very little interest in the publication of the verses" (*Letters* II, 172)—and perhaps felt that a change in his text might bring luck. If one could probe Joyce's psychological depths, one might perceive some perverse revenge on his often-rejected poems, some resentment at Yeats's patronizing but solidly based counsel, or some strange search for a co-author to share responsibility, like Joyce's later weird effort to recruit James Stephens to finish *Finnegans Wake*. There is no way to discover with rational certainty what motivations operated in Joyce's subconscious. He did accept Stanislaus's arrangement, in any case, and although that arrangement damages the "story line" of Joyce's own sequence, it offers decided advantages. In grouping the songs according to the music of the verse, and thus the mood, Stanislaus stressed the element Joyce valued most. And if a singer were to present the songs in an evening's entertainment, the arrangement by mood would be practical and effective.

But Joyce was certainly not comfortable with the book. If Stanislaus's recollection (*JJ* 270) of Joyce's wanting to cancel the publication is accurate (Stanislaus had an Irish imagination), it would be added evidence that Joyce much disliked something about the book he had so vigorously sought to publish for four years. Since Joyce often showed great affection for individual poems, since he read them to friends and critics with full confidence, and since he spoke in *Finnegans Wake* with apparent satisfaction of "all this chambermade music" (*FW* 184), I suspect that the repulsive feature may have been the arrangement that he had "perfunctorily" agreed to.

Some evidence for my suspicion seems to emerge from Joyce's description of his sequence in a letter to G. Molyneux Palmer on July 19, 1909: "The book is in fact a suite of songs and if I were a musician I suppose I should have set them to music myself. The central song is XIV after which the movement is all downwards until XXXIV which is vitally the end of the book. XXXV and XXXVI are tailpieces just as I and III are preludes" (*Letters* I, 67). Joyce still conceives of the movement rising to XIV and being "all downwards" to XXXIV, where he sees the end of something vital—I take it the end of the love affair. That description fits Joyce's arrangement to perfection, but it does not fit the published arrangement. For example, between XI (Joyce's 16), which bids adieu to virginity, and XIV (Joyce's 17), where virginity gives place to consummation, Stanislaus places XII (Joyce's 26), which weeps for the loss of girlhood. The formal tone of XII does fit well with the other poems with which it is grouped, but its motion is distinctly downward, as the poet rejects the counsel of remorse which the Capuchin moon gives to the poet's repenting lover. Again, Stanislaus's arrangement inserts, between two poems of parting (XXX and XXXII, 32 and 31 in Joyce's arrangement), a poem celebrating a uniting kiss (XXXI, 23 in Joyce's arrangement), a rude dislocation of the downward motion.

CM XVII, which speaks of the loss of a male friend because of the lady, was number 10 in Joyce's arrangement and thus appeared before the poem Joyce called "central" (his 17, *CM* XIV). In Stanislaus's rearrangement, however, *CM* XVII is placed after the original central song. Ellmann opines that Joyce retained this poem to help the "changed mood" of the later poems (*JJ* 180); but Joyce placed it among the early poems in his series, and in any case it seems to me that the poem was important to Joyce because it carries a faint echo of Shakespeare's alienation from his male friend (*FW* certainly stresses in Wildean tonality the shadowy presence of Mr. W H). If my opinion is correct, then such reference to the desertion of the male friend should belong to the upward movement, where Joyce originally put it, before the poet and his lady achieve consummation and a temporary exclusive union. The poem which follows in both arrangements (XVIII and 11) depicts the lady comforting the poet sorrowing over the loss of his friend.

But there is no certitude to be had here. Joyce did accept and publish Stanislaus's arrangement, and in effect repudiated his own previous arrangement, never published. Why not then let the matter rest there? Because, as I have experienced it, a close look at Joyce's arrangement reveals new things about the poems, and furnishes them with the kind of universal human context that Joyce found important in his works, as in his arrangement of *Dubliners* according to the development of human experience through childhood, adolescence, and maturity.

In Joyce's original conception, as I now see it, the relationship of the lovers (which begins with the appearance of the girl in 4 [II]) [3] gradually develops from the first hesitant approach up to the act of consummation (celebrated with religious tone in 17 [XIV]) and declines (with a growing intellectualizing about the nature of love and a diminishing of passion) to the death of love in 34 [XXXIV]. In an effort to reconstruct Joyce's conception, I offer the following outline of the original structure, with my own notion of each poem's theme. I will attempt to justify questionable points in my fuller discussion of the individual poems:

Ascent of the Suite

Preludes—the poet speaking to himself.
1   [XXI]—The lonely poet defies the world.
2   [I]—The poet makes music by himself, sweet but funereal.

3 [III]—The lonely poet hears a prelude to human love.
   Suite Proper—The lovers' relationship begins.
4 [II]—The lonely girl plays the piano at evening.
5 [IV]—In the evening the poet comes to her gate, singing.
6 [V]—His song: I leave my books, my loneliness, to see and hear
   you.
7 [VIII]—She brings light and love to the richly appareled spring
   wood.
8 [VII]—"My love" is now fully objectified in the light, graceful girl.
9 [IX]—He longs for the girl.
10 [XVII]—He has deserted his friend, and suffers.
11 [XVIII]—He seeks his comfort in her.
12 [VI]—Like the Bridegroom in the "Song of Solomon," he longs for
   peace in her arms, in her love.
13 [X]—Now a new lover's song, livelier than 6 [V].
14 [XX]—He longs for them to lie together in the woods (and in a
   grave).
15 [XIII]—He sends the wind as herald to the physical consummation
   of their marriage of souls.
16 [XI]—He urges the virgin to loosen her hair.

Zenith of the Suite (the noon, the summer)

17 [XIV]—His Song of Songs!

Decline of the Suite

18 [XIX]—He consoles the sad girl, shamed by unnatural dogmas.
19 [XV]—He himself hears nature's sighs and the wisdom of accepting
   mortality.
20 [XXIII]—He expresses his happiness, like the unweeping birds
   (but, like Shelley with his skylark, he is, unfortunately, *more* wise
   than they).
21 [XXIV]—Her negligence begins to justify his wisdom.
22 [XVI]—The lover wants to seek Love in a cool valley, where those
   wise choirs of birds sing (and Love may visit, as he did in the past).
23 [XXXI]—She kisses him (but overhead a bat flies).
24 [XXII]—He is allured to prison, to sleep (to death).
25 [XXVI]—She experiences the fear that only a poet can express.

26 [XII]—She has been hoodwinked into accepting the false doctrine of everlasting love, and he counsels her to be satisfied with the passing but truthful living light in her eyes.

27 [XXVII]—In his "wisdom," he suggests the true source of her fear, her own animal nature (maybe also some mysterious malice).

28 [XXVIII]—He counsels acceptance of human reality.

29 [XXV]—He more desperately calls for laughter and song.

30 [XXIX]—He complains that she is ruining their garden.

31 [XXXII]—As they prepare to part, he mounts his wise pulpit once more.

32 [XXX]—He recalls the whole course of their love.

33 [XXXIII]—Another lover's song (maybe to himself, as in the preludes): winter ends us.

34 [XXXIV]—Final lover's song: accept the sleep (which may be the "Out, out brief candle" of Macbeth).

([XXXV] and [XXXVI]—Never in Joyce's arrangement of poems, he called these "tailpieces" (*Letters* I, 67), and they are not part of the "upward-downward" movement of the other verses.)

Joyce's plot is simple enough, but the complexities within it offer many insights into his youthful notions of love, of art, and of woman. A glance at some of the points of interest in each poem might clarify Joyce's conceptions.

In the three preludial poems, the lonely poet addresses himself. In 1 [XXI], the problem, like the one which emerges occasionally in Shakespeare's sonnets, is to determine whether "his love" is subjective or objective. I incline to suppose that if the speaker really is unconsortable, then the only one he can possibly consort with is himself. In that case, "his love" is the love inside him. It is possible, no doubt, to find here what Joyce does suggest elsewhere, that he and his love become "one flesh," and then are in a position to face enemies as one being. But I find that difficult to merge with the lonely stag image which I see here, so I prefer to see this speaker "companioned" (that is, literally, "breaking bread," like a lonely Christ) with himself.

On Curran's autograph copy of the poem, given to him some months after Joyce had met Nora, the dedication "To Nora" is written, with the date September 30, 1904.[4] But while the poem found a completion in Nora, more probably, according to the evidence I can now find, the song started out like the others, expressing the lonely "desire of my youth" (*Letters* II, 237) (Joyce's reference to "my verses" seems to be inclusive of all). With this supposition, there is no difficulty in understanding the speaker's having found no soul to fellow his, and the inclusive nature of the stag image, so stressed in "The Holy Office," remains intact. Further, with this reading, the poem starts off the suite admirably, since the poet's desperate need for true companionship prepares the way for what follows.

Poem 2 [I] brings in "sweet" and "soft" music (the adjectives will be repeated *ad nauseam*), and the artist's exilic tendencies appear in the bent Narcissistic head. In 3 [III] that head assumes a more outgoing angle, looking up, longing for light and the dying fall of more "soft sweet music." The religious wind, apparently, is antiphonally causing those invisible harps to sigh for Love. The need for a soft, sweet girl is established.

Poem 4 [II] brings in the girl. The body of the suite gets under way with the girl playing an actual piano, not the fancied harp (or real penis, if Tindall's view has force) that the anemic love of 2 [I] is fingering. In a dim but lovely natural setting, she too bends her head, shyly thinking (surely of the lover she longs for) as her hands wander willfully over the keys. The trees of the avenue, lining the "way" which leads to the girl, are lighted by lamps similar to those ("like illumined pearls") which set the scene for "Two Gallants"—a grim undertone. The twilight, starting out amethyst, has at the end moved down to darker blue, approaching that violet which gives a bottom limit to the rainbow and merges with night (and which, in my imagination at least, will have a share in "violer d'amores" on the first page of *Finnegans Wake*). The girl is the central light in all this gathering dusk ("gathering" is the climactic word in 33 [XXXIII]).

The shy girl melts into the shy star of 5 [IV], which draws and guides the poet to the girl's garden. Newman's ". . . but like the morning star, which is thy emblem, bright and musical" is twice quoted in *Portrait* (116, 139), the image haunting Stephen's imagination. Mary as the morning star and as closely related to the Star of Bethlehem was even more familiar to Catholic imaginations (used to dwelling daily from earliest childhood, as Stephen demonstrates, upon the titles in her litany) than were the blessings of Guinness. To this young poet, who had probably, like Stephen, vowed not too long before he wrote this poem to be a knightly votary of his Lady Mary, the maidenly shy evening star in Song 5 [IV], like Mercedes, the lady of mercy, would surround his beloved too with the rhetorical aura reflected from New-man's undulating prose.

This modest star of *Chamber Music* receives expansion through *Dub-liners* into *Finnegans Wake*. Its potentialities as a Star of Bethlehem, drawing the Magi to that manger which had become the center of creation (as Gabriel in "The Dead" is drawn westward, and as the Evangelists with their Ass gather, in the Watches of Shaun, at the marital bed where Holy Shaun gleams forth), can be more readily perceived in this suite of poems when one reaches the climactic biblical force of 17 [XIV]. Its epiphanic role stems from the kind of emotion Joyce expressed after his visit to Nora's former room in Finn's Hotel. This was in the Advent season of 1909, leading to the season of Epiphany celebrated in "The Dead," and Joyce's feeling and words to Nora foreshadow those of Gabriel in the more elegant hotel where he and Gretta spent the night:

> Yes, I too have felt at moments the burning in my soul of that pure and sacred fire which burns for ever on the altar of my love's heart. I could have knelt by that little bed and abandoned myself to a flood of tears. The tears were besieging my eyes as I stood looking at it. I could have knelt and prayed there as the three kings from the East knelt and prayed before the manger in which Jesus lay. They had travelled over deserts and seas and brought their gifts and wisdom and royal trains to kneel before a little newborn child and I had brought my errors and follies and sins and wondering and longing to lay them at the little bed in which a young girl had dreamed of me. . . . I leave for Cork tomorrow morning but I would prefer to be going westward. . . [*Letters* II, 273].

A similar sacred bed in the Watches of Shaun is the focus of "blue-blacksliding constellations" (*FW* 405) and the scene of "How culious an epiphany!" (*FW* 508).

The solitary, young wise man of this poem (his references to his "wisdom" weigh down the second, declining half of this suite of songs), sings as a visitant drawn from afar. And she, bent in revery like the Madonna who pondered marvelous things in her heart, would surely now look up as at the visit of a seraph.

His song follows in 6 [V]. "I have left . . . I have left" probably echoes the leaving of father and mother to cleave to a wife. He leaves the book and the possibly Rosicrucean and alchemical fire to plunge into the gloom which is then pierced by her song. The merry air, a contrast to his lonely, sad studies, brings him, longing for a sight of her, to her window.

In 7 [VIII] he revels in the sight of her in the green wood. Her light and love make the whole woodland gleam with a fire, soft and golden, far superior to the fire he left behind. She is light also in her movements, graceful, virginal, calling forth all that is beautiful and good in nature, which puts on its richest apparel and its sweetest sunlight to adorn and worship her. (This springtide, alas, will have been destroyed in the final song of the suite, and this brave attire all shed and ruined in 30 [XXIX] and 31 [XXXII]).

The girl in 8 [VII] becomes one with his love, the lonely love of 1 [XXI] now objectified fully in her. They join together, in the poet's mind, as the gay winds do, joining in companies. And as the winds woo the leaves, his desires woo the graceful girl.

But there is something odd about the girl's attitude. Like the Bride of the Song of Songs (also known as the Song of Solomon and the Canticle of Canticles), she is among the apple-trees, but she seems interested in her own shadow rather than in the Bridegroom. And she goes slowly and lightly. Tindall scents creative urine, sees the sky as cup as helpful to the thematic chamber tinkling, and finds the holding up of her dress "no less prudent than relevant."[5]

It is surely true that "goes" for Joyce operated well in a context of wine and porter and urine and copulation. In a letter to Stanislaus on August 31, 1906, speaking about George Moore, he wrote: "Italy . . . where they drink nice wine and not that horrid black porter (O poor Lady Ardilaun over whose lily-like hand he lingered some years back): and then she goes (in all senses of the word) with a literary man named Ellis . . ." (*Letters* II, 154). Lady Ardilaun was one of the Guinesses, and her lily-like hand may connect with a conditioned response in young Joyce's imagination, linking cups and chamber-pots with beef-tea and sacramental white wine and porter and urine. Then indeed the dainty hand of this song gains complexity and interest.

But more immediately applicable to this poem is Joyce's Epiphany 26, in which the girl "dances with them in the round—a white dress lightly lifted as she dances, a white spray in her hair; eyes a little averted, a faint glow on her cheek. Her hand is in mine for a moment, softest of merchandise."[6] This suggests that in the song the girl's attention to her shadow may be shyness or calculation, or a combination of both, and thus might stem from a consciousness of and a reaction to her would-be lover.

In 9 [IX], the poet longs for the girl and speaks to the May winds, also

light dancers. He asks them, with Verlainian delicacy, to find his true
love and to make the divided loves of the last line truly one love.

In the midst of this longing, separated from the girl, he adverts in 10
[XVII] to his separation from his friend (like Stephen's from Cranly)
because of her. This touch of the Mr. W H element of Shakespeare's
sonnets suggests an alliance with Elizabethan sequences, and introduces the pain and betrayal motif of such interest to Joyce, enamored
of romantic suffering. The soft "merchandise" of her hand, bought
now with his betrayal of his friend, is again in his (the "again" suggests
a more definitive grasp, I suspect, after some significant encounter
with the friend). With his hand occupied, he cannot make any sign of
amendment to his friend, nor, as she sings, speak a word. Her singing
voice and willful hand have effectively destroyed his friendship with a
man who was once at his side.

He seeks comfort for the pain, in 11 [XVIII], in her soft wooing. An
immature, non-ancient mariner, he yet preaches a universal tale and
knows that words are worthless. The union of bodies can express love
as words cannot, and, like the Bridegroom, he can find in her breast
comfort for the gnawing sorrow.

He sings, in 12 [VI], the Bridegroom's song, longing for peace in her
arms, in her love. The "that" in the first line is, as Tindall beautifully
develops, a distancing word,[7] and indicates that the poet feels himself
definitely outside that sweet bosom now, with rude winds threatening
to visit him. The fourfold repetition of "that," Tindall further perceives, carries a suggestion that the poet, like Stephen in the villanelle,
is reluctant to go along with the powerful impulse to plunge into the
"lure." Thus an ironic undertone, quite alien to the Song of Song's
surface, gives a faint ominous overtone to the soft knock in line 7,
which seems to echo the Bridegroom's knocking (in Catholic liturgy
applied to Christ knocking at the heart):

> I slept, but my heart was awake.
> Hark! my beloved is knocking.
> "Open to me, my sister, my love, my dove,
>   my perfect one;
> for my head is wet with dew. . . ."
>   *Song of Solomon*, V, 2

A rogue will knock loudly in 33 [XXXIII], with murder in the background. Here the stress is on peace. Austerities (those rude south

winds) might creep in, but in that sweet softness, or soft sweetness, they would be made gentle.

He proves this, in 13 [X], by the new lover's song, livelier than the "softer than the dew" song of 5 [IV]. This song is full of motion, of gaiety, of contempt for musing dreamers who do not *act*. The lover of 1 [XXI] and 2 [I] was such a dreamer, sinking into the past, into himself. This lover, as honied as the fragrant Bridegroom, moves fast and sings boldly, with wild bees drawn to his sweet odors. But we surely note (as Bloom discovered, "Still gardens have their drawbacks" [*U* 68]), that productive and hummingly musical as they are, bees may sting.

In March, 1902, Joyce gave a Byronic—Little Chandlerish verse to John Byrne. It mourns the death of a gentle lover with (naturally) a "soft white bosom" and "no mood of guile or fear" (both moods strong characteristics in the woman of *Chamber Music*). Its last stanza fore-shadows the remarkably more mature 14 [XX]. The earlier verse reads

> I would I lay with her I love—
> And who is there to say me no?[8]

(No one says "nay" because a rhyme with "below" is called for.) In the poem in *CM*, the dark pine-wood is primarily the lovely trysting park near Dublin (quieter than the Hill of Howth with its flamboyant rho-dodendrons), but it doubles well as a coffin. Part of the wisdom of this young poet, clinging like Buck Mulligan to an adolescent rationalism, is that human love is intimately involved with the constantly changing human organism, which will inevitably deteriorate (". . . *whose mother is beastly dead*" [*U* 8]). But like Byron, and in a far more subtle way like Jonson, this poet enshrines even mundane lips and hair in an inflated religious tonality:

> Where the great pine-forest
> Enaisled is!

Interestingly, as Tindall points out, the shallowness of the religious coating trickles through the uncertain rhyming of "kiss" and "is."[9]

The ennui after the "I come" of the previous poem (13 [X]) prepares for the post-coital letdown following their actual consummation in 17 [XIV]. In 14 [XX], the long vowels delay and dwell on the rhythm, and the imagined kiss in stanza 3 descends like water as her hair, in Rossetti-like disorder, sweetly and softly endews the Bridegroom's head.

This small baptism takes place at noon. At that hour, the speaker (or dreamer) of chapter 7 of *Finnegans Wake* figures we might, through "inversions of all this chambermade music," get a glimpse (as Rebecca West did when she looked at *Pomes Penyeach* and saw Joyce for what he really was) of Shem the elusive artist, "the whirling dervish, Tumult, son of Thunder . . ." (*FW* 184). If we do link "tumult" in this poem to that liturgical (the dervish) and Evangelical (St. John) context, then this flowing hair can suggest baptismal water (so feared by Stephen), as do the letters just before the full statement of the villanelle (". . . the liquid letters of speech, symbols of the element of mystery, flowed forth over his brain" [*P* 223]); and if we compare this seemingly simple girl in the pine-forest with the luring and destructive witch of the villanelle; and if we recall the apparition of Stephen's mother in "Circe" (". . . *her face worn and noseless, green with grave mould. Her hair is scant and lank. She fixes her blue-circled hollow eyesockets on Stephen and opens her toothless mouth uttering a silent word*" [*U* 579]), then we can see why Shem is like St. John, the true Son of Thunder (". . . whom we surnamed Boanerges, that is, sons of thunder . . ." [Mark, 3:17]), celebrator of the infinite and ineffable Logos. Shem too wants to find and utter the word and needs a divining woman to that end, somewhat as St. John needed the Blessed Virgin to see and hear the true Word. Thus Stephen begged his mother, who, like Hamlet's father, had come back from the dead, for the word known to all men; thus Joyce sought a woman for his *clou* to immortality. The fear that this woman of *Chamber Music* will feel in 25 [XXVI], rising from the mystery of her own being, is the same fear that inspires that artist to express the mystery of his own being (and thus of every human being) in imperishable ink. This noon poem, for all its prettiness, contains something of the threat of death and the dark and maybe even hell, the noonday devil's horrors. (Joyce is thinking of Psalm 91:6, the destruction in wait for those who rebel against God, ". . . nor the destruction that wastes at noonday.") Shem is ". . . noondayterrorised to skin and bone by an ineluctable phantom . . ." (*FW* 184). Some such torrent of contexts brings into my mind, as I skim over the sugared surface of this sweet noontide song, the feeling of threatening possibilities swirling deep below.

Approaching the climactic moment of their courtship, the "courtly" poet, more of a Jonson than a Spenser, in 15 [XIII] sends a courteous wind as herald of his coming as the Bridegroom. The wind of spices

from the Song of Songs announces his coming, and it finds out her
little garden and her window. Noon here is the climax of their love, the
completion of the perfection of day. And the Greek "epithalamium"
mingles the ancient sexual traditions of the Greeks with the greatest of
Jewish love songs in preparation for the climactic song of this suite.

Now the voice of the lover himself, in 16 [XI], supplants that of the
herald, and the lingering adieu to virginity comes from his seraphic
lips. His address to the shy girl and his instruction to prepare for the
loss of her maidenhood (and maidenhead) is translouted into turfish in
Finnegans Wake:

> —Can you ajew ajew fro' Sheidam?
> He finges to be cutting up with a pair of sissers and to be buytings of their
> maidens and spitting their heads into their facepails. [*FW* 250]

As in *Portrait*, the lover has come as a seraph to the virgin's chamber,
and as he dreamed of her wooing in 11 [XVIII], he now woos her. The
name on the bugles of the cherubim may be just "Seraph," but more
likely, considering Joyce's eucharistic treatment of the artist as Christ,
it is "Logos," the Word. As the Word, this artist can be imagined as
overshadowing the virgin to effect through her his own conception in
transaccidentated ink (thus Joyce will deal with the Artist-Being-Made-
Word, climaxing that image on *FW* 186). I am not suggesting that the
youthful Joyce here foresees the sophisticated and faintly blasphe-
mous meanings which he later developed for Stephen and Shem, but I
do perceive that in suggesting the divine aspect of the poet (somewhat
in contrast to his "disregard of the divine" in 26 [XII]), he opens the
way for that development. The girl's veiled hair, enclosed as under the
veil of a nun or in the formal cap of Hester Prynne, must come pouring
down in what the poet sees as a sign of her surrender to him. That the
surrender is a calculated one, like Molly Tweedy's among the Howth
rhododendrons or like Hester Prynne's among the shadowy trees
where she again lured the manipulated Dimmesdale, does not appear
here—but the way is open for that too.

And now, in 17 [XIV], the climax, the celebration of Hymen! The
Song of Songs provides all the material for this ecstatic expression of
full, loving union, and the dew on the lover's lips and eyes fore-
shadows Stephen's soul "all dewy wet" as he pictures the seraph
coming to the virgin's chamber (*P* 217).

Epiphany 24, having listed a dozen elements from the Song of

Songs, focuses on "that response whereto the perfect tenderness of the body and the soul with all its mystery have gone: *Inter ubera mea commorabitur.*"[10] The mystery involved in human love (as in human poetry) is the focus of this lovely song too.

This poem corresponds to Stephen's vision of the girl in the water, a female seraph who called him to his true vocation, "to recreate life out of life!" (*P* 172). As a result of that call, he would dare, as in drunken bravery in "Oxen of the Sun," to challenge even God (*U* 391), and to call his post-creation better than the creation of God, which Stephen judges to be mere material for the artist's sublime literary Eucharist. The girl in the water shares much imagery and language with the dove of this song—e.g., "soft white down," "dovetailed," "bosom was as a bird's soft and slight, slight and soft as the breast of some darkplumaged dove" (*P* 171).

I wonder, though, if in the pale veil which lies on the poet's head (though the snood has fallen from hers), there is not some faint shadow of the demonie, some echo of the "ajew, ajew fro' Sheidam" cast backward here (*Sheidim* is Hebrew for demons), bouncing perhaps off the villanelle? There the demon-woman, the Shee, lurks in the liturgical smoke, the source of weariness for the uneasy lover. Weariness will come soon enough, in 28 [XXVIII], for this now ecstatic lover. Maybe this veil, in the fearful insecurity of the poet, is not altogether desirable.

But it would be hard to forecast, from the "beautiful one" of this song, the temptress of the villanelle, and, far more, the luscious but diseased (if that is the implication of the "injection mark" of *U* 512) Zoe of "Circe" and her enchanted days:

> (. . . *A fountain murmurs among damask roses. Mammoth roses murmur of scarlet winegrapes. A wine of shame, lust, blood exudes, strangely murmuring.*)
> Zoe
> (*Murmuring singsong with the music, her odalisk lips lusciously smeared with salve of swinefat and rosewater.*)
> Schorach ani wenowach, benoith Hierushaloim [*U* 477]

Zoe's Hebrew, I would guess, more likely emerges from Bloom's imagination recalling his father's chanting than from the actual Zoe (where would she have learned it?), but in any case it means, "I am black but comely, O ye daughters of Jerusalem" (*Song of Songs*, 1:5). It will be a long journey from this Irish girl of *Chamber Music* to the battered, depraved Zoe, but within this perfect wreath of songs ("The *Vita Nuova* of Dante suggested to him that he should make his scattered love-verses into a perfect wreath . . ." [*SH* 174]), the poems which decline from the central poem point toward the lower circles where Bella and her women wait.

Sadness has come over the deflowered girl in 18 [XIX]—not, according to Tindall, because of the deflowering (as in the "curious rite" of *U* 392), but because of what people are saying about her. Tindall refers to Yeats's "Aedh Thinks of Those Who Have Spoken Evil of His Beloved." If one judges that "all men" are actually talking about the Sweetheart of this poem, of course the text does become as puzzling as Tindall finds it. But I believe that the "lying clamour" is that which the Capuchin will whisper in her ear in 26 [XII], or a corollary to that—namely, the religious stance of Irish Catholicism (as young Joyce read it) that sexual activity is evil unless blessed by Church and State.

If that is true, then in the first stanza the poet is saying to the girl, "All men condemn you, like the woman taken in adultery, preferring the religious lie to the natural truth. But you must realize that their belief that you are a woman without honour does not make it so." "Before you" could also carry the implication, especially in light of what follows, that "they preferred that clamour before you did," thus touching the source of her sadness in herself. He appeals to her natural pride to condemn the false and wasted tears of the men, their calls to repentance, and as they deny their natures, she should, like the defiant poet of 1 [XXI], hold "to ancient nobleness" and deny their false doctrine.

In 19 [XV], the poet demonstrates his own acceptance of nature's sighs (here signs not of sorrow but, presumably, of satisfaction and fulfillment) and the wise admonitions of leaves and flowers to arise, like the Bride and Bridegroom, to a day of love. Something of the tonality of Titania and Oberon in *A Midsummer Night's Dream* accompanies those veils of gossamer and those wise choirs of faery, votaries of the natural.

"Admonisheth," with its Elizabethan formality, probably means first of all an extension of the poet's counsel to his soul to arise from sleep and death (sleep as symbol of death will be stressed in 34 [XXXIV], as it is in Shakespeare's Sonnet 73). Joyce probably composed this song originally as an address to his own soul, like Stephen's "dewy wet" soul waking from ecstatic dreams (*P* 217) or rising "from the grave of boyhood, spurning her graveclothes. Yes! Yes! Yes!" (*P* 170). But as the poem fits into the suite, following 17 [XIV], "my soul" more naturally comes to mean the beloved lady lying at his side, who has just been sighing and, no doubt, trembling in sleep. The slumber-death of love at this point still seems to be only their former loneliness, now past. And the few faeries (or at least few choirs) who faintly celebrate their present union can be heard only by attentive and wakeful ears.

"Admonisheth," however, can also carry a warning, and maybe those sighs are not totally pleasant ones after all. Maybe the faeries are "innumerous" and faint because the wisdom they sing is to some degree specious. It may even be that among the veils threatened by the rising sun is that happy veil of dew on the Bridegroom's head in 17 [XIV]. The noonday devil may be preparing his attack. These "wise" choirs may be foreshadowing the later wisdom of the lover. Nature's sighs and gentle stirrings may signal not only the dawn's epithalamium but the evening's thanatopsis.

And sure enough, the wise birds of 20 [XXIII], who do not live very long, suggest an apothegm to the yet wiser lover. Like these prudent wrens, who store treasures in their nests, he has "laid" (another word of many helpful meanings) his own treasures also in "some mossy nest." The heart of his beloved "flutters" in the first line, preparing for the propriety of picturing her as a bird. His hope and riches and happiness, which he had lost when religion and other inimical chains had taught him, like Blake, to weep, he has regained and stored in her. Thus they are—or are they?—as wise as the prudent birds. But into this wisdom of the poet creeps a question, and the possibility that evening will bring the death of love.

His beloved begins to justify that questioning in 21 [XXIV]. She had let down her hair for him in 16 [XI], and now she combs it endlessly for herself and her mirror-image. That glorious sun, which in 7 [VIII] she had made more beautiful in the woods, she now uses only as a means to admire herself more. She prefers her mirror to her lover, to natural sunlit life. Like the temptress of the villanelle, she is a witch and a lure to the lover, who "prays" her to leave her selfishness, to stop being "enchanted" by herself beneath the luring "pretty air." The charming negligence of her gestures embodies her negligence of her lover, about which he will complain more bitterly in 30 [XXIX]. Her love is declining, and she foreshadows the pretty airs of the piping poets to come (in

27 [XXVII]), airs which hide the selfish and destructive witchery beneath their enchanting praises of perfect, lasting love.

The lover in 22 [XVI], proposing to return to the valley where they once found love, reveals his uncertainty in that wavering "sometime." Now the musical and productive birds are the wise choir, calling them both away from that mirror. Almost abruptly, in proffering his pastoral invitation, he somewhat flatly asserts, "When we get there, we'll stay there." Since the lovers are not birds, who are better designed to be at home in the valley, the hesitant rhythm of the final line finds realistic justification.

She kisses him in 23 [XXXI], and sweetness and softness encompass him. But "murmuring" can be suspicious, as the idiot murmuring in Bloom's gazelle garden demonstrates (*U* 477, quoted above). Especially is this true when the murmuring educes a phrase like "O, happily!" and all the time there is a bat flying overhead. Tindall lists Joyce's numerous treatments of women as bats and of bats associated with love and sex,[11] and the vampire bat fits fairly well with the poisondart looming up in 27 [XXVII].

The witch "allures" him into the prison of her arms in 24 [XXII]. The witch of the villanelle lures seraphs from heaven, and here the "dearest" woos the lover with her soft arms, seeking to overcome the reluctance, like Stephen's, "to relent," and seeking to hold him fast, "to detain." There may have been a wooing word too, like that Joyce once heard from Nora: "I remember the first night in Pola when in the tumult of our embraces you used a certain word. It was a word of provocation, of invitation and I can see your face over me (you were *over* me that night) as you murmured it. There was madness in *your* eyes too and as for me if hell had been waiting for me the moment after I could not have held back from you" (*Letters* II, 243). Hell does wait for fallen seraphs, in Catholic as in Miltonic imaginations, and I suspect that the "lure" of the villanelle and of *Chamber Music* finds some roots in the "swallowed bait" of Shakespeare's Sonnet 129, which also lands the prey in hell.

The demonic rivulets gyrate considerably below the surface of this saccharine song, starting with "sweet" and "soft" and ending with "sleep to . . . sleep . . . soul with soul." That last coupling seems to me allied to Newman's device as cardinal, "*Cor ad cor loquitur*," heart speaks to heart. Some of the drooling prose of Stephen's dealing with

Emma, under the aegis of the Blessed Virgin, seems allied to that same device:

> She placed their hands together, hand in hand, and said, speaking to their hearts:
> —Take hands, Stephen and Emma. It is a beautiful evening now in heaven. You have erred but you are always my children. It is one heart that loves another heart. Take hands together, my dear children, and you will be happy together and your hearts will love each other [*P* 116].

Newman's "The Glories of Mary for the Sake of her Son" [12] is quoted in *Portrait* just before that passage and in length at the end of the section (*P* 138–9). And that passage, in Newman's sermon, is preceded by a quotation from the Little Office of the Blessed Virgin: ". . . and in the glorious company of the saints was I *detained*" (Newman's italics). As Atherton points out in his note to Stephen's discussion (*P* 188) of "detained" with the Dean of Studies, "Newman is translating very literally *et in plenitudine sanctorum detentio mea* (*Ecclesiasticus*, 24:16): 'My abode is in the full assembly of the saints. . . .' " [13] In this song in *Chamber Music* (24 [XXII]), the word is used as Newman uses it, and it draws in the whole complex of Newman's praise of Mary's glories, among which her virginity and her heroic determination to preserve it shine brilliantly. Now we can fully evaluate the "lying clamour" of those who, as in 18 [XIX], assert that the loss of virginity is a shameful loss (". . . those unspeakable sins by which degraded man outrages and defiles the temple of the Holy Ghost, defiles and pollutes himself" [*P* 124]). These "arms / By love made tremulous" resemble Stephen's reaction in his supposed freedom from alarms after his "penitence": "His hands were trembling, and his soul trembled . . ." (*P* 146). But Stephen's trembling stemmed from a lie, and so (we perceive as things develop) does this *Chamber Music* love. A clue lies in the ambivalence of "could" in "Ah, could they ever hold me there . . .": "I wish they could" balances with "they can't."

The basis for "I wish they could" from the artist is, I take it, his need to tap her "divining ear," to find there a *clou* to immortality. She listens, in 25 [XXVI], not to a choir of birds, but to the soft choiring of her own blood. And she hears there a sound which causes fear. The divining of this sorceress has tapped some mystery beyond her rational grasp. She may be fearing torrents of water rushing forth from grey deserts. It is her heart that fears, and north of the heart is that grey matter that, according to Molly, Bloom considered to be the actual phenomenon which some called "soul" ("he says your soul you have no soul inside only grey matter" [U 741–2]). The poet may be asking his beloved if she fears not only the vague destructive evil but also the sterile, rationalistic floods from the brain which threaten to sweep away her divination of human delight welling from the loving soul and to drown out the dulcimers of the Pleasure Dome.[14]

That it is a mystery she conjures forth, a source of fear and pain, is suggested by Joyce's cry to Nora in December, 1909: "O the sweet pain you brought into my heart! O the mystery your voice speaks to me of!" (Letters II, 273). It is the lady's *ear* that hears the mystery from that full choir where, like the Virgin, she is "detained." Her sacred river of blood brings "a mad tale," or the basis for one, into her consciousness, like that of the Ancient Mariner, frightening and ghostly. The flow may lead, when the ghosts can be conjured up, to the Sacred River to which Purchas led Coleridge, or to the oceans of blood to which Holinshed led Shakespeare. The poet, through careful scanning of her mood, hopes likewise to be led to a mad tale, maybe as mad as *Finnegans Wake*.

But his "human only" wisdom first moves him to warn her about religious sentimentality. In one of the most complex and interesting poems of the suite, 26 [XII], Joyce, among many other things, reveals most obviously his debt to Ben Jonson. Hugh Kenner, having expressed some brilliant insights on what Joyce learned from Verlaine,[15] goes on, under the heading "Ironic Elegance and Ben Jonson," to see this poem as illustrating, in its "double-writing," the aim Joyce assigned to Stephen Hero:

> But in his expressions of love he found himself compelled to use what he called the feudal terminology and as he could not use it with the same faith and purpose as animated the feudal poets themselves he was compelled to express his love a little ironically. This suggestion of relativity, he said, mingling itself with so immune a passion is a modern note: we cannot swear or expect eternal fealty because we recognise too accurately the limits of every human energy. It is not possible for the modern lover to think the universe an assistant at his love-affair and modern love, losing somewhat of its fierceness, gains also somewhat in amiableness [SH 174].

The artist as a *young* man recognized those limits more accurately than did the far more mature author of *Finnegans Wake*, who adverted to the multitude of pesky "unfacts": "Thus the unfacts, did we possess them, are too imprecisely few to warrant our certitude . . ." (*FW* 57). Youthful faith in rational science and the certitude which results still impress this young artist. With these he attempts to insert an ironic modern undertone beneath the elegant Elizabethan surface of this song, and succeeds in echoing a truly ironic Elizabethan, the witty and acerbic Ben Jonson.

The song's echo of Jonson I find quite explicitly in "plenilune." That word enjoys the fullness of its tenuous existence in English, insofar as I can determine the matter, in Jonson's *The Fountaine of Selfe-Love or Cynthias Revels* (as the title appears in the 1601 Quarto):

> . . . . Arete, behold
> Another Cynthia, and another Queene
> Whose glorie (like a lasting *plenilune*)
> Seems ignorant of what it is to wane!
> (Act V, Scene 8)

That is precisely the doctrine of Joyce's "hooded moon," itself in its waned state contradicting its dogma, namely, that the full moon demonstrates that beauty and love and glory can last forever. Jonson's "lasting" on the surface implies that Queen Elizabeth, symbolized as usual in Cynthia the moon goddess, has been and will be plenilune forever. But she was, of course, ancient when Jonson wrote his lines, so Joyce's adjective also brings out an ironic undertone of Jonson's elegant surface. Joyce refers primarily to the old Elizabethan times, when "plenilunes" were fresh and at least verbally young. Now, he implies, the times and the word are both ancient and moribund, as Elizabeth was then and as the love this suite celebrates is now. All this speculation is contingent, I am aware, on Joyce's having actually derived the word from the author he was to read exhaustively in Paris, but my guess is that he did.

The waning and waxing of the moon in Joyce's song, the narcissism of this lady, the apocalyptic glory under her feet (not "tread out," as Tindall supposes, but rather supporting and setting off her glory [16]), and her conviction, learned from the idealistic Capuchin, that there is a love that endures even to the edge of doom—these elements and others suggest Jonson's powerful influence. Further, Jonson himself, recently converted to Catholicism when he wrote those lines, would serve in excellent ways (with considerable irony also) as "the comedian Capuchin." The "elegant and antique phrase" of the following poem

(27 [XXVII]) links with the antiquity of "ancient plenilune" to stress the courtly irony of old Ben, and to find deep roots feeding the "wisdom" of this young Dublin poet. In making his Capuchin a Jonsonian comedian, the *wise* young Joyce, who is reputed to have patronized Yeats, possibly echoes the attitude of Gabriel Harvey, set down about 1600: ". . . the younger sort takes much delight in Shakespeares *Venus & Adonis*: but his *Lucrece*, & his tragedie of *Hamlet, Prince of Denmarke*, have it in them, to please the wiser sort." [17]

The glory, at any rate, passes from the unreal dogma of stanza 1 into the real sparkle in living eyes in stanza 2, which, while trembling in its ephemeral "moving and changing every part of the time" (*FW* 118), can be doubly possessed—but not for long, as the chime of "Mine, O Mine" links inevitably with "No more."

The poet's own doctrine, product of his "human only" wisdom—Shem's life transaccidentates into ink expressing a literary "chaos, perilous, potent, common to allflesh, human only, mortal" (*FW* 186)—is clearly set forth in 27 [XXVII]. In November, 1906, when he was twenty-four years old, Joyce revealed to his brother his theories on the love he had known: "Perhaps my view of life is too cynical but it seems to me that a lot of this talk about love is nonsense. A woman's love is always maternal and egoistic. A man, on the contrary, side by side with his extraordinary cerebral sexualism and bodily fervour (from which women are normally free) possesses a fund of genuine affection for the 'beloved' or 'once beloved' object" (*Letters* II, 192). This is the wisdom that falls from these "all too wise" lips, assigning categories for love according to sex, and distinguishing in the man "genuine" affection, which leaves for the egoistic though maternally tender woman a mixed, or perhaps hypocritical, or maybe more exactly, devious affection. At any rate, we see in 27 [XXVII] the rapturous satisfaction of her maternal heart operating simultaneously with the poison of her malice. The malignant and even murderous elements that may be operating in some complex and basically incomprehensible women—like Cleopatra and Hester Prynne and Molly Bloom—have in this suite developed from the lady's indifference in 21 [XXIV] to this Housmanian statement. The bat image helped to suggest it, and in his notes for "Penelope," Joyce noted "(female spider devours male after)." [18] The malice in her tenderness stems, Joyce suggests, from her own animal desires and needs, particularly the need to be inseminated and to protect and foster her offspring. This is expressed with more than Jonsonian tenderness, but with full Jonsonian irony. "I but render," I presume, echoes Shakespeare's Sonnet 125, where the rendering is mutual:

> No, let me be obsequious in thy heart,
> And take thou by oblation, poor but free,
> Which is not mixed with seconds, knows no art,
> But mutual render, only me for thee.

This *Chamber Music* poet seems to be stressing, in his rendering, that the total giving of self is all on his side, and the significant item in his confession of his complete love is the supposition that mixed in with her tender love for him is malice.

The lying Capuchin of the previous poem, with his doctrine of perfect love, has waned, but these wise lips are waxing to bring in the modern truth. His own experience brings science to the religious and false "solemnizing" of love with pastoral and lyric pipes. Some touch of the poisondart he has found in all love (love in women, that is), and so he once more warns his beloved to believe him and to face the realities of human intercourse. But the warning seems to be spoken mostly for himself, and to be sugar-coated for her sentimental and less perceptive mind. Or perhaps he is striving to spare her feelings, while at the same time expressing the Darwinian undertones of animal courtship and fulfillment. The song does not really have the definite limits I am suggesting, but, while it suggests those, leaves matters open to some unexpressed larger context. It does not finally exclude mystery, try as it will.

The poet in 28 [XXVIII] sings this same wisdom briefly, and, in more direct fashion, counsels accepting the passing nature of human love. He points to mortality and implies that death, as this wise young man tends to judge, ends all love. Mae West in her youth taught a similar doctrine when she replied to a suitor's pledge of eternal love, "Yeah, but how about your health?" Echoes in this poem of Marvell's broodings on the sleep of love in the grave prepare for the final poems of the suite. The weariness of declining love foreshadows the disillusioned "Are you not weary" of *Portrait*'s villanelle.

More desperately, the poet in 29 [XXV] calls for laughter and song. The girl's divining heart, he knows, fears the inevitability of Time's (and Death's) victory—remotely like Margaret in Hopkins's "Spring and Fall," whose heart presaged mortality. But laugh anyway, he urges—as Joyce himself fills the cosmos with laughter in *Finnegans Wake*. Do not grieve over wasted suns like that of 21 [XXIV], but run while these winds (more familiar with the lover than they were with the virgin) loosen the tumult of your hair once more. Keep it light in all senses; the clouds that will bring darkness at evening yet attend (in the sense of await) the passing of the sun and of your love. Confess, not with stern self-revelation and acceptance of defeat, but with laughing and loving song assert a human defiance to darkness and the void.

Poem 30 [XXIX] is certainly written by ". . . a certain gay young nobleman whimpering to the name Low Swine . . ." (*FW* 173). He whimpers out accusations of her destruction of the "rich apparel" of 7 [VIII], of her Titania-like despoiling of summer, of her having brought to the enclosed garden the desolate winds of autumn, soon to bring the wild winds of winter. Love is dissolving, and it's all her fault. He had loved her, too dear, not wisely but too well, as another self-satisfied hero once whimpered. But she, whose clear eyes remain unperturbed, justifies his wise insight of 27 [XXVII]. She is selfish. And so, in this song, he falls upon the thorns of life and bleeds.

But in 31 [XXXII], before the lovers finally part, he once more, as a determined preacher, mounts his wise soapbox. Rain indicates nature's empathy with their tears—his anyway, since the lady may have perceived she will do better without him—and the wet leaves, once so loving and joyful, cover their memories (which he will uncover in the following song). "Way" here is a singular, I suppose, because they have not yet parted; they will need separate ways in the next poem. They stay for a moment, to contemplate the path this whole suite has taken, before they look at the memories and part. In this moment of pause, the wise counselor returns once again to his "heart speaks to heart" pose.

In 32 [XXX], he recalls the whole course of their love. The main memory is the opening action of the suite in 4 [IV], where she shyly played the piano and he fearfully stood near—like Bloom, less shy, turning the pages for young Molly. "Grave" has something of the atmosphere of "The Dead" about it, as do all these dripping trees and soggy leaves. The sweetness is gone, and the anapest "at the last" suggests the almost stumbling speed of the painful yet welcome parting. The plodding hesitancy of the final line, similar to the movement in the final line of *Paradise Lost*—"Through Eden took their solitary way"—suggests the return of loneliness.

Two lover's songs end the suite. The poet may be singing just to comfort himself, as he did in the opening poems. At any rate, he takes the advice which he gave to her in 29 [XXV], to laugh and sing though heavyhearted—or at least he tries. Having expressed his resentment and hurt in 30 [XXIX], and his sorrow and resignation and determination in 31 [XXXII], he now sings, and his music contrasts with the "sweet" music of Love at the beginning. Love now (in 33 [XXXIII]) is neither the lonely harpist nor the happy lover nor the possibly divine figure softly knocking at the heart in 12 [VI], but is a "fool in motley" like the one Jaques met in the forest (like Buck Mulligan in motley), now loudly knocking perseveringly at the tree—no doubt the garden's apple tree. Loneliness has returned to them, now loveless, but nature, not really malignant but only indifferent, carries on in its merry determination to have propagation by fair means or foul. *Macbeth*, indeed, is somehow involved in that knocking, as the next and last poem makes explicit. The fall, which takes the ungrieving leaves, goes into the gathering of winter, as night seals their sad parting. But the repetition of "year" in the final line may go with the ambivalence of gathering, which means both a collection of force for a deadly attack and a preparation for new things to come. It may more specifically imply, too, at the close of the suite, a harvest of the good things in their love. He urges her, or at least (if she has already gone) his memory of her, to imitate the leaves and go the way nature calls her. The ending has some faint hint of the immensely powerful tonality of the ending of "The Dead."

But all hopeful possibilities disappear or are at least muffled in the final song, almost a lullaby. It is more likely that the poet is alone here, as in the opening poems, speaking once again to himself. The unquiet of the girl in 25 [XXVI] now settles in him (if she herself, as I imagine to be the case, is not actually present), and the voice which urged her to sleep in union with him in 24 [XXII] now sounds only in his own unquiet heart. "The voice of the winter" has replaced the lovely voice of the turtle once heard in the land ("voax of the turfur is hurled on our lande" [*FW* 39]), and it is likely the wintry voice emerges from that rogue (Jack Frost?) knocking in the previous poem. Here the sinister voice echoes the cry which Macbeth heard, and it sounds in the heart which has murdered love—"Glamours hath moidered's lieb . . ." (*FW* 250).

In the final stanza, we run into what Tindall calls "pronominal confusion." [19] "My kiss" operating on "your heart" would argue that the lady is still there. I settle it by supposing that she is there in his imagination, and that his unquiet heart can be viewed by him as his or hers or both. Shem (as Mercius) does something like this in regard to himself and Justius (and their mother) at the end of chapter 7 in *Finnegans Wake,* mixing pronouns as he and his brother mingle in his mind and merge into the fluid mother. But in any case, the suite ends in some confusion, in frustration, incomplete and uneasy, with a wish for peace stymied by that fateful knocking.

Joyce, having just received the proofs of *Chamber Music,* told his brother, about March 1, 1907, that he might finally determine to become a writer: "Yet I have certain ideas I would like to give form to: not as a doctrine but as the continuation of the expression of myself which I now see I began in *Chamber Music*" (*Letters* II, 217). With this Wildean attitude in his mind, he goes on to say, "It is not a book of love verse at all, I perceive" (*Letters* II, 219). Stanislaus's arrangement had treated the poems as just scattered love-verses. Joyce, as I understand him, perceived his poems, with his own suite in mind, as an attempt at a portrait of himself as artist, as a projection of the woman he desired to meet in the world outside himself (something like Stephen's "green rose"), and as a large philosophy dealing with human love.

Joyce's portrait of himself looms largest, of course, but if one listens to and stares long enough at the poems in Joyce's own imaginative scheme, not Stanislaus's, then behind that rather precious, self-centered, verbal musician emerges the outline of a woman, like the lovely Eve peering curiously out from under God's other arm in Michelangelo's "Creation of Adam." Joyce shows the woman of *Chamber Music* fulfilling Shakespeare's prophecy about his love:

> 'Gainst death and all oblivious enmity
> Shall you pace forth. . .
>
> (Sonnet 35)

Joyce's woman, as I attempt to unify these fragmentary glimpses, emerges for me a clear Irish figure—lovely, graceful, shy, talented, passionate, affectionate, selfish, sensitive, possessive, intuitive, guilt-ridden, resentful, cold, determined—a woman of infinite variety. She has the Jewish beauty and passion of the Bride in the *Song of Songs,* of the Queen of Sheba, of Anastashie. She has the glory of Mary, the source of the human Word; the happy purity of Beatrice; the shy virginity of Stephen's Mercedes, Lady of Mercy. She has the sensual taint of Zoe (Jewish at least in Bloom's imagination), sterile source of life, like the Dead Sea. She has the witchery of the villanelle's Temptress, of the Shee, of Circe, of Titania. She has the malice of the Vampire, seeking the poet's mouth like the Pale Vampire of *Ulysses*, the complete inversion of the *Song of Songs'* opening line: "Let him kiss me with the kisses of his mouth. . . ." She is contradictory and tantalizing and mysterious, but full of life and energy. She deserves to be restored to the ordered if fragmentary world in which Joyce placed her. Then, in spite of the flaws with which adolescent certitudes and artistic uncertainties left her, she will still do all that a girl composed of ink can do to make defect perfection.

NOTES

1. So A. Walton Litz points out in his preface to the invaluable first volume of *The James Joyce Archive* (New York: Garland Publishing Company, 1978), p. xxxii. Mr. Gilvarry did not permit reproduction, but Litz examined and describes the MS.

2. William York Tindall, in his excellent edition of the poems (*Chamber Music* [New York: Columbia University Press, 1954], hereafter Tindall), uses the Roman numeral for Stanislaus's numbering and Arabic for Joyce's, as I do, putting Joyce's number first.

3 Tindall. It will be obvious in this paper how much I owe to Tindall's careful work with the MSS. I have, of course, learned a great deal from Tindall's interpretations and insights—offensive as many of those seemed to me, as to many others, in 1954. I have since learned far greater respect for Tindall's judgment. His fine edition has long been out of print—a shame! My hope is that he (or some worthy successor) will bring out an equally valuable edition based on Joyce's arrangement rather than on Stanislaus's.

4. *Ibid.*, p. 83.

5. *Ibid.*, p. 74.

6. *The Workshop of Daedalus*, ed. Robert Scholes and Richard M. Kain (Evanston, Ill.: Northwestern University Press, 1965), p. 36. Hereafter *Workshop*.

7. Tindall, p. 188.

8. *Workshop*, p. 191.

9. Tindall, p. 204.

10. *Workshop*, p. 34.

11. Tindall, pp. 217–18. See also Elaine Unkeless, "Bats and Sanguivorous Bugaboos," *James Joyce Quarterly*, 15 (Winter, 1978), 128–33.

12. John Henry Cardinal Newman, *Discourses Addressed to Mixed Congregations* (London: Longmans, Green, 1906), pp. 342–59. Joyce owned this book, now in the Buffalo collection of Joyce's library.

13. *A Portrait of the Artist as a Young Man*, introduction and notes by J. S. Atherton (London: Heinemann Educational Books, 1964), p. 252.

14. Compare Hopkins's treatment in *The Wreck of the Deutschland* of the perceptive heart intuiting what the rational brain cannot perceive. *The Poems of Gerard Manley Hopkins*, ed. W. H. Gardner and N. H. MacKenzie (London: Oxford University Press, 1967).

15. Hugh Kenner, *Dublin's Joyce* (Boston: Beacon Press, 1962), pp. 27–33.

16. "If the Creator comes on earth in the form of a servant and a creature, why may not His Mother, on the other hand, rise to be the Queen of heaven, and be clothed with the sun, and have the moon under her feet?" Newman, *Discourses*, p. 355.

17. *Gabriel Harvey's Marginalia*, ed. G. C. Moore Smith (Stratford on Avon: Shakespeare Head Press, 1913), p. 232.

18. Phillip F. Herring, *Joyce's "Ulysses" Notesheets in the British Museum* (Charlottesville: University Press of Virginia, 1972), p. 504.

19. Tindall, p. 222.

FLORENCE L. WALZL

*D*ubliners: Women in Irish Society

Dubliners is the book in which Joyce examines the middle-class Irish society from which he originated. It is also the work which presents his most comprehensive picture of the condition of women in Ireland. This collection of fifteen short stories has a deliberately planned structure, covering a range from youth to age, moving from studies of individuals to tales of men and women in relation to cultural groups, and picturing both men and women in typical situations, religious and ethical, social, economic, or political. Moreover, as a work of fiction, it reflects certain of Joyce's early convictions of this period (1900–1910) about the artist and society. One is his belief that the survival of the artist depends inevitably upon his escape from the constrictive conditions of bourgeois society, including bonds to women and the family. Another is his early view that the artist must in his life and work not only repudiate societal stereotypes and conventionalities, but also affirm a call to a new society. For example, in "A Portrait of the Artist," an essay written in January, 1904, Joyce described how the artist must first proclaim his *"Nego"* (I deny) in defiance of Church and State and then as moral, intellectual leader enunciate his *Credo:* "To those multitudes not as yet in the wombs of humanity but surely engenderable there, he [the artist] would give the word: Man and woman, out of you comes the nation that is to come, the lightning of your masses in travail. . . ."[1] In midsummer of that same year, Joyce began writing *Dubliners,* a book in which his role as critic-reformer is explicit. He said *Dubliners* was a "looking-glass" in which the Irish people could see themselves and their paralysis. The book comprised "a chapter of the moral history" of Ireland, concentrating on Dublin because that was the "centre of paralysis," and covering in the stories the range of "childhood, adolescence, maturity and public life." It was written in "a style of scrupulous meanness" (*Letters* I, 63–4; II, 134). Joyce's term "scrupulous meanness" has mainly been interpreted as a stylistic label, but it also carries an implication that *Dubliners* mirrors Irish social conditions with accuracy and realism. Therefore, Joyce's treatment of women in *Dubliners* should be examined against the background of these assertions: that *Dubliners* is an anatomy of Irish society and that, as an analysis, it is scrupulously realistic.

The aim of this study is to examine the life pattern Joyce outlines as characteristic of women in Dublin and to ascertain from various social records whether the typical fictional situations of his women characters are accurate depictions of Irish family mores and of social and economic conditions as they affected women in Dublin at the turn of the century. Some comments will be made about the relationship between Joyce's social theories and his view of women in this book. Certainly, the large volume of criticism dealing with feminine characterization in *Dubliners* is evidence that these portraits are memorable but complex, since there is marked disagreement in interpretation of characters and their situations.

First, the social background. Though autobiographical elements in *Dubliners* have been well explored, the degree of social realism of the background has not been as fully studied. Certainly, it has been taken for granted that *Dubliners*, begun in midsummer, 1904, presents some of the conditions which motivated Joyce to leave Ireland in October of that year. Thus it lays the groundwork for the *apologia* of the rebel-artist of *A Portrait of the Artist as a Young Man*. Also, *Dubliners* clearly presents a life pattern of Irish society, as the careful arrangement of the stories into successive chronologies shows.[2] For example, in the first chronology, comprising the stories of childhood, adolescence, and maturity, each protagonist (or set of main characters) seems older and more paralyzed than the one in the previous story. In a second, minor chronology beginning at the middle of *Dubliners*, the effects on children of the second generation are traced.

Throughout, as has often been observed, *Dubliners* seems a set of social case histories. Children are stunted in their development, youths are frustrated socially and economically, and adults are trapped in sterile and unproductive lives. The total society, pictured as materialistic and provincial, inert and insensitive, is both betrayed and betraying. Failure to feel and to apprehend is pervasive. This most social of weaknesses, the inability to communicate or understand, is repetitive and is associated with a prevailing communion imagery. For the idea especially of human communion is central to this book, and the role of woman is quintessential in Joyce's exploration of the relations of human beings: of mothers and children, fathers and daughters, sisters and brothers, and especially of men and women in their sexual relationships from early courtship to old age. In its treatment of women, *Dubliners* needs examination as a social document, since historically women have been particularly vulnerable to societal pressures. At issue are the questions of Joyce's accuracy in depiction of the social milieu of his women characters and of the realism of his portraits of women as social entities.

In *Dubliners*, Joyce neither glosses over nor sentimentalizes situations.[3] That his picture of the middle-class Irish family is generally accurate can be supported by sociological studies and statistics.[4] Some of the social conditions that produced the harshness of Irish family life at this period are too well known to need documentation; however, several need comment in terms of their importance to *Dubliners*. The first is lack of economic opportunity. For a full century after 1845, the year of the great Famine, economic deprivation drove millions abroad.[5] For those who remained, poverty was widespread, jobs few and precarious, salaries meager, and opportunities for advancement rare. It normally took a young man fifteen to twenty years to achieve a modicum of security. *Dubliners* reflects this, especially in the companion tales of youth, "Two Gallants" and "The Boarding House," which deal with young men in their thirties. Lenehan, the protagonist of "Two Gallants," is knocking about town jobless, nearly penniless, longing, without prospects, for a "good job," and a "good simpleminded girl with a little of the ready," and a "home of his own" (*D* 58). Robert Doran's career in the office of a wine merchant in "The Boarding House" is typical: at thirty-five, after "long years of service," he is able at last to afford marriage, but he is being pressured into an unsuitable alliance because of his fear that gossip may lose him his position (*D* 66). The effects of such conditions upon women were severe. Economic opportunities for young women were extremely limited, and marriages were few and late.

A second major social condition radically affecting women's lives is that for over a century following 1841, Ireland had the lowest marriage and birth rates in the civilized world. As a natural concomitant, it also had the highest rate of unmarried men and women in the world.[6] During Joyce's youth and young manhood, the marriage rate underwent its greatest decline. From 1881 to 1891, it was at its all-time low of

4 percent per 1,000 population. Even by 1908, when *Dubliners* was finally completed, it had not yet risen to 5 percent.[7] Only comparisons make clear the severity of the situation: throughout the first third of the twentieth century, the marriage rate in Ireland ran less than half that of England and Wales and of Denmark, a country of comparable size and type on the continent.[8] *Dubliners* throughout reflects these adverse conditions in the few marriages depicted and in the number of unmarried characters. For example, in the four stories devoted to youth, only one has marriage as its outcome and that one involves coercion. Of the four tales of "maturity," two depict the lives of lonely celibates.

A third set of statistics involving the late ages of marriage for both sexes is also characteristic of Ireland during the century following the Famine and is reflected significantly in *Dubliners*. In 1841, the time of highest population, the marriage age was a normal one: for example, in that year only 43 percent of males between twenty-five and thirty-five were unmarried. In contrast, by 1911 that figure was above 70 percent.[9] Social commentators and sociologists agree on the rigidity and persistence of the marriage patterns that developed after 1845.[10] Marriage before or at the age of twenty-five became rare. For most men, marriage was delayed until the period between thirty-five and forty-five years, when a man was established in a secure position or had inherited family land, money, or a business. Men tended to marry women ten years or more younger than themselves. Women began marrying in significant numbers only after thirty; men after thirty-five, frequently not before forty. Meantime, in some cases, there might be "understandings" or engagements of as long as ten to fifteen years, but more commonly men avoided any commitments, preferring the company of their own sex. Moreover, the statistics show that most women who reached forty-five and men who reached fifty-five without marrying would remain single all their lives. Bachelors outnumbered spinsters in large numbers, though the percentages of both continued to be the highest in the world.

These marriage practices remained deeply entrenched throughout the first half of the twentieth century. For example, Seán O'Faolain, the Irish novelist, in an essay "Love among the Irish" in 1953, describes correspondence he received after writing a series of articles about late marriages in Ireland for a popular newspaper. Among quotations from letters sent him, he included one on "how one young Irishman approaches wedlock":

> I am a bachelor, aged 38. I am in no hurry to get married. Next September, or the September after, I will take a holiday with an object at Lisdoonvarna, County Clare. I will inform some of the priests on holiday that I am on the lookout, and that I am a bachelor of some substance who requires a wife with a dowry of a certain minimum figure. The good priests will pass the word around. In due course a girl will be selected and the wooing will proceed on a sane plane. At Christmas my people will visit her people, and her people will investigate my background, credentials and relatives. I will meet the young lady again on some such occasion as the Rugby International in Dublin during the following Easter. In due course the nuptials will take place. If I marry at 40 on the lines I have indicated I will guarantee that at 60 my wife and myself will be fonder of one another than any couple of the same age who married in their youth for what Hollywood miscalls love, but which is in fact *lustful infatuation.*[11]

This letter is instructive: marriage is a deliberate, unromantic business involving acquisition of money and property on the bridegroom's part in exchange for presumed security on the bride's. Indeed, romantic love is denounced as "lustful infatuation." It might be noted that Joyce once described such an approach to love in *Stephen Hero* as moral "simony" (*SH* 202).

The authenticity of Joyce's picture of courtship and marriage in Dublin becomes evident. Not only does *Dubliners* have many wary bachelors, but it has its own feminine variant of O'Faolain's deliberate wooer. She is the formidable Mrs. Kearney of "A Mother," who as a well-educated young woman and an accomplished pianist, had at "the age of marriage" been "sent out to many houses where her playing and ivory manners were much admired." "Pale and unbending," she had long sat "amid the chilly circle of her accomplishments," waiting for a proper "suitor to brave it." But the young men were "ordinary," and when she drew "near the limit" of age and her friends had begun to talk, she had "silenced them" by marrying an elderly bootmaker. She well "knew the small number of his talents," but she appreciated his "abstract value as a male," and she respected him "as she respected the General Post Office as something large, secure and fixed." After the first year of married life, she "perceived such a man would wear better than a romantic person" (*D* 136–37, 141). Her talents as a mother will be dealt with later.

It is also clear that *Dubliners* pictures a society overweighted with unmarried people. Bachelors are legion. Among marriageable younger bachelors are such important characters as Eveline's sailor-suitor, Frank, Jimmy Doyle of "After the Race," Lenehan and Corley of "Two Gallants," Gallaher of "A Little Cloud," and Mr. Power of "Grace." By Dublin standards of marriageability, the wizened Mr. Browne of "The Dead"; bald, middle-aged Mr. Alleyne of "Counterparts," said to be "sweet" on Miss Delacour's money; and elderly James Duffy of "A Painful Case," who, Captain Sinico thinks, is courting his young daughter—all are highly eligible as suitors. Most noticeable are all the bachelors in the many group scenes of *Dubliners:* the all-male party on Farley's yacht in "After the Race," the numerous young men who gathered round the piano in Mrs. Mooney's Boarding House, the pub crawlers of "Counterparts" who twit Farrington for being a married man, many of the political hacks of "Ivy Day in the Committee Room," and at the party in "The Dead," the gallery of unmarried young men—Browne, Freddy Malins, Bartell D'Arcy, and many more.

Dubliners is also full of unmarried women—young Eveline Hill, who, in timidity, rejected a romantic suitor and so made spinsterhood her choice in life; the seduced slavey of "Two Gallants," whose choices seem less voluntary; and the little old maid, Maria, of "Clay," who had no choice at all. "The Dead," the climactic story of the book, takes place in the home of two old maids and a spinster niece, and its range of women characters includes a youthful servant girl bitter about men, a bevy of flirtatious young girls, unmarried schoolmistresses and music teachers, and an old widow. In fact, Gretta and Gabriel Conroy, the principal characters, are apparently the only married couple attending the Misses Morkan's party.

The last general social condition requiring comment seems paradoxical. In Ireland, a country with a falling birthrate and a declining population during this entire period, the fecundity of its women remained extremely high. Families of four to five children and more were usual in Ireland.[12] *Dubliners* reflects this commonplace facet of Irish life in the large families of the stories, "Eveline," "Grace," and especially "Counterparts," in which Farrington, coming home drunk from a night in the pubs, has trouble distinguishing between two of his sons and beats one of them violently (*D* 71, 97–98). Arland Ussher, the critic and Gaelic scholar, in an essay, "The Boundary between the Sexes," discusses the situation of a wife in such circumstances, pointing out that the typical Irishman prefers a life of "male camaraderie" with "the boys" and likes to spend his money "like a gentleman." But the "Irish wife, at grips with a numerous family in a rather comfortless home, with a not-too-generous housekeeping allowance comes off less well." [13] Certainly, Joyce was aware of the difficulties of life for the mother of a large household. On August 29, 1904, he wrote Nora Barnacle, whom he was courting, an unsparing account of his own family background: "How could I like the idea of home? My home was simply a middle class affair ruined by spendthrift habits. . . . My mother was slowly killed, I think, by my father's ill-treatment, by years of trouble, and by my cynical frankness of conduct. When I looked on her face as she lay in her coffin . . . I understood that I was looking on the face of a victim and I cursed the system which had made her a victim. We were seventeen in family" (*Letters* II, 48). But Joyce knew that women were not the only victims in Irish society. The psychological effects of the social conditions I have outlined were felt by the entire middle-class society, male and female.

Such conditions, however, were more serious for women because women's vocational choices were so much more limited than men's. Most girls in economically depressed Ireland, facing long delays in marrying and perhaps eventual spinsterhood, had to work in the home, in family enterprises, or at outside jobs. Exactly how limited were women in their vocational choices? In order to judge the authenticity of Joyce's picture in *Dubliners*, one needs to know whether the type and range of women's occupations that he describes were really characteristic of urban Ireland in 1904–06—data that are not readily available. The observations that follow are based on two main sources: *Open Doors for Irishwomen: A Guide to the Professions Open to Educated Women in Ireland*, a little-known publication which appeared early in 1907 and is, therefore, contemporaneous with the composition of *Dubliners*, and the "Trades' Dictionary, Dublin and Suburbs" section of *Thom's Official Directory . . . for the Year 1904 . . . , Dublin City and Dublin County.*

Open Doors for Irishwomen is a publication issued by the Irish Central Bureau for the Employment of Women. Its introduction indicates that this is the only organization in Ireland which deals "as a class, without distinction of creed or politics with women of good birth and education, who, for lack of means, are forced to take up remunerative work"—a class that in Ireland "is by no means a small one." It is aimed to aid women embarking on a "professional career." Each article is written by an expert in a given field and gives summaries of the "qualifications, preliminary education and professional training" necessary for the work and estimates of the "remuneration and prospects" to be expected. It is clearly a pioneer work and one of its experts rejoices that "the girl of the twentieth century has a wide range of professions from which to choose nowadays—very different to that of her mother, for whom the one opportunity of earning a livelihood was as the everlasting governess." [14]

There are some twenty-five main occupations described, with a number of subheadings under *Nursing* and *Teaching*. The range is from cookery and domestic positions of a supervisory nature such as housekeepers, "Lady-Cooks," and "Lady-Nurses" (nannies) to office work, journalism, civil service, nursing, and teaching. (This directory is not for unskilled labor such as slaveys and laundresses.) In this brave new world, educational qualifications are high and remuneration low. For example, for an ordinary clerk in the Civil Service, the requirements include two foreign languages; for secretaries, as distinguished from typists, there were expectations of the usual secretarial skills, at least two foreign languages, and if possible a university degree; for nursing and teaching, advanced diplomas or degrees plus unpaid experience. Though this book shows that women could theoretically qualify for a variety of professions, actual positions were sometimes remote possibilities. Moreover, a number paid so badly as not to be practical undertakings. For instance, openings in the Civil Service were so few that a "candidate" might pass "the age limit before having a chance to compete for a vacancy." As for "dispensing chemists" (apothecaries), there were "practically no openings in Ireland for Women Dispensers"; moreover, the profession was not "remunerative." As for office clerks (typists and shorthand writers), "hundreds respond to any advertisement of a vacancy in an office . . . , competition is extremely keen and the demand far less than the supply." [15] (No wonder the chief clerk of Crosbie and Alleyne in "Counterparts" had no qualms about harrying Miss Parker in her typing—she dared not object.)

In this book, the only real "open doors for Irishwomen" of the middle class were at the bottom and top of the categories, that is, for the least and best trained. There were ample openings for the "lady-domestic"—the housekeeper and supervisor—presumably in the well-off households of the Establishment. Matronships of institutions were also in "fair demand," though positions as matron-housekeepers were "oftener required" and "ladies . . . liked them." [16] (This seems precisely Maria's post in the Dublin by Lamplight Laundry in "Clay"— and she liked it too.)

For ambitious girls undertaking careers in such professions as scientific work, nursing, and teaching, there were good possibilities, but not even the most extensive preparation guaranteed jobs. Nurses were especially in demand because of the great variety of types of nursing, but advancement was limited. The most promising field, however, was teaching. At this period a broad spectrum of instruction in specialized areas was rapidly developing. In music, dancing, art, elocution, kindergarten work, and physical education, prospects were good: e.g., *The Open Door* states that "fields" were "widening" (elocution); demand was "growing" (kindergarten); and need exceeded supply (gymnastics). Music was an especially good field. Though "a first-rate [vocal] artiste could probably not make a decent livelihood" in Ireland by performance alone, good music teachers, especially of piano and violin, were "always [in] steady demand," and if in addition they were "good performers," they could command much "higher fees." These details fit the Misses Morkan of "The Dead" exactly. Old Aunt Kate gave piano lessons to beginners for lesser fees; Aunt Julia was "still the leading soprano in Adam and Eve's" church, and she supplemented by teaching too; but their niece, Mary Jane, who had been through the Academy and was both teacher and performer, was "the main prop of the household." She held the post of organist at Haddington Road Church and had many piano pupils belonging to "better-class families" (*D* 176). The main educational system offered the best prospects for young women teachers, but only at the lower level. The most certain career for women was in primary school teaching, where the demand regularly exceeded the supply. [17]

Unfortunately, the brightest and most ambitious young women encountered their most formidable barriers at top levels, in both nursing and education. In Ireland most hospitals have always been run by religious orders or organizations, and according to Arland Ussher, the key positions such as "*theater* sisters and senior sisters" have generally been held by nuns, although nuns were not the only occupants of high rank. "Promotion . . . beyond a certain point" was "likely to be barred." [18] For the woman who wished to enter secondary teaching in

1907, the prospects were even more hazardous. The main article on "The Teaching Profession" by the Lady Principal of Alexandra College urges that such a candidate should have especially rigorous preparation. She should "begin her education at a good public school [in Ireland, as in Britain, elitist, expensive, and private] from which she should proceed to a woman's college," and after this training, obtain her degree either at the Royal University or at Trinity College. What then? The article concludes thus: "The prospects for teachers in Ireland are not very good. There are not many large Protestant schools, and as the education of Roman Catholic girls is almost entirely in the hands of the religious orders, the number of openings for highly-qualified women teachers is small." [19]

Given such a situation, it is evident that Molly Ivors, the teacher in "The Dead," had achieved a considerable educational position. Most readers do not realize that the tension that arises between Miss Ivors and Gabriel Conroy lies in part in his realization that she is his professional equal. "They were friends of many years' standing and their careers had been parallel, first at the University and then as teachers: he could not risk a grandiose phrase with her" (D 188).

Open Doors for Irishwomen makes clear how limited vocational choices were for women in Ireland and how difficult advancement was. Its information confirms the accuracy with which Joyce treats the professional background of a number of his women characters. However, it highlights one important group of professional women he omits completely—nurses. This omission is the more surprising in view of his extensive representation of working women in the other main professions.

The women characters of *Dubliners* clearly represent the middle class, and the range of their occupations lies within that class also. (The exceptions are few; Lily, the maidservant of "The Dead," the slavey of "Two Gallants," and the magdalen-inmates of the Dublin by Lamplight Laundry are all lower class.) *Dubliners* includes women shopkeepers and shop assistants, office clerks and typists, the operator of a lodging house and the housekeeper of an institution, schoolteachers, and especially musicians—pianists, vocalists, and music teachers. Since one of Joyce's principal goals in *Dubliners* was the presentation of social types, he may have aimed at typicality of occupations for women also.

Thom's Directory for 1904, which has long been a source of helpful information about Dublin for Joyce readers—as it was for Joyce him-self—has data which support this view.[20] The Dublin "Trades' Direc-tory" section lists alphabetically hundreds of occupations, pro-fessions, and businesses, and under each heading gives a list of com-panies and individuals in the category by name and address. Because the list is overwhelmingly masculine, it is easy to discern the occupa-tions in which women are important or numerous. Marital status is indicated by use of *Miss* or *Mrs.* Women cluster in relatively few occupational groups. Five groups that are especially prominent are (1) operators of businesses that make women's and children's clothes and of shops that sell them; (2) owners of neighborhood food stores (dairies, butcher shops, groceries, bakeries, and fruit stores); (3) lodg-ing-house keepers and tavern owners; (4) teachers; and (5) musicians. To give some slight sense of the economic importance of women in these areas, the following observations may be helpful. In 1904, *Thom's Directory* shows that women monopolized dressmaking, millinery, and sewing enterprises; owned 30 percent of the bakeries, fruit stores, and dairies and over 10 percent of the butcher shops and groceries; operated all the boarding houses listed, 75 percent of the lodging houses, and 20 percent of the hotels; were approximately a third of the teachers of dancing, elocution, and languages; made up a majority of all professional musicians; and, finally, were directors or owners of all the "Seminaries for Young Ladies" in Dublin. The most surprising statistic among these groups is the high percentage of women owning or operating shops in Dublin. Arensberg and Kimball, who devote two chapters of *Family and Community in Ireland* to shopkeeping, describe the great number of small family businesses in Ireland and show that when children grew up, they might be set up in shops in other areas, and that when the father of the family died, the widow frequently continued the enterprise. These practices partially explain the high percentage of women owners of small shops in Ireland.[21]

Within the compact limits of the brief tales in *Dubliners,* Joyce could not deal with the scope of such material. However, even a cursory view of the book shows how accurately he knew his native city and how tellingly he used selective details. As a first example, let us examine the career of the redoubtable Mrs. Mooney of "The Boarding House." She was a butcher's daughter who had "married her father's foreman and opened a butcher shop" elsewhere. (Such a familial and occupational pattern is one that Arensberg and Kimball describe as commonplace, and Mrs. Mooney in real life would have been one of their statistics.) Later, after his father-in-law died, Mr. Mooney took to drink, "plundered the till, [and] ran headlong into debt." So Mrs. Mooney, a "determined woman," shed her alcoholic husband and the butcher shop simultaneously and set up a boarding house in central Dublin, where she presided as "The Madam" (D 61–62). (In life, her name and address would have appeared in *Thom's Directory* under the heading of "Lodging Houses.")

A second example is Joyce's accurate knowledge of the musical background of Dublin, which is demonstrated in his stories. *Thom's Directory* of 1904 lists over two hundred performers and teachers of music and allied arts such as dancing, elocution, and languages, over half of whom were women. Joyce used the names of many Dublin musicians in his work. In "The Dead," Joyce pictured members of his own family and recognizable friends. Indeed, "the Misses Flynn school" at 15 Usher's Island was listed in Thom's and had been for many years. These ladies, Joyce's great-aunts, were the originals of the Misses Morkan, and in life, his mother had taken dancing and music lessons from them. The climax of *Dubliners* is the musical party at their home, and as a social event it represents Joyce's final comment on Dublin in this book. *Dubliners* is full of musicians. No other group of women in the book is comparable in size. In 1900, apparently, no career was as promising for a young woman or as secure for a mature woman as music. In "A Painful Case," Mrs. Sinico's daughter, though still in her teens, is already launched as a music teacher. Kathleen Kearney aims higher at a concert career. Mary Jane Morkan, a little older, is established as an organist and teacher. Her aunts' school is old and successful. Music was also a career that could sustain one in adversity. Mrs. Fanny M'Coy, once a professional soprano but now come down in the world, "taught young children to play the piano at low terms"; and even poor old Madam Glynn, who wailed like a banshee when she sang, was still able to get engagements (D 110, 147, 158).

Dubliners also shows women responsive to the new cultural developments associated with the Irish Renascence at the turn of the century— drama, verse, and language study. In the story "A Mother," Mrs. Kearney, well aware of the publicity value of the "Irish Revival" for her musical daughter Kathleen, has "brought an Irish [language] teacher to the house" to teach the girl Gaelic; and at the ill-fated concert that is the core of this story, a "stirring patriotic recitation" is delivered—no doubt with suitable elocutionary gestures—by a young woman interested in "amateur theatricals" (*D* 137, 147). The concert of this story, mediocre and stereotyped, becomes a portrait of the society.

All this evidence seems to indicate that Joyce aimed at more than fictional verisimilitude. His intent seems to have been realistic accuracy and typicality in his characterization of women and in depiction of their occupations. Throughout *Dubliners*, Joyce tends to view his women as types. His later feminine trinity of woman as virgin, mother, and temptress can be seen in incipient form in a story as early as "Araby." However, the main typology is of women as societal figures. One example of the linkage between Irish social types and the occupations these women engage in involves a deliberate parallel between the important first story of *Dubliners*, "The Sisters," and the famous final story, "The Dead." The similarity between the scenes has been noted by a number of critics: each story presents a social group in the home of a pair of elderly spinsters. "The Sisters" describes a wake at the home of the Misses Eliza and Nannie Flynn; "The Dead," a party at the home of the Misses Julia and Kate Morkan. The narrative parallels are obvious, but what is not so evident is that each pair is associated with one of the two leading professions for women at this period, shopkeeping and music teaching. Thus they portray contrasting but complementary facets of Dublin life: one economic, the other artistic. Both pairs are made highly characteristic of the professions they represent.

Eliza and Nannie Flynn seem the very stereotype of the woman shopkeeper who emerges from the statistics of *Family and Community in Ireland* and *Thom's Directory*. They run a small neighborhood shop that specializes in children's shoes. Their choice of life work probably results from an Irish social pattern involving the "internal dynamics of the Irish family," the practice of shopkeeping fathers to "establish unmarried daughters in small businesses of their own," often at the time their brothers are married or otherwise settled in life. In this case the occasion might have been their brother's ordination. The fact that the sisters are unmarried fits the statistics on ownership of shops operated by women. In Ireland overall, of women shopowners approximately 20 percent were married, 35 percent widowed, and 44 percent unmarried.[22] The significance of Joyce's title "The Sisters" for this opening story thus becomes evident. There has been much critical conjecture as to Joyce's retention of this title through the long process of revision that placed the focus of the story on the relations of an ailing priest and a young boy.[23] But Joyce in this story is presenting the two sisters as typal figures of one segment of Irish society. At this level their ultimate role goes beyond mere social definition to present an important facet of Irish life. Not only do they represent the Ireland that is a nation of small shopkeepers, living meagerly off a narrow range of merchandise, but also, pious and hardworking, they exhaust themselves supporting their brother, an invalid priest. The plot in which they function is thus typal in that it images the historical role of the Irish Church and its supporting laity. In Joyce's view, their straitened lives and spinsterhood are visible signs of the sterile and empty lives of their cultural sphere.

In contrast, the Misses Morkan represent an affluent level of society and an intellectual and artistic sphere far above that of the impoverished Flynn sisters. In "The Dead," Joyce apparently intended to make partial amends for the omission in the early version of *Dubliners* of certain Irish virtues, the ingenuousness and hospitality of the people. So these old ladies are made pleasingly hospitable, but also, as is characteristic of Joyce's ambivalence, their ingenuousness borders on ignorance. They too are flawed types. Like the concert in "A Mother," their party is the image of their culture. In viewpoint, the people are provincial and intellectually limited. The young men leave for a drink when Mary Jane plays her "Academy" piece, and Gabriel Conroy fears that a Browning quotation in his after-dinner speech is above the heads of his audience. Their taste in music is for florid operatic arias and sentimental ballads. Though the conversation is largely about music, it dwells on the past; "grand old operas" and "good voices" are no more. The guests are conformist and stuffy: their pleasures are good food and drink, dancing, singing, and chitchat, in that order. The emptiness and sterility of the Flynn sisters' parlor at the wake find their counterpart in the drawing room of the Misses Morkan. It is interesting that in life the originals of the Misses Morkan both were married and had families. Significantly, Joyce makes them old maids in the story.

It is clear that *Dubliners* accurately reflects the social conditions of Ireland at the turn of the century and presents a realistic picture of middle-class life. Additional analysis of the stories demonstrates that in *Dubliners* Joyce also traces the paralytic effects on his characters of life in such a constrictive environment. Human relationships become distorted and human communion is destroyed.

Since *Dubliners* in its narrative design presents a life pattern, to deal merely with the stories concerned with women fragments this work and mutilates its meaning. Men in 1905 tended to be the initiators of action in the relationships between the sexes; therefore, I shall discuss first the effects of these social conditions on men in Ireland. There is agreement among social commentators that the economic pressures that prevented marriage at normal early ages, combined with the stringent views of the puritanical Irish Church on the moral depravity of sex except for procreative purposes in marriage, led to great male tensions. The high degree of alcoholism among Irishmen is commonly attributed to this repression. *Dubliners* is virtually a gallery of alcoholics. In the early stories like "Araby" when the uncle comes home late, inebriate and forgetful, or in "Eveline" when Mr. Hill arrives home "bad" and threatens "to go" for his daughter, the results of drunkenness are generally seen in connection with children (*D* 38). In the middle and later stories like "Counterparts" and "Grace," the effects of intemperance on both children and wives are shown. Farrington bullies his wife and beats his children. The Kernan children are growing up neglected and unruly. The family suffers in another respect in that men under such pressures seek their pleasures outside the home with male companions in pubs and elsewhere. One of Seán O'Faolain's female correspondents complained that Ireland is "a land made for the male—card playing, horse racing, coursing, fishing. It is a paradise" for men.[24] The scenes in the bars of "A Little Cloud," "Counterparts," and "Grace" reflect this masculine world. Irish social life was clearly not centered in the family. Moreover, the family was further demoralized by a third effect: the high degree of homosexuality in Ireland. Maura Laverty, Irish journalist and playwright, in an essay "Womanshy Irishmen," writes as follows: "I know . . . we have a shocking number of 'queers,' too many of them practicing homosexuals, the others unconscious perverts. I know, too, that cowardice in one form or another has caused others . . . to become addicted to . . . little-boy habits." Other men are "completely indifferent to sex in any . . . form." This large "mixed collection" of men are, she says, known in Ireland as "ould Mary Annes." [25] Joyce knew this problem well: in "After the Race," he depicts an all-male party where men dance with each other and, in "An Encounter," deals frankly with a pederast in a scene that caused much trouble with publishers.

The results of abnormally delayed marriages, of sexual abstinence or guilt over illicit sex, and of long years of primarily male company led many men to take a cold-blooded, unromantic view of marriage.[26] Their attitudes toward marriage were openly mercenary.

The results for women were often most unhappy. Girls, generally reared with a ladylike abhorrence of sex and with their emotions channeled into a frustrated romanticism, were ill prepared for the realities of marriage. They had little opportunity for normal social relationships with men since even "company keeping" was denounced as a "danger to chastity."[27] Normal relationships between young men and women are never depicted in *Dubliners*, and the causes for this are not solely socioeconomic.

Maternal domination of both daughters and sons also distorted the relationships that should develop between young people contemplating marriage. This fact introduces necessity for some consideration of the matriarchy common in Irish families. Mary Frances Keating, Irish journalist, describes this type: "The Irishwoman has had to become the 'dominant' female, a role which suits her ill and makes her quite frequently dislike herself heartily. It earns for her, too, the dislike of the man. . . . In marriage, . . . the woman has to be the driving force. . . . Often denied the protection, affection, and tenderness of marital love, she placates herself with a strangle hold on her children."[28] Daughters she disposed of "round the place" as useful. Sons were kept dependent financially and otherwise. Maura Laverty agrees, noting that "mothers prize their sons far above their daughters" and have "no compunction in showing this favoritism." The result is that the "Irish boy grows up with an exaggerated affection for and dependence on his mother and with a contempt for all other females." In fact, the "Irishman is the world's prime example of the Oedipus complex."[29] Joyce knew this type well. He drew two extraordinary portraits of the dominant female in Mrs. Mooney of "The Boarding House" and Mrs. Kearney of "A Mother." In *Dubliners*, he carries the typology further to make this dominant female a central figure in his picture of Irish society—the determined, conventional upholder of bourgeois standards and ideas and strong supporter of the establishment, both church and state, when it suited her purposes.

Mothers in *Dubliners* tend either to use their daughters or to vent their own frustrations through them. In their stories, the paralysis theme is important. This motif is exemplified in repeated pictures of people living dull rounds of existence that eventually turn them into figures of death in life. Throughout, Joyce uses circle images to depict the sterile circle of these lives. In the tales treating primarily mothers and daughters, this motif of the vicious round is projected into the actual plot pattern: the frustration of Dublin's women—a consequence of their dull, empty rounds of existence—results in a circular plot in which the evils of the first generation are visited upon the second. Mothers so influence or manipulate their daughters that, in effect, the young women relive their mothers' lives. With development of this plot motif, Joyce introduces into *Dubliners* a theme he was to emphasize greatly in *A Portrait of the Artist as a Young Man*: "Ireland is the old sow that eats her farrow" (*P* 203). At worst mothers destroy their daughters; at best they maim them. Two stories of youth, "Eveline" and "The Boarding House," illustrate this motif.

"Eveline" and "The Boarding House" are matched stories which respectively open and close the tales of adolescence. A number of similarities are obvious. The heroines, Eveline Hill and Polly Mooney, are both nineteen years old, both are the daughters of alcoholic fathers, and both hold jobs that reflect the limited economic possibilities for women in Ireland. Eveline works for meager wages in a department store, where she is exploited and miserably treated. Polly has been sent by her mother to work as a typist in an office, with the express purpose of finding a suitor, but when this stratagem fails, her mother brings her home to work without pay in the family boarding house. Finally, both girls are placed in plots dealing with courtship.

Joyce's differences are as significant as his similarities, especially in the handling of the courtships. In "Eveline," the heroine is ardently wooed by a young Irishman who has emigrated and is well settled in the New World. But Eveline's decision is difficult because her irascible father has taken an unreasonable dislike to her suitor, and her loving, protective mother, worn out by the rigors of life with a violent, alcoholic husband, is dead. To marry, Eveline will have to elope and leave Ireland. In contrast, Polly's suitor is reluctant, and her determined mother, whose boarding house has deservedly acquired "a certain fame," abets her daughter at every turn. With tacit connivance, she has observed Polly entice Robert Doran, an industrious and ambitious young man, into a relationship. As a suitor for marriage, he is most reluctant, but Polly and her mother are determined on matrimony as the only reparation for Polly's presumed pregnancy. The really striking contrast is that in the end each girl makes a life choice that insures her a repetition of her mother's life. Eveline, conditioned by her mother's sense of duty, exhausted by her own hard work in the stores and at home, and haunted by a deathbed promise to her mother to take care of the younger children and "keep the home together," chooses a death-in-life, rejection of the man who loves her and can offer her a new life. Joyce makes the point explicit: "As she mused the pitiful vision of her mother's life laid its spell on the very quick of her being—that life of common-place sacrifices closing in final craziness" (D 40). When later, at the gangplank of the embarking ship she turns away from her lover, the life she returns to is a repetition of her mother's life of commonplace sacrifices and confusion. The amnesic trance she experiences portends her final breakdown. Eveline's spinsterhood represents in Dubliners the fate of the large portion of Irish women who will never marry.

In contrast, Mrs. Mooney, by social pressures and economic threats, brings the unwilling Mr. Doran to terms and to the altar. Polly's future is only hinted at in Dubliners, but the story of her marriage to Doran is continued in Ulysses. On June 16, 1904, Bob Doran is on his great "annual bend" of boozing and women, driven to this excess by his demanding "little concubine of a wife," who with her mother, the "old prostitute," makes him "toe the line" the rest of the year (U 167, 303, 314). The family pattern of the dominant wife and inebriate husband is repeated. Polly's "managed" marriage to a man older than herself reflects an Irish social pattern in which marriages are late and carefully calculated.

In contrast to these companion stories dealing with mothers in relationship to their daughters' romances, "A Mother" deals with maternal influence on a girl's career. This story depicts, as we have seen, two intrinsically Irish situations affecting women: for the mother, a marriage to an older commonplace man, entered into out of desperation at the prospect of spinsterhood; and for the daughter, a chance at one of the few professional careers open to women at this period, music. The mother, Mrs. Kearney, is a frustrated romantic who in youth had "learned French and music" at a "high-class" school and had hoped for a "brilliant life." However, she had to settle for a safe marriage to a dull bootmaker. Her disappointment in her own marriage finds outlet in her maneuvering her daughter toward a concert career. She sends Kathleen to the Academy to learn "French and music," in preparation for a career as pianist and popular vocalist. But in the end, the mercenariness and unwillingness to take chances which Mrs. Kearney had exhibited in her own life choice overcome her ambition for her daughter. She orders the girl out of a theater rather than risk her not being paid for a concert. The final words applied to the girl augur her fate: "Kathleen followed her mother meekly"—out to the same empty life of frustration. The newspaper reviewer speaks the requiem to her career: "Miss Kathleen Kearney's musical career was ended in Dublin" (*D* 136–37, 147, 149).

As mothers, so daughters. It is clear in these stories that the situation of the first generation becomes the condition of the second and that mothers tend to transform their daughters into replicas of themselves.

The relations of mothers and sons are equally destructive because of the matriarchal system in Ireland. The psychological effects on men in Ireland have been carefully studied. A Dublin psychiatrist writing in the *Journal of the Irish Medical Association* describes a typical situation:

> If there is a picture characteristic of Irish culture, this is probably it. The male, doted on by his mother, reared in a monosexual atmosphere in school, who has never learned to form a friendship with the opposite sex of his own age—then marries and takes a "housekeeper" into his home—while he continues his friendship with his male friends —"the lads". She goes on to become the mother of his children, invests her life in these and so carries on the pattern into the next generation.[30]

Dubliners illustrates the first stages of this pattern in the story, "A Little Cloud." Little Chandler, a timid clerk and would-be poet, discovers he is "a little man" who has been trapped by marriage in a little life in a "little house" by a "little wife." The irony of the ending is that his wife, rejecting her ineffective husband, turns to their infant son, whom she fondles as "My little man! My little Mannie!" (*D* 70–85). The child's future as the coddled son who will replace her husband in her affections and for whom every sacrifice will be made is thus forecast. He will grow up an incomplete human being, unable to sustain a meaningful relationship with anyone other than his mother.

The relationships between the sexes are not attractive in this book. Victim and victimizer alternate. Girls flirt with men to get minimal attention from them—for example Polly Mooney and the boarders, Miss Healy and the music critic in "A Mother," and all the belles at the Morkans' party. They must "play their cards right" and trap a husband—by hook or by crook. Bachelors are no better. In "Two Gallants," the plot of "The Boarding House" is exactly reversed: here two corrupt men connive to seduce a servant girl and cheat her of her savings. Here woman is victim both of society and of individual men.

With such maneuvering by both men and women as a prelude to marriage, marital life is not likely to be happy. In "Counterparts," Ada Farrington "bullied her husband when he was sober and was bullied by him when he was drunk" (D 97). Mrs. Kernan of "Grace," after three weeks of marriage, had "found a wife's life irksome and, later on, when she was beginning to find it unbearable, she had become a mother." Her affections then focused on her children, and she "accepted [her husband's] frequent intemperance as part of the climate" (D 156). The celibate life was no better. Maria, the little spinster of "Clay," who lived her lonely life as housekeeper-matron among unruly women in a reformatory, never had any chance at the love and romance she longed for. Mr. James Duffy, the old bachelor of "A Painful Case," who spent his life among men in a bank, rejected his chance at romantic love because it was unconventional. Maria could not consciously face the barren reality of her life. James Duffy's epiphany was a realization that he was utterly "alone."

Love does not easily cross the ineluctable barriers between human beings in such a society. Most of the characters never realized their insularity in this book. But one did. In "The Dead," the story Joyce wrote later as a new ending for *Dubliners*, he presents the only intellectual in the book—his protagonist Gabriel Conroy, a teacher and book reviewer. Gabriel alone comes to an understanding of the nature of his society and what it means to be a Dubliner in a society like this. Essentially, the story contrasts Gabriel with the commonplace guests at a party. It is significant that the plot progresses by a series of confrontations Gabriel has with women.[31] In the opening, Lily, the young maidservant, startles him by responding bitterly to his perfunctory wish that she will soon be getting married: "The men that is now is only all palaver and what they can get out of you." Later, his uneasiness among the guests and worry over the appropriateness of quoting Browning in his after-dinner speech are aggravated by a sharp encounter with Molly Ivors, his academic colleague. She unnerves him by her challenge of his reviews as "West Briton" and her insistence that he ought to visit the Aran Islands to learn Gaelic instead of taking holidays abroad. Even a stray memory of his dead mother's opposition to his wife, Gretta, who came from the West of Ireland, disturbs him. But his main confrontation is with his attractive wife who, despite years of

marriage in Dublin, is still a natural, lively, and spontaneous person—
the only woman in *Dubliners* so depicted. After the party, Gabriel
approaches Gretta amorously, and at this point the one certainty in his
life, his comfortable relationship with his wife, is shattered. Explaining
her reluctance, Gretta tells him of a lover of her youth whose memory
she reveres. And suddenly Gabriel sees himself as he probably seemed
to Gretta that evening: "a ludicrous figure . . . orating to vulgarians"
in a dead society. But that is not all.

Gretta tells Gabriel that hearing an old ballad sung that evening had
reawakened in her the vivid memory of her dead love, Michael Furey,
who, when she was about to leave Connacht for Dublin, had "braved
death" to come to say farewell to her. "He did not wish to live" without
her. Gabriel's discovery that for Gretta this vibrant memory of a shade
is more real than the bodily presence of her husband beside her
precipitates the climactic epiphany of "The Dead" and of *Dubliners*—
Gabriel's realization that he has never fully loved and so has never
fully lived. He feels one of the shades admidst the "vast hosts of the
dead." At the end, the final protagonist of *Dubliners* understands that
he has not understood—and that is the beginning of knowledge. In the
final story, there is enlightenment and it has come about through a
woman (*D* 178, 188–89, 219–23).

At the end one asks, What is Joyce's view of women and the relationships between the sexes? It seems an essentially masculine attitude. The study of point of view as technique in *Dubliners* is complex
and beyond the scope of this essay. However, it should be noted that
most of the stories are either narrated through a male consciousness or
related by an omniscient narrator who tends at times to identify with a
male protagonist. That does not necessarily mean that Joyce has anti-
feminine attitudes or that he does not sympathize with women. The
autobiographical approach to literary material was an intrinsic part of
his early aesthetic and of his early processes of composition. The
problem of definition of Joyce's attitudes is further complicated by his
aims in *Dubliners* and his *schema* for accomplishing them. A brief
description of the groups of stories in this context will illustrate the
difficulties.

Dubliners begins characteristically with three stories of young boys—
perhaps the same boy—all autobiographical in origin. These stories are
told in the first person and told at successively later ages. In them the
boy gradually learns about women and sex. In the second story, "An

Encounter," the boy as young adolescent is shocked by sexual abnormality in an adult. In the third story, "Araby," the youth has his first disillusioning experience of romantic infatuation. By this point, in this patterned collection of stories, a very special "point of view" has been developed. It is one that is open and receptive, scrutinizing, seeking meaning and reflecting it in the narration. It is more receptor than initiator of action. It always holds itself at a certain distance, and there is an ironic turn to the observations. It carries a masculine signature.

In assessing Joyce's treatment of both women and men characters in the three later groups of stories, it is imperative to keep in mind Joyce's main aim: *Dubliners* was to be "a chapter of the moral history" of Ireland and Dublin, the "centre of paralysis." His pattern for the book required that the successive stories mark a progressive deterioration of personality and moral fiber in the characters. All must suffer destruction of psyche and character through denial of basic needs and rights, social and familial restrictions, personal frustrations and deprivations. A note of pity runs through the tales of adolescence, especially evident for Eveline, who is too frightened to grasp her chance at life and love, and less so for Jimmy Doyle as dupe of fast-talking financiers. In "Two Gallants" and "The Boarding House," Joyce attempts to be evenhanded in his matching but inverted plots: in the first story, two corrupt men deceive a girl; in the second, two conniving women trap a man. But the fact that from this point on in *Dubliners* the stories are told prevailingly through a narrator identifying himself with the male characters tends to tip the balance away from the women of his stories.

In the two final groups, the tales of maturity and public life, the characters show the inexorable degeneration that Joyce's design demands. Men are pictured as weak (Little Chandler of "A Little Cloud"), venal (the politicians of "Ivy Day in the Committee Room," the retreatants of "Grace," and Gallaher of "A Little Cloud"), irascible and violent (Farrington and Mr. Alleyne of "Counterparts"), and arbitrary and demanding (Alleyne and Mr. Duffy of "A Painful Case"). Women tend to be either insecure, weak, pitiable, and deprived (Kathleen Kearney, Maria, and Mrs. Sinico) or domineering and dictatorial (nagging wives like Mrs. Chandler and Mrs. Farrington or a dominating mother like Mrs. Kearney). Even the stories "Eveline" and "Clay" where Joyce shows great compassion, in the first, for a young girl who chooses a barren life and, in the second, for an old woman who has lived one, there are problems of ambiguity of language and imagery and important questions of interpretation.

Joyces's picture of the relationships between men and women is not a pleasant one; but because these characters are harshly vivid and because Joyce ensures that we know their difficulties and suffering, we feel sympathy for them. Yet not in the same degree for all. The reader is allowed many more glimpses into the minds and emotions of the men characters than of the women. This has two effects: a greater empathy with the male characters than with the female, and a tendency to be tolerant of the men's failures and weaknesses and critical of the women's frailties and arrogance. However, I believe that if Joyce had been challenged on grounds of partiality, he would have denied he was making such a sexual distinction. Such an admission would have invalidated the main thesis of *Dubliners*—that the morbidity of Irish society is all-encompassing and progressive and that it embraces all segments of the society. Yet the fact remains that the narrative mode Joyce employs results in a prevailingly masculine viewpoint.

Dubliners has emerged as a major achievement in the Joyce canon and its reputation continues to grow. In conclusion, I would like to suggest that my study provides one reason for *Dubliners'* renown: Joyce's picture of Dublin social life is solidly based on historical reality. His description of the lives and careers of different women of different ages and types can be authenticated in full, verifiable detail from a variety of sociological sources. In short, when Joyce pits men against women in his tales, it can be proved that drastic economic and social pressures actually forced Dubliners into such situations of frustration, deprivation, and hostility. He spares neither sex; he sympathizes with both, but not to the same degree. These stories thus bear what I have termed a masculine signature. The style Joyce himself characterized as one of "scupulous meanness" is, in actuality, the ultimate of a scrupulous realism. Thus it is evident that even in *Dubliners*, Joyce's first work of fiction, the portraiture of women is very complex. That Joyce felt sympathy for women caught in restrictive social conditions is clear, but it is a sympathy often tempered by ironic dissection of feminine weakness or hypocrisy or sometimes biased by male ambivalence or even hostility to the smothering role of women in the various developing phases of their lives. In these stories of women, the complexities of motivation, shifts in point of view, and uncertainty of interpretation, especially of conclusions, all reveal in Joyce a subtle, elusive artist standing ambivalently behind his characters—like a man, not a god— alternately biting and paring his fingernails.

Joyce in *Dubliners* was also faithful to the artistic dicta he defined in the *Portrait* as the essential conditions of the writer—silence, cunning, and exile. As narrator he remains enigmatically apart in one story after another, manipulating image and symbol and making suggestions, but avoiding statements. In short, Joyce remains Joyce, subtle, masculine, and ironic. His silences are deliberate, his cunning too consummate for simplistic answers, and his distances as artist too great for the narrator ever to reveal himself fully. It is this extraordinary combination of factual social reality and artful technique that gives *Dubliners* its unique quality.

NOTES

1. James Joyce, "A Portrait of the Artist" in *"A Portrait of the Artist as a Young Man": Text, Criticism, and Notes*, ed. Chester G. Anderson (New York: Viking Press, 1969), pp. 265–66.

2. Florence L. Walzl, "The Life Chronology of *Dubliners*," *James Joyce Quarterly*, 14 (Summer, 1977), 408–15.

3. If Joyce erred, his errors are of omission of certain agreeable aspects of Ireland—a possibility he admitted: "Sometimes thinking of Ireland it seems to me that I have been unnecessarily harsh. I have reproduced (in *Dubliners* at least) none of the attraction of the city. . . . I have not reproduced its ingenuous insularity and its hospitality. . . . I have not been just to its beauty" (*Letters* II, 166).

4. A major source for my data has been Conrad M. Arensberg and Solon T. Kimball, *Family and Community in Ireland*, 2nd ed. (Cambridge: Harvard University Press, 1968). This important monograph is a study primarily of rural Ireland, but for purposes of comparison gives relevant data about Ireland in general and Dublin.

5. In 1926, 30 percent of native-born Irish were living abroad. See Arensberg and Kimball, p. 95.

6. John A. O'Brien, ed., *The Vanishing Irish: The Enigma of the Modern World* (New York: McGraw-Hill Book Company, 1953), pp. 25–28; Arensberg and Kimball, pp. 99, 221–22; S. H. Cousens, "Population Trends in Ireland at the Beginning of the Twentieth Century," *Irish Geography*, 5, no. 5 (1968), 389, 399.

7. See data in O'Brien, p. 25. The marriage rate in 1891–1901 was 4.4; in 1901–11, 4.8; and 1911–26, 5.0.

8. See data in Arensberg and Kimball, pp. 99–101, and O'Brien, pp. 16, 27.

9. For tables showing the marriages of both sexes, 1841–1926, consult Arensberg and Kimball, p. 151. See also pp. 99–101, 221–22.

10. Arensberg and Kimball (p. 221) point out that "the release of the 1936 census figures in 1939 showed conclusively that the demographic trends that have marked Ireland since Famine times continue to persist. . . . Ireland continues to hold its record of possessing the highest percentage of unmarried men and women in the world."

11. Sean O'Faolain, "Love among the Irish," in O'Brien, pp. 111–22.

12. O'Brien, p. 32; Arensberg and Kimball (pp. 102–103) note that even as late as 1926 for every 100 married women under forty-five in Ireland, there were 131 children under five years of age in contrast to seventy-seven in the United States, seventy-one in England, ninety-three in Denmark and seventy-five in Germany.

13. Arland Ussher, "The Boundary between the Sexes," in O'Brien, p. 160.

14. Myrrha Bradshaw, ed., *Open Doors for Irishwomen: A Guide to the Professions Open to Educated Women in Ireland* (Dublin: Irish Central Bureau, 1907), pp. 2–4, 40.

15. *Ibid.*, pp. 6, 10, 60.

16. *Ibid.*, p. 27.

17. *Ibid.*, pp. 37–39, 70–77.

18. Ussher, p. 163.

19. Bradshaw, pp. 62–63.

20. *Thom's Official Directory of the United Kingdom of Great Britain and Ireland for the Year 1904* (Dublin: Alexander Thom and Company, 1904).

21. Arensberg and Kimball, pp. 332–60, 380–85.

22. *Ibid.*, pp. 337–38, 379–80.

23. For a summary of various interpretations of the sisters as characters, see Florence L. Walzl, "Joyce's 'The Sisters': A Development," *James Joyce Quarterly*, 10 (Summer, 1973), 375–421.

24. O'Faolain, in O'Brien, p. 116.

25. Maura Laverty, "Woman-shy Irishmen," in O'Brien, pp. 58–59.

26. See O'Faolain, in O'Brien, pp. 120–21, and Ussher, p. 158.

27. See Bryan MacMahon, "Getting on the High Road Again," in O'Brien, p. 217. MacMahon points out that even in the *New Catechism*, "company keeping" is retained as a "danger to chastity" in a long list of evils that includes "intemperance, bad companions, improper dances, immodest dress, . . . and indecent conversation. . . ."

28. Mary Frances Keating, "Marriage-shy Irishmen," in O'Brien, pp. 173–74.

29. Laverty, in O'Brien, p. 57.

30. Cited in J. B. Lyons, *James Joyce and Medicine* (Dublin: Dolmen Press, 1973), p. 93.

31. The earliest and most influential study of the structure of "The Dead" is that of David Daiches in *The Novel and the Modern World* (Chicago: University of Chicago Press, 1939), pp. 91–100. It analyzes the plot as a series of confrontations of the protagonist, Gabriel Conroy, with characters and situations that

are "assault[s] on the walled circle of Gabriel's egotism," and that eventually lead to self-realization. This interpretation of essential structure has been accepted, with individual modifications, by many later critics, including Allen Tate, "Three Commentaries," *Sewanee Review*, 58 (Winter, 1950), 10–15; Kenneth Burke, "Three Definitions," *Kenyon Review*, 13 (Spring, 1951), 186–92; Hugh Kenner, *Dublin's Joyce* (1956; rpt. Boston: Beacon Press, 1962), pp. 62–68; William York Tindall, *A Reader's Guide to James Joyce* (New York: Farrar, Straus and Giroux, 1959), pp. 42–49; and others. The fact that all the main confrontations of "The Dead" are with women has not received as much critical attention. An exception is Edward Brandabur's study "Arrayed for the Bridal: The Embodied Vision of 'The Dead,'" which gives a detailed psychological analysis of Gabriel's contacts with women throughout the story and argues that these encounters effect an ultimate realization of paralysis. See *Joyce's "The Dead,"* ed. William T. Moynihan (Boston: Allyn and Bacon, 1965), pp. 108–19. This essay was later incorporated into Brandabur's *A Scrupulous Meanness: A Study of Joyce's Early Work* (Urbana: University of Illinois Press, 1971), pp. 115–26.

BONNIE KIME SCOTT

Emma Clery in *Stephen Hero:* A Young Woman Walking Proudly Through the Decayed City

Aside from a few women like Eveline and Maria, whose viewpoints appear centrally and directly in *Dubliners*, Joyce's female characters are rarely studied or understood thoroughly as human beings. Complete, objective representation of women may have been beyond Joyce's capabilities or designs. As demonstrated in his probing letters to Nora, Joyce liked to think that women had secret lives of their own, unique though trivial.[1] This idea served as an aphrodisiac to Joyce, but hardly encouraged his development of serious-minded female characters. Archetypal characters like Molly Bloom and Anna Livia Plurabelle are important and independent, but fail to come across as complete, individualized women. Usually, Joyce's flower girls, peasant women, nursemaids, prostitutes, and college girls are met briefly at a party, passed on a street, glimpsed on a beach, or flashed in a dream or vision. Joyce typically filters their identities through the biased point of view of one of his male characters; indeed, the structuring of point of view is one of his most essential ironic techniques. Even in his early novel *Stephen Hero*, Joyce uses the shortcomings and preoccupations of his primary observer to show how these distort Stephen's experience of the world and of women. What is true for Stephen also holds for Gabriel Conroy, Mr. Duffy, Leopold Bloom, Buck Mulligan, and HCE. As readers, we should be aware of the inadequacy of these men's views of women. A sense of what Joyce's male characters miss or misinterpret is vital to understanding Joyce's depiction of women and the male-female relationship.

An excellent character to focus on in investigating relationships between men and women in Joyce's work is Emma Clery, a young college woman from the Catholic middle class who is seen through

Stephen's eyes in both *Stephen Hero* and *A Portrait of the Artist as a Young Man*. Emma is an unusual woman in Joyce's canon because she has intellectual aspirations. We can also get to know her better than most of his women because she exists in two versions created over a period of some ten years. Most critics disapprove of what Joyce has done to Emma in the later version. As Theodore Spencer puts it, he converts a "living personality" to an "anonymous girl" usually known only by her initials.[2] Bernard Benstock finds this "overly refined extension" of *Stephen Hero*'s Emma "at best a failed heroine: her timidity of spirit and conventional demeanor disqualify her as a person."[3] It is largely Stephen Dedalus who does the disqualifying through his restrictive, symbolic interpretation of Emma's "demeanor" in thought and poetry. Joyce presents Stephen as an unbalanced, preoccupied observer of E——C—— in *A Portrait*. Charles Rossman has considered some of the probable causes for Stephen's flawed vision of Emma. He feels that, as a symptom of Stephen's alienation from his physical being, the young man subjects the potentially warm relationship with Emma to his "spiritual-heroic refrigerating apparatus."[4] Paradoxically, he also transforms the real Emma into an ideal "masculine erotic fantasy" in his "Villanelle" and an earlier poem. This symptom of his discomfort with external reality is very much out of keeping with Stephen's life-centered aesthetic.[5]

Emma asserts herself even in *A Portrait*, in which she utters only two sentences and is seen in fleeting glimpses. She resists Stephen's efforts to refrigerate her, idealize her, or assign her to a pigeonhole. Rossman notes that her literal presence intrudes on Stephen even as he attempts to reduce her to a satisfying poetic image.[6] In addition, her identity is reflected in other characters like the wading bird-girl, the flower girl, and Davin's peasant woman, all of whom haunt Stephen.[7] As readers, we may not be satisfied with Stephen's evaluation of her. We wonder what brought Emma to the library steps, what interest—if any—she had in the priest, and what was discussed in those quiet, gay conversations with her companions. In order to capture the "whatness" of Emma that Stephen seems to have missed, we must turn to her fuller representation in *Stephen Hero* and to the Dublin background from which she was created.

In *Stephen Hero*, Emma Clery is participating in a genteel and quiet women's revolution, and she may well be experiencing conflicting emotions. Undergraduate education for Catholic middle-class women was only twenty years old. It was still the accepted pattern for a young woman to attend a convent school for a few years, learning some Latin and French, music, dancing, and needlework, and then to retire to marriage and motherhood. This was the pattern followed by Stephen's ladylike mother. Mary Dedalus plays the piano beautifully for parlor entertainments, but she submerges her cultural interests when her husband does not share them. Stephen is amazed that she once read "all kinds of new plays" and that she wants to read and discuss Ibsen with him (*SH* 85–87). Stephen's sister Isabel seems destined to be a typical, pious wife once she emerges from her convent (*SH* 126); she seems devoid of intellectual interest and ability. His sister Dilly in *Ulysses* has the desire to be educated, but no family backing. It may be symbolic of the new woman that Dilly uses the money she has pried from Simon Dedalus for domestic purposes to buy a French primer.

If Stephen Dedalus had problems being a young artist in Dublin at the turn of the century, Emma had problems of her own merely being a student. Catholic women could expect at best a fourth-class college education in Dublin. The finest instruction went to the Protestant men at Trinity College—a true lecturing institution with a three-century tradition, an excellent faculty, an extensive campus ("the grey block of Trinity" [*P* 180]), a library, athletic fields, and extracurricular activities. Catholics argued "the University Question" in this era in an effort to obtain equal facilities. What they had was a twenty-year-old "Royal University," an institution which supplied limited building funds, administered examinations, gave cash awards, and rather indiscriminately granted degrees to students of member colleges.[8] None of the colleges had dining halls, libraries, or athletic fields. One member institution, Joyce's own University College, offered a standard higher than that in other colleges for Catholic men, despite the limited resources and authority of its administrators. U. C. D. had a fifty-year tradition, dating back to its founding by Cardinal Newman. Its campus consisted of three stately, graceful eighteenth-century mansions facing St. Stephen's Green. There were active and reasonably stimulating extracurricular groups like the Literary and Historical Society and the student journal, *St. Stephen's*. The Jesuit instruction commanded respect. However, there does seem to have been a real basis for Joyce's criticisms of the faculty, shown in Stephen's interviews with the College President in *Stephen Hero* and the Dean of Studies in *A Portrait*, and in the dull physics lecture, also in *A Portrait*.[9] The Jesuits were disturbingly pious and their tastes did not run to the modern continental literature that fascinated young Joyce. There is no question that Trinity College offered a sounder program of studies, more extensive lectures, and a more prestigious and competent faculty.

Institutions for Catholic women had all of the disadvantages of the Catholic men's U. C. D. and fewer advantages. The women's colleges Emma could have attended were Alexandra College (founded 1866), St. Mary's University and High School (founded 1882 by Dominican nuns), and Loreto College (founded in 1895 by the Irish Loreto Sisters). "Undenominational" Alexandra College was predominantly a Protestant institution once the Catholic women's colleges opened. In this era Protestant women were not admitted to Trinity, but depended on it for borrowed faculty. Trinity resisted all attempts at alliance made by the women's college.[10] The women in the Catholic colleges took the same national examinations as the Catholic men and, like them, studied at the National Library. Thus the college education of Catholic men and women was similar in many ways. Mary Colum asserts that she and Joyce had been "educated in the same way."[11] Gabriel Conroy notes in "The Dead" that his career and that of Miss Ivors "had been parallel, first at the University and then as teachers" (D 188). It seems telling, however, that women graduates of the Royal University and its successor, the National University—Mary Colum included—never seem to identify their college; University College men never fail to do so.

There were notable inequities which may have contributed to this difference in attitude. Like the Protestant women, the Catholic female students depended on "visiting faculty." Thus one might expect that Emma would have a harder time finding a faculty member with whom to discuss aesthetics than Stephen did. Though Emma expresses an interest in the paper Stephen is to deliver in his society, she would have been barred from attending. Father William Delaney, president of University College, strenuously opposed admitting women to his school's lectures. If a Loreto woman had a contact (often a brother), she might be asked to write a trivial column called "Girl Graduates' Chat" for St. Stephen's. In Stephen Hero, a friend of Emma's writes for a similar column, "The Female Fellow" (SH 187), and "Glynn's sister" contributes an article in Irish (SH 182). Both efforts receive Stephen's scorn.[12]

Women were also restricted in their residential lives. If they came from outside Dublin, they could live in inexpensive hostels run by nuns like Mother Patrick, the prioress of St. Mary's. Though Emma lives at home, some of her friends must reside in these facilities: Stephen watches a group of them "returning to the convent—demure corridors and simple dormitories, a quiet rosary of hours" (*SH* 184). Former residents of hostels, like Mary Colum, report that curfews and restrictions of theater attendance were imposed, frustrating the interest in theater shared by many young women.[13] Parents imposed their own curfews on women living at home, as Emma's father does in *Stephen Hero* (*SH* 152). The nuns who ran the women's colleges must have provided very different role models from those of the Jesuits who controlled the men's college. Mary Colum contrasts the "self-sacrificing" nuns who administered her convent education with the occasional learned Jesuit who would be brought in to explain important issues.[14] Both of the Catholic women's colleges were extensions of the traditional convent schools for younger girls; domesticity and piety were part of the tradition.

Despite the inequities in educational opportunities, the examination system of the Royal University placed women into competition with men, and they did surprisingly well. Francis Skeffington, Joyce's respected friend and a champion of women's education, used evidence of female performance on exams to argue women's rights to equal facilities and advantages in any plans for the reform of Catholic education. In the essay he published privately alongside Joyce's equally controversial "The Day of the Rabblement," Skeffington tabulates the number of honors won by women students. By 1900, women were earning 28.5 percent of all the honors granted, a figure that had climbed steadily since 1884.[15] In the 1894 competitions, St. Mary's had come in a very presentable third behind Queen's College, Belfast, and University College.[16] Especially in the modern languages—Joyce's specialty, but usually the area chosen by the women instead of the "masculine" classics—men were feeling pressured by the women. Though indifferent himself, Stephen is aware of the examination rivalry:

> Stephen who did not care very much whether he succeeded or failed in the examination was very much amused observing the jealousies and nervous anxieties which tried to conceal themselves under airs of carelessness. . . . [The students'] excitement was so genuine that even the excitement of sex failed to overcome it. The girl students were not the subject of the usual sniggers and jokes but were regarded with some aversion as sly enemies. Some of the young men eased their enmity and vindicated their

superiority at the same time by saying that it was no wonder the women would do well seeing that they could study ten hours [all] a day all the year round [*SH* 130–31].

Even outside of the examination situation, male and female students did not associate with one another easily. Mary Colum reports that "male and female students at the university in those days paid little attention to one another, as such relations were frowned on by the authorities."[17] Her anecdotes about some women undergraduates' opinions of James Joyce show that there was a large gulf between him and at least the college women of her acquaintance. One student, who rebuked Joyce for supposedly sending her a postcard with an unacceptable message, received a "haughty reply, phrased with extreme politeness but conveying to her that it was foolish to imagine that he, James A. Joyce, would have perpetrated such a missive, as he never remembered to have seen her, and anyhow never communicated with girl students unless they were family friends."[18] Another companion pointed Joyce out to Mary Colum, labeling him sarcastically a self-proclaimed genius, and a specialist in girls' studies (modern languages). The young Colum was not impressed by his appearance or his reputation for giving up his religion and frequenting evil places.[19]

Indeed, if James Joyce had not been a close friend of Eugene and Richard Sheehy, he might never have observed young Catholic college women closely enough to have created E——C——. By the time Joyce was in college, his family had sunk too far on the social and economic scales to provide social entertainments for young people. Stanislaus Joyce considers Joyce's relationship with the Sheehys "practically the only experience of what might be called social life" his brother had in Dublin.[20] Joyce sang, played parlor games, danced, and occasionally discussed art or politics with the mixed group. He was probably much less out of sympathy with the Sheehys than Stephen is with their counterpart, the Daniels, in *Stephen Hero*. Joyce carefully observed the people and activities at these gatherings. No fewer than five of his collected "epiphanies" are located "at Sheehy's, Belvedere Place." Many of them involved one of the four lively Sheehy daughters, Hanna, Margaret, Mary, and Kathleen. They and their female friends were undoubtedly Joyce's best models for E——C——. All but Margaret were students of the Royal University, attending classes at St. Mary's or Loreto. Stanislaus Joyce has suggested that Mary was the inspiration for two of Joyce's early romantic poems, and that he held some form of undeclared passion for her.[21] In *Stephen Hero*, Stephen seems to feel that the Daniels have attempted to set a Catholic marriage trap in their home, inviting promising young men to meet their "marriageable daughters" (*SH* 42). Stephen gazes with mistrust at the emblem of the Catholic family, the picture of the Sacred Heart, and at the daughters' performances (*SH* 44). In fact, Hanna and Mary Sheehy eventually did marry young men brought to the parlor by their brothers. But they were not the young dolts pictured by Stephen; they were the students Joyce respected most at University College, Francis Skeffington and Thomas Kettle. The Sacred Heart certainly did not overshadow the Sheehy-Skeffington marriage; they eventually "thought themselves out of the Catholic church,"[22] just as Joyce had done.

Our knowledge of the extracurricular activities of the Sheehy daughters allows us to speculate about the kinds of activities that were open to young women like Emma Clery. All of the Sheehy women did some form of writing. During the time Joyce spent with them, Margaret was the most active. She gave recitations in the Literary, Dramatic and Music Society and wrote *Cupid's Confidante*, in which Joyce played the leading role.[23] Under a pseudonym, Kathleen Sheehy O'Brien wrote the farce *Apartments*, which was performed in the Abbey Theatre in 1923.[24] Mary Sheehy Kettle published a long memoir of her husband's life to preface his collected essays. Hanna Sheehy-Skeffington wrote political and suffragist essays and helped publish a feminist weekly. Other young women joined AE's poetic circle or wrote for Arthur Griffith's *The United Irishman*; their numbers included Ethna Carbery, Lizzy Twigg, Ella Young, Alice Milligan, and Susan Mitchell, women of widely varying abilities.

Nationalism, which often could not be separated from literary activity during the Irish Literary Revival, was perhaps the most popular interest to which young women devoted themselves. Mary Colum describes the efforts of her schoolmates to re-create the dress of ancient Celtic women; Joyce may have gotten the idea for the austere bodice and patriotic pin worn by the nationalist Miss Ivors in "The Dead" from the usual dress of Kathleen Sheehy (*JJ* 256).[25] Hanna Sheehy-Skeffington proved a more ardent nationalist than her pacifist husband and even tried to carry messages to the insurgents in the G. P. O. during the Easter Rising.[26] Still an active nationalist in the mid-1920s, she organized the patriotic women's protest against Sean O'Casey's

The Plough and the Stars and defended her position against the play-wright in letters and an open debate.[27] The Ladies' Land League, founded by Fanny Parnell in 1881, had set the precedent for women's nationalistic groups, and organizations of its type were renewed by turn-of-the-century female leaders like Maud Gonne.[28] The Gaelic League also welcomed women and, as we see in *Stephen Hero*, taught the language in coeducational classes, where the women often were brighter and less embarrassed by the presence of the opposite sex than were some of the men (*SH* 60–61).

Feminism was another major interest of young college women of Emma's era and can again be illustrated by the Sheehy family. Hanna Sheehy-Skeffington shared the feminist causes that her husband sure-ly brought to Joyce's attention with "A Forgotten Aspect of the Uni-versity Question" and in discussion. In *Stephen Hero*, McCann, con-stantly labeled "the feminist," is modeled on Skeffington. When Fran-cis and Hanna married in 1903, they "each took the other's name as a gesture of belief in equal status for women,"[29] and in 1904, Sheehy-Skeffington resigned his position as registrar of University College rather than give up his campaign for the admission of women. The Sheehy-Skeffingtons eventually joined another couple that Joyce knew in his youth, James and Gretta Cousins, in founding the militant Irish Women's Franchise League and an incendiary suffrage weekly, the *Irish Citizen*.[30]

This new female tradition is a part of Joyce's world which has been largely neglected in previous background studies. It is the tradition in which Emma Clery is trying to operate when she meets Stephen in the Daniels' parlor in *Stephen Hero*. Joyce, still working within established practices of the novel, sets up a conventional series of encounters for his young couple, who try to know and evaluate each other and establish a relationship. The situation is further complicated by the fact that, like Emma, Stephen is also attempting to transform social con-ventions. With increased understanding of the background for Emma Clery, we can better evaluate Stephen as an observer and more fully appreciate Joyce's irony in the creation of Stephen's solipsistic, male point of view. We suspect Emma of awkwardness, naiveté, and gaps in knowledge. But we suspect Stephen of hypocrisy, blindness, and insensitivity in his assessment and treatment of her.

From Emma's first appearance in *Stephen Hero*, her energy and initiative are attractive. Breaking with traditions in her own way, Emma dispenses with ceremony and assumes control of the situation:

> Without waiting for Miss Daniel's introduction, she said:
> —I think we know each other already.
> She sat beside him on the sofa and he found out that she was studying in the same college with the Miss Daniels and that she always signed her name in Irish. She said Stephen should «learn Irish too» and join the League. A young man of the company, [with] whose face wore always the same look of studied purpose, spoke with her across Stephen addressing her familiarly by her Irish name. Stephen therefore spoke very formally and always addressed her as 'Miss Clery.' She seemed on her part to include him in the «general scheme of her nationalising charm: and when he helped her into her jacket she allowed his hands to rest for a moment against the warm flesh of her shoulders» [SH 46–47].

Emma may "know" Stephen from childhood (from their talk on the tram steps in *A Portrait*)—a partial justification for her informality. She spontaneously discloses her interest in the Gaelic Revival, and she is direct and affirmative about her idea that Stephen should learn Irish. Stephen assumes an air of formality in order to feel superior to a competing young man. He seems passive in the conversation and cautious about its implications. However, Stephen is quick to respond to Emma's physical attractions. He may already be projecting a "temptress" image onto Emma, who is said to be using "charm" because "she allowed his hands to rest for a moment against the warm flesh of her shoulders." She may have felt he was rather awkward in helping her on with her coat.

In their successive meetings, Emma remains energetic and seems in control of the situation. Stephen is often attracted by her appearance, her full, warm body, and his static and distilled "impression of her when she was at her finest moment." At other times, he is repelled by her manners and even by her mind. Emma does persuade Stephen to begin learning Irish, but if she is trying to convert him to nationalism, she has not succeeded. Stephen is interested in Emma, not in nationalism. Emma remains her own agent, failing to grant Stephen the preferential treatment he deems appropriate: "Emma allowed him to see her home several times but she did not seem to have reserved herself for him. The youth was piqued at this for above all things he hated to be compared with others . . ." (SH 66).[31] He waits jealously to walk Emma home while she converses with a popular young priest, Father

Moran. Now, more definitely than before, Stephen sees Emma as an encouraging, desirable temptress. Even the priest accuses her of flirtation: "One must not believe all the complimentary things the ladies say of us. . . . The ladies are a little given to—what shall I say—fibbing, I am afraid" (*SH* 65). As Stephen watches Emma and the priest, he attributes biological drives to Emma as well as to Moran. "Father Moran's eyes were so clear and tender-looking, Emma stood to his gaze in such a poise of bold careless «pride of the flesh» that Stephen longed to precipitate the two into each other's arms . . ." (*SH* 66). Stephen is outraged by what he deems "Irish ineffectualness," or the religious and cultural inhibitions of both the young woman and the priest.[32] The rebellious artist is reading his own theories about Irish Catholic puritanism as well as his own erotic interests into the situation.

The account of the subsequent conversation between Stephen and Emma shows Stephen's growing dissatisfaction with Emma's manners and mind:

> Her loud forced manners shocked him at first until his mind had thoroughly mastered the stupidity of hers. She criticised the Miss Daniels very sharply, assuming, much to Stephen's discomfort, an identical temper in him. She coquetted with knowledge, asking Stephen could he not persuade the President of his College to admit women to the college. Stephen told her to apply to McCann who was the champion of women. She laughed at this and said with «genuine dismay» "Well, honestly, isn't he a dreadful-looking artist?" She treated femininely everything that young men are supposed to regard as serious but she made polite exception for Stephen himself and for the Gaelic Revival. She asked him wasn't he reading a paper and what it was on. She would give anything to go and hear him: she was awfully fond of the theatre herself and a gypsy woman had once read her hand and told her she would be an actress. She had been three times to the pantomime and asked Stephen what he liked best in pantomime. Stephen said he liked a good clown but she said that she preferred ballets. Then she wanted to know did he go out much to dances and pressed him to join an Irish dancing class of which she was a member. Her eyes had begun to «imitate the expression» of Father Moran's—an expression of tender «significance» when the conversation was at the lowest level of banality [*SH* 66–67].

It is interesting to note that Stephen is most critical of qualities in Emma that he himself has displayed. She has "loud forced manners"; he sometimes breaks into a loud fit of laughter (*SH* 52) and is a master of aloof manners. She criticizes the Misses Daniels "very sharply" and passes McCann off as a "dreadful-looking artist." He is extremely

critical of the Daniels circle (*SH* 43–46) and has his own criticisms of McCann's methods and causes. Emma has perhaps perceived
Stephen's critical attitude accurately. She is wrong, however, to
assume that he will abandon his aloofness and share in her raillery.[33]
Stephen's general charge of "stupidity" is also suspect. Is it coquetting
with knowledge to want the benefits of University College? In treating
femininely what most young men were supposed to consider serious,
Emma may be responding to Stephen's own behavior. With the exception of literature (his special interest), he considers the interests of his
fellow students trivial. He pretends to have an interest in the Gaelic
League and perhaps in women's rights for the sake of his own flirtation
with Emma. Even Emma's sympathizers would have to admit that her
recorded remarks hardly reveal intellectual depth. She may miss
Stephen's sarcasm. Does he really like a good clown? She moves
rapidly from one subject to the next, never really developing a topic.
This does show energy, however. Perhaps Emma is too lively for
Stephen, controlling the conversation more than he wishes, and again
encouraging him into popular activities. It should also be noted that
what appears in *Stephen Hero* is an edited version of the conversation
designed primarily to reveal Stephen's assessment, not the event
itself. A fuller version might show greater depths to Emma.

These first two conversations between Emma and Stephen set the
pattern for their relationship, revealing both its intellectual and emotional possibilities and its potential for failure. Four areas of serious
discussion which Emma and Stephen might pursue are social criticism
(focused so far upon student acquaintances), the Irish Revival, aesthetics as examined in Stephen's paper, and women's rights. Emma
repeatedly provides provocative introductions to these subjects.
Stephen seems unable or unwilling to pursue them with her.

Emma tries again in the third conversation to discuss student acquaintances with Stephen, expressing her amusement "that McCann
should have a desire for matrimony" (*SH* 153). Stephen is bound to
share her amusement, having already aimed his "agile bullets" at
McCann's sexual purity (*SH* 51). The related subjects of sex and marriage are social topics which Stephen and Emma might well discuss.
They miss an innocuous opportunity in this case. Stephen saves his
student criticisms for his own internal monologues or occasional pro-
nouncements to his brother Maurice and the few male students he
respects. Emma seems to him an inferior critic, bound up in the "toy

life" (*SH* 187) he objects to. But he fails to see her own objections to that life. He observes that she plays their parlor games and participates in their "enthusiasms." She praises things that Stephen considers inferior, like Hughes's poetry, Moran's singing, and her friend's writing in the "Female Fellow" column. She fails to single him out as superior to the young man "whose face wore always the same look of studied purpose" at the Daniels' (*SH* 46), or the two stupid men in their Irish class, or Father Moran. He has seen her give "the same expression of tender solicitude" (*SH* 189) too often; it is comparable to the "soft seriousness" given indiscriminately by one of the "studious" but (in his opinion) unintelligent Daniels daughters (*SH* 46). In equating Emma with others, Stephen does the very thing that he most resents having done to him. He also seems unaware of the biases created by his own engagement in male rivalry.

Emma seems sincere in her interest in the Irish Revival. She attends Gaelic classes regularly, visits the Aran Islands, and works on Old Irish at the National Library. Still, Stephen never has a "severe" discussion of nationalism with her; this he reserves for his male colleague, Madden (Davin in *A Portrait*). Their debate is straightforward, lively, and fully reported (*SH* 62–65). Stephen feigns interest in learning Gaelic only to gain access to Emma's attentions. He sings Irish songs to curry her favor. He never lets her suspect that he makes a distinction between the "compact body of national revivalists" and those with "ideas of their own" (*SH* 38–39). He never tries to learn about her studies or her travels to rural Ireland.[34]

In contrast, Emma is eager to discuss Stephen's great interest in aesthetics. On both their second and third walks, Emma encourages Stephen to talk about his paper. But Stephen is never willing to discuss it or any other aesthetic matter with her. These debates are reserved for Madden, McCann, Dr. Dillon, and Cranly. Because of his need for "sympathy from a friend," Stephen reads his paper to one woman, his mother. Mrs. Dedalus's reception of the paper is recorded in suspicious tones, which reflect Stephen's own attitudes. She is supposed to have an inadequate definition for beauty and to have ulterior motives for hearing the paper:

> His mother who had never suspected probably that "beauty" could be anything more than a convention of the drawingroom or a natural antecedent to marriage and married life was surprised to see the extraordinary honour which her son conferred upon it. Beauty, to the mind of such a

woman, was often a synonym for licentious ways and probably for this reason she was relieved to find that the excesses of this new worship were supervised by a recognized saintly authority. However as the essayist's recent habits were not very re-assuring she decided to combine a discreet motherly solicitude with an interest, which without being open to the accusation of factitiousness was at first intended as a compliment [*SH* 84].

Mrs. Dedalus goes on to a careful reading of several of Ibsen's plays, demonstrating greater concentration than her husband is capable of. She is open-minded enough to pronounce them "magnificent plays indeed," and even Stephen has to recognize "genuine sentiment" in her praise of Ibsen's depiction of human nature. Stephen thinks this a "well-worn generality," but it actually represents one of Joyce's most important criteria for art.

Though Stephen discusses Ibsen rather haughtily with his mother, he is loathe to share his knowledge of the playwright with one of the Daniels daughters, put off by what he interprets as her reaction to his artistic authority: "she was impressed by a possible vastness of the unknown, complimented to confer with one who conferred directly with the exceptional" (*SH* 46). When Emma appears immediately after this incident, her coming is mystically termed an "advent," and we sense that Stephen has definitely lost all interest in teaching Ibsen to women. But Emma repeatedly brings up aesthetics. She says she would give anything to hear Stephen's paper and, once it has been aired, she baits him with the charge, "I hear you read a dreadful paper in the college—all kinds of ideas in it." Emma's tone does not ingratiate her with Stephen because the reception of the paper has been hostile and now it is a sore subject. Stephen has no inclination to explain his ideas to Emma or even to try to elicit her sympathy. The male students, Madden and Cranly, are the only people from whom he accepts this kind of comfort.

After failing in their third conversation to elicit a response from Stephen on artistic ideas, Emma returns to another of her interests, women's rights.

> —But I'm sure you're a woman hater. You've got so stand-offish, you know, so reserved. Perhaps you don't like ladies' company?
> Stephen pressed her arm a little by way of a disclaimer.
> —Are you a believer in the emancipation of women too? she asked.
> —To be sure! said Stephen.
> —Well, I'm glad to hear you say that, at any rate. I didn't think you were in favour of women.

—Oh, I am very liberal—like Father Dillon—he is very liberal-minded.
—Yes? Isn't he? she said in a puzzled manner . . . [SH 153].

Initially, Emma is criticising Stephen's manner toward her. The question about not liking ladies' company indicates that she already senses the inadequacy of their previous conversations. Stephen's expression of belief in "the emancipation of women" may pertain only to sexual liberation—a mockery Emma is too naive to apprehend. Stephen's thoughts about the lives of his mother and sister indicate some desire to emancipate women from the sterility of their environment and their subservience to the church, but he is hardly an advocate of female political liberation, and Emma seems to detect his irony. She responds to Stephen's comparison of himself and Dr. Dillon "in a puzzled manner." According to an earlier discussion between Stephen and Emma, the president of Stephen's College (Dillon) needs to be persuaded to admit women. Also, Dillon hardly qualifies as a liberal in Stephen's interview with him about his paper.[35] As was the case with the Irish Revival, Stephen pretends to be more sympathetic with Emma's interests than he actually is. His true opinions come out in a debate with a male, "the feminist, McCann."

McCann's interpretation of the emancipation of women is clearly set forth in *Stephen Hero*. It is in fact a condensation of Francis Skeffington's "A Forgotten Aspect of the University Question": "He believed that the sexes should be educated together in order to accustom them early to each other's influences and he believed that women should be afforded the same opportunities as were afforded to the so-called superior sex and he believed that women had the right to compete with men in every branch of social and intellectual activity" (SH 49).[36] Instead of politely agreeing with McCann, as he does with Emma, Stephen "delighted to riddle" McCann's theories "with agile bullets" (SH 49). It would have been interesting to see Stephen pose his objections to Emma, instead of to another man, and good for Emma to have developed agile responses. Stephen's challenges are indeed less clever and agile than he thinks. McCann is finally troubled by Stephen's flippancy toward the church, not by his suggestions of activities unsuitable to women—some of which McCann agrees with (SH 50). Joyce treats both McCann and Stephen ironically in their debates and should probably not be identified exclusively with either side.

Stephen's failure to respond to the subjects of discussion introduced by Emma suggests that he has different plans for their relationship. He does not wish to share ideas and activities with a "female fellow." He may feel that, at best, Emma's genteel feminine revolution will only make her like the commonplace male students he finds futile and intolerable. He would prefer to involve her in his own revolution—a resistance of social and religious strictures and an assertion of natural human sensuality or "pride of the flesh." Unfortunately, Stephen is as inept at introducing his own subjects of discussion as he is at entertaining Emma's. Emma replies to those of Stephen's ideas that he expresses, but he is unable to handle her responses sensibly.

Once we recognize the nature of Stephen's revolutionary ideas, we can also understand that his preoccupation with religion and sensuality has affected his perceptions of Emma and his behavior toward her from the start of their relationship. Their effect becomes particularly strong in the later interviews. The church has taught Stephen to idealize and love (even sensually) a female image, "a «weaker and more engaging vessel»" (*SH* 112), the Virgin Mary. This is a habit that he readily transfers to earthly women, including Emma. Both Emma and Stephen have been taught, in the tradition of Aristotle, Aquinas, and St. Paul, that male as well as female chastity is essential to virtuous conduct. In Emma's era, society, enforcing the double standard, made chastity the *sine qua non* of Catholic maidenhood. But Stephen resents the church's control over human lives. He wants to believe that sensuality is not sinful. Specifically, he objects to the church's control over women—his sister's pious, purposeless life and his mother's allegiance, which even impels her to report her son's deeds to her confessor. He makes a special point of getting Father Moran to agree that women are important helpers of the church (*P* 220). He goes into his relationship with Emma prepared to believe that she will have greater loyalty to the church than to him. But he is just as convinced of the primacy of "pride of the flesh" in all human beings, including Emma.

Equipped with these notions, Stephen tries to read Emma's intentions and motivations in her manners and reaches some questionable conclusions. He recalls a scene of departure after an evening walk: "They smiled at each other; and again in the centre of her amiableness he discerned a [centre] point of illwill and he suspected that by her code of honour she was obliged to insist on the forbearance of the male and to despise him for forbearing" (*SH* 68).[37] Again preferring to communicate with a male, Stephen discusses Emma's sensual nature at greatest length with Lynch. Stephen believes that Emma has been encouraging his advances and bends religious terminology to suit his purposes:

—Jesus said "Whoso looketh upon a woman to lust after her hath already committed adultery with her in his heart": but he did not condemn "adultery." Besides it is impossible not to commit "adultery."
—Quite impossible.
—Consequently if I see a woman inclined for oracle I go to her: if she has no inclination I stay away.
—But that girl has an inclination for oracle.
—That's the tantalising part of it: I know she has. It's very unfair of her to tantalise me. I must go to where I am sure of my ground [SH 191].

Stephen uses another religious adaptation, his own version of the confessional, to express to Emma his interest in her private life:

—I wish you would go to confession to me, Emma, said Stephen from his heart.
—That's a dreadful thing to say . . . Why would you like that?
—To hear your sins.
—Stephen!
—To hear you murmur them into my ear and say you were sorry and would never [do] commit them again and ask me to forgive you. And I would forgive you and make you promise to commit them every time you liked and say "God Bless you, my dear child."
—O, for shame, Stephen! Such a way to talk of the sacraments!
Stephen had expected that she would blush but her cheek maintained its innocence and her eyes grew brighter and brighter.
—You'd get tired of that too.
—Do you think so? said Stephen making an effort not to be surprised at such an intelligent remark.
—You'd be a dreadful flirt, I'm sure. You get tired of everything so quickly—just the way you did in the Gaelic League.
—People should not think of the end in the beginning of flirtations, should they?
—Perhaps not [SH 154].

This topic is of true interest to Stephen: thus his words come "from his heart." The scheme is satisfying to Stephen because it allows him to modify what he considers woman's unfortunate subservience to the church; by usurping the priest's role, he diverts woman's attention from the church to himself and his sensual interests. He uses women just as he believes the priests do, thus falling into the church's own patriarchal scheme of male authority. Emma's playful reaction indicates that she is not prudish or obsessed with religious proprieties. Her "for shame" seems more a typical taunt than a reprimand. She goes on to make a remark about satiety that surprises Stephen with its "intelligence" (a surprise he tries to conceal). She also brings up the idea of flirtation, perhaps aware that her supposed flirtations have troubled Stephen throughout their relationship. Stephen, in his final response, is as romantic as he ever has been. This discussion, rather than shocking and alienating Emma, produces the sweetest closing of any of their meetings in *Stephen Hero*. They are listening to each other and adjusting their responses. Thinking over the situation later, Stephen has tenuous hopes for their relationship:

> He remembered the first mood of monstrous dissatisfaction which had overcome him on his entrance into Dublin life and how it was her beauty that had appeased him. Now she seemed to offer him rest. He wondered did she understand him or sympathise with him and was the vulgarity of her manners only a condescension of one who was consciously playing the game. He knew that it was not for such an image that he had constructed a theory of art and life and a garland of verse and yet if he could have been sure of her he would have held his art and verses lightly enough. The longing for a mad night of love came upon him, a desperate willingness to cast his soul away, his life and his art, and to bury them all with her under fathoms of «lust-laden» slumber. . . . The spirits of the tame sodalists, unsullied and undeserving, he would petrify amid a ring of Jesuits in the circle of foolish and grotesque virginities and ascend above them and their baffled icons to where his Emma, with no detail of her earthly form or vesture abated, invoked him from a Mohammadan paradise [*SH* 158–59].

After witnessing Stephen and Emma achieving a moment of tenuous communication, the reader may be astonished by the end of this passage. Stephen leaps from a real and promising situation to an erotic, mystical scheme of his own, a plan which even renounces his artistic aspirations. He will bury the frustrations of Dublin in sex. Emma will serve him as both sex object and replacement deity. There is no way to enact the plan immediately. Emma goes away. Dublin becomes more oppressive as Stephen witnesses the purposeless death of his sister. He tries to overcome thanatos with eros, and again imagines committing fornication with Emma (*SH* 162).

When Emma and Stephen meet months later, Stephen's provocative notions begin their destructive work. Emma starts a discussion in her familiar manner of mock accusation, probably hoping to know Stephen better. She gets less—and more—than she expects:

—Everyone says you have dreadful ideas, that you read dreadful books.
You're a mystic or something. Do you know what I heard a girl say?
   —No. What?
   That you didn't believe in God.
   They were walking along the Green inside the chains and as she said this
she gave more of her body's warmth to him and her eyes looked at him with
an expression of solicitude. Stephen looked into them steadfastly.
   —Never mind God, Emma, he said. You interest me much more that that
old gentleman does.
   —What gentleman? said Emma frankly.
   —The middle-aged gentleman with the aviary—Jehovah the Second.
   —You must not say such things to me, I told you that before.
   —Very good, Emma. I see you are afraid you will lose the faith. But you
need't be afraid of my influence [SH 187–88].

For the first time, Emma definitely recoils from Stephen, imposing a
form of puritan censorship. But Stephen does change the tone and
direction of the discussion with bewildering suddenness. He risks
alienating Emma from his revolution instead of involving her. Following this exchange, Stephen is suddenly put off by Emma's rebuff, her
imagined "solicitude," and perhaps by the symbolic chains that are on
the periphery of their walk through the Green. He resolves never to
see her again. Emma is more resilient. She halts in the shadow of the
trees—a position which Stephen finds "equivocal." She is willing to
continue the conversation on a theme which Stephen has introduced.
She tries to get him to clarify and define his terms.

   —Do I interest you so much as that? she said, speaking at last in a rich
significant voice.
   —Of course you do, said Stephen trying to match her tone. I know that
you are alive and human.
   —But so many people are alive.
   —You are a woman, Emma.
   —Would you call me a woman now? Don't you think I am still a girl?
   . . .
   —No, Emma, he said. You are not a girl any longer.
   —But you are not a man, are you? she said quickly for pride and youth
and desire were beginning to inflame her cheek even in the shadow.
   —I am a hobbledehoy, said Stephen.
   She leaned a little more towards him and the same expression of tender
solicitude appeared in her eyes. The warmth of her body seemed to flow
into his and without a moment's hesitation he put his hand into his
pocket and began to finger out his coins [SH 188–89].

Stephen is no longer participating in the discussion. In matching her
tone, he falls into the hypocritical habits of agreement demonstrated

earlier. The accurate "hobbledehoy" slips out almost unconsciously, perhaps making it all the more valid. Stephen is far from expert in explaining himself to a young woman. His terms are not unique or pleasing: there is nothing very select about being alive, human, or a woman. Emma cannot possibly feel appreciated for herself. Emma is warm, but Stephen turns cold, fingering his coins. As he leaves the scene, Stephen's fickle allegiance is quickly diverted to a strange woman in a black straw hat. After hearing her "Good night, love," and her request that he walk with her, Stephen offers all of his coins to her. Knowing nothing about her, he creates an archetypal identity for her and allows her to take over Emma's place in his "religion" of moral revolution.

Despite his mental dismissal of Emma, Stephen is tempted by her physical appearance once again. He sees her in a perfect moment, contrasted to the decay around her, and posed against the trees in the rain, conditions which have proved alluring to him in the past.

> —Do you know, Emma, even from my window I could see your hips moving your waterproof? I saw a young woman walking proudly through the decayed city. Yes, that's the way you walk: you're proud of being young and proud of being a woman. Do you know when I caught sight of you from my window—do you know what I felt?
>
> . . .
>
> —I felt that I longed to hold you in my arms—your body. I longed for you to take me in your arms. That's all . . . Then I thought I would run after you and say that to you . . . Just to live one night together, Emma, and then to say goodbye in the morning and never to see each other again! There is no such thing as love in the world: only people are young . . . [*SH* 197–98].

The reader has been prepared for this moment by sharing Stephen's thoughts, but as far as Emma is concerned, Stephen makes a mad, unpredictable leap in their relationship. Instead of communicating on a reasonable level, Stephen gives fragmentary explanations. His attempt to "liberate" Emma paralyzes her; she murmurs her unimaginative responses as if from memory.

Stephen tries to re-create the event and his motivations in a conversation with Lynch. Stephen's poorly articulated theory makes marriage a form of simony, "monstrous because it revolts our notion of what is humanly possible." Stephen considers it impossible to "swear to love, honor and obey" until his dying day. Both Lynch and Stephen assume that Emma would demand marriage, though she has never been consulted; Stephen also assumes that the woman in the black straw hat would make no demands and he consequently declares her Emma's spiritual superior. Marriage certainly was Emma's cultural norm, and we have no reason to believe that she planned to depart from it. But Emma's failure to single out Stephen for her attentions eliminates him from immediate candidacy and makes his proposal to her seem irrational as well as abrupt. With his suggestion, Stephen overthrows not only the marriage custom, but also the principles of selectivity and individual preference. Emma has been given no reason to feel preferred to any other young woman in a raincoat. The brief explanation, given after the proposal, "There is no such thing as love in the world," is cryptic and ill-timed. The discussions of marriage reform with Lynch are not relevant to the event itself. Certainly when thoughts of lust with Emma ran through Stephen's head earlier, he was motivated by a desire to escape "the decayed city," not to modify marriage customs. Stephen's thoughts and actions in this final interview with Emma are wildly disjointed. He is hopelessly out of touch with Emma; he is surprised to see her tears. The reader can imagine her terrible epiphany. She has failed to establish herself with Stephen as a person worthy of an exchange of impressions, feelings, and ideas. She is preferred as an anonymous sex object. She feels insulted, angry, hurt, humiliated, but still proud. It is not what Stephen terms pride of the flesh, however, that makes Emma hide her tears, but pride in her individuality.

In the final parting, manners, the forms that have covered their feelings throughout the relationship, fall away. Salutes are ignored; good-byes go unuttered. Stephen characterizes the situation with symbolic suggestiveness: "As he watched her walk onward swiftly with her head slightly bowed he seemed to feel her soul and his falling asunder swiftly and for ever after an instant of all but union" (*SH* 199).

Stephen's soul and its capacity to fall remain persistent themes in *A Portrait of the Artist as a Young Man*. His soul must fall in order for him to become an artist, an exile, a revolutionary. But in *Stephen Hero*, two souls fall asunder; a young man and a young woman must each fall—Stephen to attempt an artistic, moral revolution and Emma to attempt a feminist, intellectual revolution. That any "union" or "all but union" is achieved is questionable, unless it is a brief recognition of differing aims. They manage some accommodation in a few conversations, but they cannot supply each other's basic intellectual and emotional needs; they depart in mutual bewilderment.

The idea of uniting the two seems to have been important to Joyce, however. The development of their relationship figures prominently in half of the surviving chapters of the novel; three chapters culminate with dramatic events in their relationship. Lynch is probably right in assuming that Emma is not "nothing" to Stephen at the end of the novel (*SH* 234). *Stephen Hero* is a flawed novel, as Joyce acknowledged by abandoning it. It seems likely that the Emma-Stephen relationship was something that Joyce, like Stephen himself, was not ready to handle. At this point in his own life, Joyce took Nora as a partner, establishing a union with a woman, while avoiding the marriage trap Stephen scorned. In letters preceding their elopement, Joyce plays the priest with Nora, as Stephen had with Emma, and describes his rejection of the social and Christian order (*Letters* II, 48, 49, 53). However, the union with "simple-minded, excitable" Nora (*Letters* II, 51) was not one in which Joyce had to cope with a Catholic woman who sought an education and had interests and plans of her own. Emma's rare combination of physical attractiveness and mental ambition is seldom glimpsed in Joyce's subsequent fiction. Miss Ivors in "The Dead" and Beatrice in *Exiles* are exceptional cases. In rewriting *Stephen Hero*, Joyce's easier path was to focus on the character closest to his own identity, to internalize his conflicts, and to concentrate on his artistic processes. For this new emphasis, it was advisable to make E—— C—— a faint, peripheral image instead of a lively, interfering, and admirable foil. After making this decision, Joyce needed only to follow one adolescent through momentous choices in life. And, like a wise parent, he postponed (and indeed never treated) Stephen's serious union with a woman, insisting that Stephen first establish his aesthetic vocation and life values; quick glances at a number of women were easier to handle. Stephen's talents and causes probably interested Joyce more than did Emma's.

The mature James Joyce seems to have been sympathetic with Emma's efforts at intellectual emancipation. He argued her position in a discussion with Arthur Power:

—As I say, repeated Joyce, you do not understand him [Ibsen]. You ignore the spirit which animated him. The purpose of *The Doll's House*, for instance, was the emancipation of women, which has caused the greatest revolution in our time in the most important relationship there is—that between men and women; the revolt of women against the idea that they are the mere instruments of men.

—And the more pity, I [Power] replied, for the relationship between the sexes has now been ruined; an intellectualism has been allowed to super-cede a biological fact, and the result is that neither is happy.

—The relationship between the two sexes is now on a different basis, but I do not know whether they are happier or unhappier than they were before; I suppose it depends on the individuals.[38]

As a character, Emma Clery compares favorably with her male counterpart, Stephen, especially when we make allowances for the inequalities of her education, her country's treatment of women, and the novel's emphasis on the male point of view. Emma is far less knowledgeable than Stephen, but Joyce ended by mocking mere facts in *Finnegans Wake*, and even in *Stephen Hero* treated Stephen's intellectual superiority ironically. Stephen is inhumane. He makes his female acquaintance the victim as well as the subject of his art. Stephen has achieved little at this point in his career; though his analytical powers and artistic direction offer promise, his intellectual pride and his artistic manipulations are inappropriate. Emma may be overly enthusiastic about the Gaelic Revival, but she does not jump to conclusions or lose touch with reality the way Stephen does. She has control over her pride. Her self-confidence in undertaking a relationship with this difficult young man is admirable. Even if she does fall short of understanding Stephen, she has a far greater respect for the individual than he does.

The creation of Emma Clery was a noble experiment, an effort in part to provide a female counterpart to Stephen. But Joyce apparently felt incapable of sustaining the portrait at this early stage and then passed beyond similar conception in his later works. Though she is immature intellectually and emotionally, and present only in the remnant of a book about someone else, Emma Clery still presents a challenge. She resists a young man's stereotypes and bold manipulations. She calls for understanding. She may even suggest an equal union of man and woman, an ideal too rarely found even in the world of her great-grandchildren.

NOTES

1. Mark Shechner, *Joyce in Nighttown: A Psychoanalytic Inquiry into Ulysses* (Berkeley: University of California Press, 1974), 243. In the recently published

letter of December 3, 1909, Joyce claims to have told Nora "everything" about his past and requests details of her love life previous to their union. He wants to know "the smallest things about yourself Nora so long as they are obscene and secret and filthy" (*SL* 182, 183, 186).

2. Theodore Spencer, "Introduction," *Stephen Hero*, ed. John J. Slocum and Herbert Cahoon (New York: New Directions, 1959), p. 12.

3. Bernard Benstock, "James Joyce and the Women of the Western World," in *Litters from Aloft*, ed. Ronald Bates and Harry J. Pollock (Tulsa: University of Tulsa Press, 1971) p. 101. Benstock expands his remarks on Emma in *James Joyce: The Undiscover'd Country* (Dublin: Gill and Macmillan; New York: Barnes and Noble, 1977), pp. 8–12.

4. See Charles Rossman, "Stephen Dedalus and the Spiritual-Heroic Refrigerating Apparatus: Art and Life in Joyce's *Portrait*," in *Forms of Modern British Fiction*, ed. Alan Warren Friedman (Austin: University of Texas Press, 1975), pp. 101–31.

5. Charles Rossman, "Stephen Dedalus' Villanelle," *James Joyce Quarterly*, 12 (Spring, 1975), 284, 287–88.

6. *Ibid.*, p. 287.

7. See Benstock, "James Joyce and the Women of the Western World," p. 102.

8. Kevin Sullivan, *Joyce among the Jesuits* (New York: Columbia University Press, 1967), pp. 148–52. A few students prepared for the exams privately.

9. Sullivan, pp. 158–60, and C. P. Curran, *James Joyce Remembered* (New York: Oxford University Press, 1968), p. 8, offer their criticism of the University College curriculum.

10. Norman Atkinson, *Irish Education* (Dublin: Allen Figgis, 1969), pp. 116–17. Additional information from interview with Eileen Breathnach, graduate student at University College, June 21, 1977. Ms. Breathnach is preparing an M.A. thesis on Irish women's education, 1860–1909. See also her article, "Women and Higher Education in Ireland (1879–1914)," *The Crane Bag*, 4 (1980), 47–54.

11. Mary and Padraic Colum, *Our Friend James Joyce* (Garden City, N.Y.: Doubleday, 1958), p. 14.

12. Feminist Francis Skeffington considered the "Girl Graduates' Chat" trivial and an affront to women. See *St. Stephen's*, February, 1902, p. 75. Students at St. Mary's did have the Literary Society (founded 1889, with Father Tom Finlay of University College as its first president) and an obscure journal, *The Lantern*. Eileen Breathnach interview.

13. Mary Colum, *Life and the Dream* (Garden City, N.Y.: Doubleday, 1974), pp. 91–92. According to *Stephen Hero*, male boarders had some, though probably lighter, restrictions. They were kept from attending *Othello* "on the ground that there were many coarse expressions in the play" (*SH* 29).

14. *Ibid.* pp. 40–42.

15. Francis J. C. Skeffington, "A Forgotten Aspect of the University Question," in *Two Essays* by Francis J. C. Skeffington and James Joyce (1901; rpt. Minneapolis: McCosh's Book Store, 1957), p. 6.

16. Atkinson, p. 117.

17. Colum, *Our Friend*, p. 14.

18. *Ibid.*, p. 13. This aloofness with educated young women and Stephen's criticisms of Emma's manners are echoed in Joyce's exaggerated statement to Nora in a letter of August 21, 1909. He confides, "I never could speak to the girls I used to meet at houses. Their false manners checked me at once" (*Letters* II, 161).

19. *Ibid.*, pp. 11–12.

20. Stanislaus Joyce, *My Brother's Keeper: James Joyce's Early Years*, ed. Richard Ellmann (New York: Viking Press, 1958), p. 72.

21. *Ibid.*, p. 259. Mark Shechner speculates (with no proof) that Joyce might have "carried on an imaginary affair with her for years after his elopement with Nora" (*Joyce in Nighttown*, pp. 76–77). Audrée Sheehy-Skeffington (daughter-in-law of Francis and Hanna Sheehy-Skeffington) describes her husband's Aunt Mary as "the most conservative of the four" daughters. She may have "bantered" with Joyce, but she was "very distant" and "shocked by him." Interview, Dublin, June 18, 1977.

22. Owen Sheehy-Skeffington, "Francis Sheehy-Skeffington" in *1916: The Easter Rising*, ed. O. Dudley Edwards and F. Pyle (London: Routledge and Kegan Paul, 1968), p. 136.

23. *Irish Figaro*, February 10, 1900, p. 85. According to the *Figaro*, Margaret "gave a very humorous representation of 'Nothing to Wear,' verses better suited to a male reciter."

24. Elisabeth Young-Bruehl and Robert Hogan, "Conor Cruise O'Brien: An Appraisal," *The Journal of Irish Literature*, 3, no. 2 (May, 1974), 6.

25. According to Audrée Sheehy-Skeffington, Kathleen was the most ardent nationalist among the Sheehy girls. She helped prevent an eviction and was involved with the people of the West of Ireland. Interview, June 18, 1977.

26. Owen Sheehy-Skeffington, p. 145.

27. Young-Bruehl and Hogan, p. 6.

28. Ironically, Charles Stuart Parnell put an end to his sister's organization for the sake of a political compromise.

29. Owen Sheehy-Skeffington, p. 145.

30. See James Henry and Margaret Cousins, *We Two Together* (Madras: Ganesh, 1950), pp. 164–65, 203–205.

31. Stephen is also "piqued" by the indifference Miss Howard displays toward him in the Mullingar fragment of *Stephen Hero*. He is similarly critical of her manners in general, and especially of her conduct with other young men (*SH* 240, 242). Some of Joyce's letters exhibit the same complaint about Nora. He protests to Aunt Josephine on December 4, 1905, "Nora does not seem to make much difference between me and the rest of the men she has known and I can hardly believe that she is justified in this" (*Letters* II, 129).

32. Throughout *Stephen Hero*, Stephen shows scorn for eunuch priests and tries to imagine the sex life of the priesthood and of Jesus.

33. Mary Sheehy may have been Joyce's model for this section. Stanislaus Joyce records that "Jim says Mary Sheehy seems to him like a person who had a

great contempt for many of the people she knew." *The Complete Dublin Diary of Stanislaus Joyce*, ed. George H. Healey (Ithaca: Cornell University Press, 1971), p. 24.

34. Much greater respect is given to Madden's experiences; the story he tells of the peasant woman's invitation provides Stephen with a lasting image.

35. It is interesting that a form of emancipation dearer to Stephen than women's emancipation is a central topic—emancipation of the poet (*SH* 95). Dillon's real-life counterpart, Father Delaney, was far from liberal-minded about female students.

36. A comparable section of Skeffington's original essay states: "The two sexes, in equal and untramelled intercourse, exercise the strongest beneficial influence on each other; the predominant faults of each are restrained, the nobler qualities of both are fostered, and men and women of the best type are the result. . . . The life of school and college is brought more closely into accord with the natural order the more it approximates to the conditions of a large family circle of brothers and sisters. . . . It is not on behalf of women alone that the claim for coeducation is made; for men also, this system is the only wholesome and natural one. Mentally and morally, the unrestrained companionship, the intellectual and social comradeship between man and woman which is thus produced cannot fail to rebound to the advantage of both sexes and to the future well-being of the race" (pp. 9–10). Skeffington, with his "brothers and sisters" concept, is as unconcerned with the physical attraction between male and female as Joyce is preoccupied with it. The polarities are preserved in McCann and Stephen.

37. Stanislaus Joyce's assessment of Mary Sheehy may be relevant here. He sees her as "romantic but clever and sensible and therefore dissatisfied. She wants Hero." *Complete Dublin Diary*, p. 23.

38. Arthur Power, *Conversations with James Joyce*, ed. Clive Hart (New York: Barnes and Noble, 1974), p. 35.

SUZETTE HENKE

Stephen Dedalus and Women:
A Portrait of the Artist as a Young Misogynist

Mother and Child

Female characters are present everywhere and nowhere in *A Portrait of the Artist as a Young Man*. They pervade the novel, yet remain elusive. Their sensuous figures haunt the developing consciousness of Stephen Dedalus and provide a foil against which he defines himself as both man and artist. Like everything in *A Portrait*, women are portrayed almost exclusively from Stephen's point of view. Seen through his eyes and colored by his fantasies, they often appear as one-dimensional projections of a narcissistic imagination. Females emerge as the psychological "other," forceful antagonists in the novel's dialectical structure. They stand as emblems of the flesh—frightening reminders of sex, generation, and death.

At the dawn of infantile consciousness, Stephen perceives the external world in terms of complementary pairs: male and female, father and mother, politics and religion, Davitt and Parnell. Baby Tuckoo's cosmos is organized in binary structures that set the stage for a dialectic of personal development. From a psychological perspective, the mother seems to be in touch with the overwhelming chaos of nature. The father, in contrast, offers a model of logocentric control.[1]

Stephen sees his father as masculine and aloof, visually separated by a glass monocle and a hairy face. The male parent is bearer of the word; he tells a story that appeals to the child's imagination and awakens him to a sense of individual identity. The female parent relates to the boy primarily as caretaker; she satisfies her son's physical desires and encourages his artistic expression by playing the piano. This sweet-smelling guardian is closely associated with sensuous comfort and bodily joy:

> When you wet the bed first it is warm then it gets cold. His mother put on the oilsheet. That had the queer smell.

His mother had a nicer smell than his father. She played on the piano the sailor's hornpipe for him to dance. He danced [*P* 7].

At the outset of *A Portrait*, Stephen perceives his mother as a powerful and beneficent source of physical pleasure. She ministers to each of the five senses.[2] It is the "nice" mother, however, who is one of the women principally responsible for introducing Stephen to a hostile external world and to the laws of social conformity. The first of the many imperatives that thwart the boy's ego, "apologise," is associated with matriarchal threats:

He hid under the table. His mother said:
—O, Stephen will apologise.
Dante said:
—O, if not, the eagles will come and pull out his eyes [*P* 8].[3]

Dante and Mrs. Dedalus both represent the inhibitions of a reality principle that begins, at this point, to take precedence over the gratifications of infantile narcissism. They mutually demand the repression of libidinous tendencies and a conquest of the id in favor of a developing social ego. As Dorothy Dinnerstein explains in *The Mermaid and the Minotaur*, it is usually a woman who serves as "every infant's first love, first witness and first boss. . . . The initial experience of dependence on a largely uncontrollable outside source of good is focused on a woman, and so is the earliest experience of vulnerability to disappointment and pain."[4]

According to Freudian theory, the primordial conflict between male and female takes root in the infant's early discovery of a world alien to his sensibilities and antagonistic to the demands of his omnipotent will. As the child begins to distinguish between ego and environment, between self and other, he becomes aware of a dangerous threat to his own struggle for individuation. In a process of psychological transference, he symbolically equates the mother or a mother-surrogate with the enemy that frustrates his desires and threatens to engulf his newly-acquired sense of self. The female takes on extraordinary and mysterious powers. A goddess in her authority, she is unconsciously identified with the hated flesh that eludes the infant's control.[5]

As Simone de Beauvoir explains in *The Second Sex*, the male child associates his mother, and consequently his image of the female, with the viscosity and "immanence" of physical existence. He develops a conviction that women are bound by the generative demands of the species, and the presence of his mother becomes an ominous reminder of the shame of his animal nature and the reality of personal extinction. "The uncleanness of birth is reflected upon the mother. . . . And if the little boy remains in early childhood sensually attached to the maternal flesh, when he grows older, becomes socialized, and takes note of his individual existence, this same flesh frightens him . . . calls him back to those realms of immanence whence he would fly.[6]

"Reproduction is the beginning of death" (P 231). So argued Hegel, and so argues Stephen's friend Temple. The Manichean dichotomy between flesh and spirit, body and mind, has long been allied in the writings of male philosophers with the basic polarity between the sexes. Stephen vies with Nietzsche and with Schopenhauer when, in *Stephen Hero*, he proposes a misogynist "theory of dualism which would symbolise the twin eternities of spirit and nature in the twin eternities of male and female" (SH 210). According to Simone de Beauvoir, man's symbolic association of woman with the flesh reflects a disdain for human corporality. The male identifies himself as "spirit" by virtue of his own subjective consciousness; he then perceives the female as "the Other, who limits and denies him." [7]

The antagonism of these "twin eternities" is impressed on Stephen at an early age. He disdains his mother's feminine vulnerability and thinks that she is "not nice" when she cries. Like most young boys, Stephen begins to interpret his relationship with his mother as an obstacle to more grown-up ties with his own sex. Armed with ten shillings and his father's injunctions toward a code of masculine loyalty, he "manfully" enters the competitive joust of life at Clongowes. He determines to adopt an ethic of male stoicism because "his father had told him . . . whatever he did, never to peach on a fellow" (P 9).

In a world of social Darwinism, Stephen defines himself as both literally and figuratively marginal. Caught in a stampede of "flashing eyes and muddy boots," he is horrified by the bestial fury of the crowd— "fellows . . . struggling and groaning . . . and stamping" (P 10). The boy mentally takes refuge in artistic evocations of the family hearth, protected by beneficent female spirits—Mother, Dante, and the servant Brigid. As he relives the horror of being shouldered into a urinal ditch by the bully Wells, Stephen projects himself beyond the rats and the scum to an apparently dissociated reverie. He recalls his mother sitting by the fire in hot "jewelly slippers" that exude a "lovely warm smell" (P 10). Alienated from a brutal male environment, Stephen longs to return to his mother. In true Oedipal fashion, he focuses on the fetishistic symbols of her warm feet, sexual totems that offer both kinesthetic and olfactory satisfaction in compensation for the stench and the slimy touch of the chilling water.

Incarcerated in the infirmary, Stephen hallucinates his own death and burial. He also reverts to infant attachment and imagines writing a letter begging his mother to "come and take me home" (P 23). "He longed to be at home and lay his head on his mother's lap" (P 13). But he distinguishes between this maternal sanctuary and "his father's house," "cold and dark under the seawall" (P 17).

In a confused way, Stephen tries to fathom the mysteries of Oedipal attraction. He is unable to differentiate between filial and erotic love and feels perplexed when Wells unites the two in a sexual conundrum: "Tell us, Dedalus, do you kiss your mother before you go to bed?" (P 14). Stephen desires the soft wetness of his mother's lips, but is baffled by the moral implications of a riddle that would challenge the saintliness of Aloysius Gonzaga. Later, in chapter 5, when Cranly asks Stephen whether he "loves his mother," the young man is still unable to respond. "I don't know what your words mean" (P 240), he replies.

As the curious child stumbles toward manhood, he feels compelled to cast off allegiance to maternal figures. His childhood educator Dante, "a clever woman and a wellread woman" who teaches him geography and lunar lore, is supplanted by male instructors: "Father Arnall knew more than Dante because he was a priest" (P 11). The Jesuit masters invite Stephen to ponder the mysteries of religion, death, canker, and cancer. They introduce him to a system of male authority and discipline, to a pedagogical regimen that will insure his "correct training" and proper socialization. Through examinations that pit red rose against white, Yorks against Lancastrians, they make education an aggressive game of simulated warfare. The students, like soldiers, are depersonalized through institutional surveillance.[8]

At home for Christmas dinner, Stephen assimilates the knowledge that rabid women like Dante Riordan support ecclesiastical authority in the name of moral righteousness. Like the "sow that eats her farrow," Dante is willing to sacrifice Parnell as a political scapegoat. In the face of Mr. Casey's Fenianism and Simon's contemptuous snorting, she declares the Catholic clergy "the apple of God's eye" (P 38). Like a perverted Eve, Dante defends the ecclesiastical apple against

Ireland's republican leader, that "devil out of hell" crushed by an irate populace. She suggests a formidable alliance between the Catholic church and bourgeois respectability.

In the battle between male and female, Mother Church emerges as a bastion of sexual repression defended by hysterical women. Dante's own credibility is negated by spinsterhood and involuntary celibacy. Stephen "had heard his father say that she was a spoiled nun and that she had come out of the convent in the Alleghanies when her brother had got the money from the savages for the trinkets and the chainies" (*P* 35). Stephen's male role models, Simon Dedalus and John Casey, assert masculine prowess through acts of republican fervor. Hence Casey's braggadocio in recounting his triumph over the hag who screamed "whore": "I had my mouth full of tobacco juice. I bent down to her and *Phth!* says I to her like that . . . right into her eye" (*P* 36–37). In this tale of heroism, Casey conquers the malevolent crone—the folkloric witch, hag, or "mother-in-law" who caricatures female dementia. Spitting in her eye, he symbolically achieves a talismanic victory through sexual violation of the phallic mother. Casey expects women to function as docile bodies—peacemakers like Mary Dedalus and mollifying agents of social arbitration.

When Stephen again returns to Clongowes, he realizes that his mother cannot offer a viable sanctuary from the male-dominated power structure that controls the outer world. He must learn to survive in a society that protects bullies like Wells and sadists like Father Dolan, that condones brutality, and that takes advantage of the weak and the helpless. The pandybat incident at the end of chapter 1 symbolically reinforces the rites of objectification characteristic of Jesuit training. Father Dolan's authority is absolute and unquestioned. He relies on patriarchal privilege and assumes a "panoptical" vision: "Father Dolan will be in to see you every day" (*P* 49).[9] Branded as a "lazy little schemer," Stephen must endure the ignominy of being misnamed and robbed of subjective identity.

The young boy is being socialized into what Philip Slater identifies as a culture of male narcissism. According to Slater, single-sex education and the separation of male children from the emotional refuge of the family promotes misogyny, narcissism, and a terror of the female. Boy children suffer from an "unconscious fear of being feminine, which leads to 'protest masculinity,' exaggeration of the difference between men and women." [10] Once the child is deprived of maternal affection, he "seeks compensation through self-aggrandizement—renouncing love for admiration—and in this he is encouraged by the achievement pressure placed upon him, and presumably by the myriad narcissistic role models he finds around him. He becomes vain, hypersensitive, invidious, ambitious, . . . boastful, and exhibitionistic." [11]

Stephen's appeal to Father Conmee is motivated not only by optimistic faith in a male-controlled world, but by personal vanity and a tendency toward exhibitionism. His youthful vision is blurred, idealistic, and Panglossian. He naively believes that he will be exonerated simply by presenting his case before a higher patriarch. In his confrontation with the rector, Stephen makes a symbolic rite of passage through the primordial chambers of racial and ecclesiastical history. He asserts his budding manhood against totalitarian power and is acclaimed a revolutionary hero by "the Senate and the Roman people." But the triumphant child later discovers the aftermath of his rebellion: Dolan and Conmee, in smug condescension, "had a famous laugh together over it" (P 72). Stephen has unwittingly played the ingenuous fool at the court of his Jesuit masters. In a bold attempt to assert masculine independence, he has served merely as an object of paternal amusement.

Virgin and Whore

In chapter 5 of A Portrait, Cranly asks Stephen if he would deflower a virgin. His companion replies by posing another question: "Is that not the ambition of most young gentlemen?" (P 246). Figuratively, it is Stephen's ambition throughout the novel to "deflower" the Blessed Virgin of Catholicism. He wants to supplant the Catholic Madonna with a profane surrogate, an aesthetic muse rooted in sensuous reality.

In chapter 2, Stephen vainly searches for the romantic figure of a woman who will mediate his artistic transfiguration. Identifying with the Count of Monte Cristo, he conjures up adolescent fantasies of a beautiful Mercedes, whom he stalks in the suburbs of Blackrock. He longs "to meet in the real world the unsubstantial image which his soul so constantly beheld. . . . They would meet quietly as if they had known each other and had made their tryst. . . . He would fade into something impalpable under her eyes and then in a moment, he would be transfigured. Weakness and timidity and inexperience would fall from him in that magic moment" (P 65). It is essential that the figure of

Mercedes be "unsubstantial" and free of physical dross. She must obliterate any palpable connection with the corporeal prison of the body. The semi-religious scene suggests beatific transformation in the darkness and silence of a moonlit garden. The romantic heroine, however, releasing her lover from the shackles of youthful inexperience, blesses him with nothing less than the power of refusal. In spiritualizing his life, she paradoxically endows him with sufficient grace to transcend the demands of sexual love.

When Stephen dreams of himself as Edmond Dantes, he identifies with a man betrayed by his friends and his mistress, unjustly exiled and imprisoned, but eventually able to wreak revenge on those who failed him. Monte Cristo's adventures culminate in a "sadly proud gesture of refusal": "Madam, I never eat muscatel grapes" (P 63). Mercedes is an "untouchable" mistress, tainted by collaboration with her lover's enemies. Stephen admires the self-sufficiency of Dantes, the isolated hero who conquers the woman he loves by rejecting his amorous need for her body.

Art promises to invest Stephen with the powers of priest and shaman—the ability to confront the mysteries of creation while tasting the "joy of loneliness." Before the tantalizing face of Emma, "cowled" in nun's veiling, Stephen forces himself to remain calm and controlled, "a tranquil watcher of the scene before him" (P 69). "He saw her urge her vanities, her fine dress and sash and long black stockings, and knew that he had yielded to them a thousand times. Yet a voice within him spoke above the noise of his dancing heart, asking him would he take her gift to which he had only to stretch out his hand" (P 69). In Stephen's imagination, Emma becomes a nubile temptress—Mercedes in Dublin garb, Eve in nun's habit. He interprets her gestures as "flattering, taunting, searching, exciting his heart" (P 69) and speculates: "She too wants me to catch hold of her . . . and kiss her" (P 70).

To the reader, the adolescent Emma is hardly a Circean figure. She seems shy and coy, gaily flirtatious and mildly seductive. "She came up to his step many times and went down to hers again between their phrases and once or twice stood close beside him for some moments" (P 69). Like Stephen, Emma probably feels confused by the excitations of a budding sexuality. Her gestures of affection are limited to the subtle patterns of courtship available in nineteenth-century Ireland to a young girl who wants to attract a suitor but to remain pure, chaste, and respectable.

Like the Count of Monte Cristo, Stephen turns away from Emma in proud abnegation. He will possess his mistress wholly through art. In Byronic verses written to E——C——, "the kiss, which had been withheld by one, was given by both" (*P* 71). Poetry offers aesthetic compensation for frustrated erotic desire. The stirrings of adolescent sexuality are deftly sublimated through lyrical fulfillment beneath the "balmy breeze and the maiden lustre of the moon" (*P* 70). The artist's mind is cold, chaste, and detached, like that of the virginal muse Diana. His disciplined verses statically embalm the moment of romantic epiphany. Emotional mutuality has been restricted to art: Stephen feels fulfilled, but Emma is left to pine in her nun-like shroud. Her desires are safely crystallized in Byronic verses framed by two Jesuit mottoes.[12]

The night of the Whitsuntide play, Stephen remembers the touch of Emma's hand and the sight of dark eyes that "invited and unnerved him" (*P* 82). When Emma eludes him after the play, he feels the pang of "wounded pride and fallen hope and baffled desire" (*P* 86). Dashing to an alley behind the Dublin morgue, he soberly takes comfort in the "good odour" of "horse piss and rotted straw" (*P* 86). The enigmatic scene psychologically gives vent to Stephen's terror of the female. As the source of physical generation, woman serves as a reminder of animality, bodily decomposition, excrement, and death. Stephen's sentiment is Thomistic and medieval, reminiscent of religious triptychs that portray a woman first at the height of beauty, then aged and wrinkled, and finally as a skeleton bedecked in morbid finery. Stephen mentally projects onto Emma images of decay and corruption. He is accosted by his carnal connection with the world; and, like the medieval fathers of the church, he tries to rebel against mortality by renouncing the fires of lust. As Saint Augustine wryly noted, "We are born between feces and urine" [*Inter faeces et urinam nascimur*]. Joyce's young artist is well on his way to developing a similar excremental vision of sex.[13] Birth and death are so closely linked to physical nature that they are easily allied in the misogynist mind. Rotting bodies in the morgue and rotting straw convince Stephen that "reproduction is the beginning of death."

Simon Dedalus nostalgically believes that *"Tis youth and folly/ Makes young men marry"* (*P* 88). Stephen, freed of his father's notions about youth and innocence, confines his erotic activities to "monstrous" reveries, wild orgies of the imagination in which the female is reduced to a powerless object of male fantasy. Stephen is horrified at seeing the word "Foetus" scrawled on a desk, perhaps because it suggests frustrated sexuality and the souls "impossibilised" by his onanistic rites; or perhaps because it links him with the rude, lascivious males of his father's generation. "Nothing stirred within his soul but a cold cruel and loveless lust" (*P* 96). "He wanted to sin with another of his kind, to force another being to sin with him and to exult with her in sin" (*P* 99–100).

The image of Mercedes traverses the background of Stephen's memory, but the transfiguration he once sought is consummated in the embrace of a Dublin whore. Stephen is no longer the Count of Monte Cristo when the "holy encounter" occurs. The sexual imagery at the end of chapter 2 is ironically inverted. As Stephen feels the shadow of a streetwalker "moving irresistibly upon him," he figuratively suffers the "agony of its penetration" and surrenders to a "murmurous . . . flood" of physical desire. The fusion of erotic and romantic imagery degenerates into a vague ritual of sexual initiation, celebrated before a phantasmal altar illumined by "yellow gasflames" (*P* 100). Traditional symbols are reversed, and Stephen envisions himself in the role of sacrificial virgin, raped by a phallic figure and flooded with seminal streams.[14] His "cry for an iniquitous abandonment" again evokes an excremental vision of sex. The sound is "but the echo of an obscene scrawl which he had read on the oozing wall of a urinal" (*P* 100).[15]

When Stephen yields to the prostitute's solicitations, he resembles a child about to "burst into hysterical weeping." The perfumed female recalls his "nice-smelling" mother. Clothed in a long pink gown, she leads him into a womb-like chamber, "warm and lightsome." Her round arms offer a maternal caress. Soothed like a baby by the "warm calm rise and fall of her breast," Stephen momentarily retrieves the illusion of infant satiety: "He wanted to be held firmly in her arms, to be caressed slowly, slowly, slowly. In her arms he felt that he had suddenly become strong and fearless and sure of himself. But his lips would not bend to kiss her. . . . He closed his eyes, surrendering himself to her, body and mind, conscious of nothing in the world but the dark pressure of her softly parting lips" (*P* 101).[16]

Stephen feels, at last, transfigured by a woman. "He was in another world; he had awakened from a slumber of centuries" (*P* 100). His vision of the female, however, has remained essentially unchanged.

The traditional dichotomy between virgin and whore, madonna and temptress, breaks down in the young man's imagination. For him, all women encompass both roles. As a child, he feared the sexual implications of his mother's kiss. He proudly spurns the romantic Mercedes and finds temporary salvation in the arms of a prostitute, who exacts the kiss earlier withheld from Emma. All the women in Stephen's life are both nurturant and demanding. They are sporadically aloof, solicitous, and sexually receptive. Emma tempted Stephen and fled—only to be transformed into a lyrical muse, then to be rejected in a cathartic scene of ascetic renunciation. The whore is an ambivalent figure of masculine aggression and feminine protection. She demands erotic surrender, yet shelters her adolescent charge in a tender, maternal embrace.

The Catholic Virgin

Like Sartre's hell in *Huis Clos*, the notion of damnation that Stephen gleans from the priest's retreat sermon involves other people—bodies crowded together after death in noisome, rotting putrefaction. "All the filth of the world, all the offal and scum of the world, we are told, shall run there as to a vast and reeking sewer. . . . And then imagine this sickening stench, multiplied a millionfold, . . . a huge and rotting human fungus" (*P* 120).

As the "jeweleyed harlots" of Stephen's sins dance before his fevered imagination, the boy is horrified that he has besmirched the sacred figure of Emma by making her the object of his masturbatory fantasies: "The image of Emma appeared before him and, under her eyes, the flood of shame rushed forth anew from his heart. If she knew to what his mind had subjected her or how his brutelike lust had torn and trampled upon her innocence! Was that boyish love? Was that chivalry? Was that poetry?" (*P* 115). At the same time, Stephen believes that Emma has "erred" by serving as erotic stimulus for his nightly orgies.

He feels that he has violated both Emma's honor and his own code of chivalry—not to mention the rigorous ethic of purity enforced by Irish Catholicism. Emma, he decides, shall serve as his envoy to the Blessed Mother. He imagines a scene of heavenly confrontation with the Catholic Virgin, who enjoins them to "take hands. . . . You have erred but you are always my children" (*P* 116). With the help of Emma,

Stephen plans to recoup his spiritual losses. He and his beloved, under the aegis of the Virgin Mary, will embark on a journey toward forgiveness and salvation.

Without the innocent and virginal Emma, Stephen is as "helpless and hopeless" as the souls of the damned (P 123). He hallucinates a vision of the libidinous inferno prepared especially for him: "That was his hell. God had allowed him to see the hell reserved for his sins: stinking, bestial, malignant, a hell of lecherous goatish fiends. For him! For him!" (P 138).

To escape the threat of damnation, Stephen must be willing to purge himself of erotic desire. He must triumph over carnal concupiscence by refusing the impure thoughts that stimulate erection. Terrified not only of woman, but of the body and its sexual needs, Stephen is moved simultaneously to renounce Satan, the female, and his own genitalia. Catholicism demands that he psychologically castrate himself by consenting to a guilty dissociation of ego and id. He cannot identify with the antagonistic penis that seems to operate with a will of its own: "Was that then he or an inhuman thing moved by a lower soul than his soul? His soul sickened at the thought of a torpid snaky life feeding itself out of the tender marrow of his life and fattening upon the slime of lust" (P 140). Haunted by grotesque fantasies of sexual alienation, Stephen feels "possessed by a magic not of himself. . . . That organ by which he thought to assert himself does not obey him; heavy with unsatisfied desires, unexpectedly becoming erect, . . . it manifests a suspicious and capricious vitality." [17]

In order to confess his sins of impurity, Stephen must revert to a state of childhood innocence. He allows himself to be infantilized, "for God loved little children and suffered them to come to Him. It was a terrible and a sad thing to sin. But God was merciful to poor sinners who were truly sorry" (P 143). Stephen resolves to amend his life for the sake of "atonement" with the Christian community and re-integration into a state of grace and beatitude: "He would be at one with others and with God. He would love his neighbor. He would love God Who had made and loved him. He would kneel and pray with others and be happy" (P 143).

Stephen determines to repress the emergence of adolescent sexuality and to repent of the one sin that mortifies him even more than murder. The female temptress has reduced his soul to a syphilitic chancre, "festering and oozing like a sore, a squalid stream of vice" (P

144). Repelled by the lurid imagery of venereal disease, Stephen humbles himself before the "old and weary voice" of his father-priest-confessor. The church's medicine man will cure his wound, rescue him from the siren, and offer a "life of grace and virtue and happiness" (*P* 146). The priest invokes the Blessed Virgin Mary as spiritual guardian of Christian "manliness." Chanting simple declarative sentences that echo catechetical instruction, he exhorts his charge to renounce the sins of the flesh, especially masturbation: "It is a terrible sin. It kills the body and it kills the soul. It is the cause of many crimes and misfortunes. Give it up, my child, for God's sake. It is dishonorable and unmanly. . . . Pray to our mother Mary to help you. She will help you, my child. Pray to Our Blessed Lady when that sin comes into your mind" (*P* 144–45).

In his repentance, Stephen turns back to the woman emblematic of Catholic worship. As prefect of Our Blessed Lady's Sodality, he will cling to purity, spiritualize his life, and engage in prolific acts of piety. With the help of the Virgin Mary, Stephen will sublimate his sexual needs and attempt to recapture the prepubescent calm characteristic of juvenile innocence.

The Bird-Girl: Aesthetic Muse

In his return to ritualistic devotion, Stephen has actually become involved in an aesthetic love affair with his own soul. The anima, the feminine aspect of the psyche, has won his passion and holds him enthralled. Like Narcissus, Stephen has fallen in love with his projected self-image clothed in female garb.[18] "The attitude of rapture in sacred art, the raised and parted hands, the parted lips and eyes as of one about to swoon, became for him an image of the soul in prayer, humiliated and faint before her Creator" (*P* 150). In the glorified female, "man also perceives his mysterious double; man's soul is Psyche, a woman."[19] The feminine side of Stephen's identity, personified as the soul, swoons in erotic ecstasy before her creator, as the young man once swooned in the arms of a prostitute.

The Catholic priesthood offers Stephen a chance to consummate this narcissistic love affair with his psyche. It bequeaths on the soul the magical power of transubstantiation. And it promises a rite of passage into male mysteries that successfully counteract female authority: "No angel or archangel in heaven, no saint, not even the Blessed Virgin

herself has the power of a priest of God" (*P* 158). A Jesuit vocation
would guarantee Stephen ascendancy over the Catholic matriarch. By
virtue of the "secret knowledge and secret power" of an exclusively
masculine fraternity, he would be admitted to the inner sanctum of
male religious privilege.

But the price of this "awful power of which angels and saints stood
in reverence" is the "grave and ordered and passionless life" of Jesuit
conformity. Stephen is convinced that his destiny is to be unique and
isolated, "elusive of social or religious orders" (*P* 162). And so he
chooses "the misrule and confusion of his father's house" (*P* 162) over
the pomp and ceremony of religious ritual. He will commit himself
to the pagan priesthood of Father Daedalus, "the fabulous artificer,
. . . a symbol of the artist forging anew in his workshop out of
the sluggish matter of the earth a new soaring impalpable imperishable being" (*P* 169).

Stephen's artistic vocation seems to be confirmed by an encounter
with a woman who evokes a luminous vision of earthly beauty: "A girl
stood before him in midstream, alone and still, gazing out to sea. She
seemed like one whom magic had changed into the likeness of a
strange and beautiful seabird. Her long slender bare legs were delicate
as a crane's and pure save where an emerald trail of seaweed had
fashioned itself as a sign upon the flesh. Her thighs, fuller and soft-
hued as ivory, were bared almost to the hips where the white fringes of
her drawers were like featherings of soft white down" (*P* 171).

The woman revealed in Stephen's epiphany amalgamates the images of pagan and Christian iconography. She is both mortal and
angelic, sensuous and serene. Her soft-hued, ivory thighs recall Eileen's ivory hands and the figure of the Catholic Virgin, Tower of
Ivory. Her avian transformation harks back to the Greek myth of Leda
and the swan. And her bosom, like "the breast of some darkplumaged
dove," suggests the Holy Ghost, traditionally represented as a dove in
Christian art. Stephen, as purveyor of the Word, imaginatively begets
a surrogate Holy Spirit in his ecstatic vision of the bird-girl.[20]

At this point in the novel, Joyce's ironic gaze is subtle but implicit. If
Stephen feels sexual arousal in the presence of the exposed girl, he
quickly sublimates erotic agitation beneath effusions of purple prose.
The young man catches sight of an attractive woman and immediately
detaches himself from participation in the scene. His reaction is static,
purged of desire or loathing. Aesthetic fantasy quenches any impulse

to approach the girl, to reach out and touch her, or to establish physical contact. Stephen must distance and "depersonalize" the tempting figure by making her into a species of aesthetic prey.

As the young woman rises out of the sea, she is reminiscent of Venus, the goddess of love born of the ocean foam. She is pure and virginal, yet "an emerald trail of seaweed" functions as a sign of mortality stamped on her flesh. She belongs to the mundane world of decay and corruption, and the vegetation clinging to her flesh suggests a viscous image of entrapment. The woman appears as an "angel of mortal youth and beauty, an envoy from the fair courts of life" (P 172). It is significant that Joyce, in his 1904 essay "A Portrait of the Artist," uses similar phrases to describe a phantasmal image evoked by the Dublin red light district: "Beneficent one! . . . thou camest timely, as a witch to the agony of self devourer, an envoy from the fair courts of life" (P 263).[21]

Like an Irish Circe, the nymph in *A Portrait* has the potential to drag Stephen down into the emerald-green nets of Dublin paralysis.[22] As a realistic figure, the wading girl implicitly threatens Stephen with the institutional bondage of courtship and marriage associated with physical attraction. The young man knows that he may look but not touch, admire but not speak. He glorifies the woman as an angelic messenger from the "fair courts of life," but he never considers joining her in the teeming ocean waters.

Afraid of the "waters circumfluent in space" that symbolize female fluidity, Stephen is determined to control the world of physiological process by "freezing" life in the stasis of art. His "spiritual-heroic refrigerating apparatus" has already begun to implement this flight from woman. As an artist, Stephen can capture and crystallize the "eternal feminine" in the sacramental but icy realm of aesthetic consciousness. "Her image had passed into his soul for ever and no word had broken the holy silence of his ecstasy" (P 172).[23]

At nightfall, Stephen feels his soul "swooning into some new world, fantastic, dim, uncertain as under sea, traversed by cloudy shapes and beings. A world, a glimmer, or a flower?" (P 172). His spirit seems to embark on an archetypal journey through Hades to the multifoliate rose of Dante's beatific vision.[24] The bird-girl has served as Stephen's profane virgin, a Beatrice who ushers him into the circle of heavenly experience. The Dantesque underworld may, in fact, symbolize the artistic unconscious. And the pre-Raphaelite rose imagery, popular with the early Yeats and with the Rhymers of the nineties, surely casts a satirical light on Stephen's romantic self-indulgence. As the young man attempts to "still the riot of his blood," he swoons in languorous ecstasy. He poetically envisions an "opening flower": "Glimmering and trembling, trembling and unfolding, a breaking light, . . . it spread in endless succession to itself, breaking in full crimson and unfolding and fading to palest rose, leaf by leaf and wave of light by wave of light, flooding all the heavens with its soft flushes, every flush deeper than other" (*P* 172).

Sublimating the sexual component of his experience, Stephen vividly imagines a metaphorical rose engulfing the heavens. Certainly, to readers familiar with the psychology of Freud and the poetry of D. H. Lawrence, this "language of flowers" suggests an exercise in erotic displacement. The boy's fantasy re-creates a repressed vision of the female genitalia, spreading in luxuriant rose-pink petals before the aroused male consciousness. Stephen's active libido summons images of a woman's body erotically revealing its sexual mysteries and palpitating with the "crimson flush" of physical stimulation. His florid prose imitates the orgasmic rhythms of sexual excitement, as tension mounts until the dream climaxes in a flood of "soft flushes." Stephen may believe that he has purified his sensuous encounter by making it into an object of art. But even his Dantesque vision is founded on sexual passion, thinly disguised by the language of romantic sublimation.

Flight from the Mother

The gates of salvation open at the end of chapter 4. In chapter 5, Stephen finds himself exiled from the Garden of Eden. Chewing crusts of fried bread, he remembers the turf-coloured water in the bath at Clongowes—a spectral image that resonates with associations of death, drowning, and claustrophobia.[25]

The young artist escapes from the sordid reality of Dublin by taking shelter in a world of words.[26] His soul is struggling to fly beyond the nets of family, nationality, and religion. As Stephen proclaims his proud *Non Serviam*, however, he continues to rely on his mother for service and for nurturance. Mary Dedalus washes her son's face and ears, enjoins him to receive communion, and packs his second-hand clothes in preparation for his journey. Having magically transmuted the power of the female into a static object of art, Stephen is again accosted by harsh reminders of Mother Church and Mother Ireland. And so he feels compelled to reject all three "mothers"—physical, spiritual, and political. His refusal to take communion at Easter is as much a gesture of liberation from the pleas of Mary Dedalus as it is a rejection of ecclesiastical authority. The image of woman metonymically absorbs all the paralyzing nets that constrain the artist. Hence Stephen's rejection of Cranly's romantic exaltation of "mother love." Unlike his companion, Stephen resolves to detach himself from "the sufferings of women, the weaknesses of their bodies and souls"; he refuses to "shield them with a strong and resolute arm and bow his mind to them" (P 245). He determines, instead, to "discover the mode of life or of art" that will allow his spirit to "express itself in unfettered freedom" (P 246). In casting off the yoke of matriarchy, Stephen asserts his manhood in fraternal collusion with Daedalus, his classical mentor.

The male artistic spirit is symbolized by birds that wheel above the sensuous world and become emblems of a disembodied consciousness. Like Swedenborg, Stephen is convinced of "the correspondence of birds to things of the intellect" (P 224). Swallows careening in the evening air become symbols of the unfettered spirit of the male artist. The female, in contrast, is depicted either as a water bird, immersed in the fluidity of sensuous life, or as a "batlike" creature mired in the dark secrets of a primitive race.[27] The peasant woman who solicits Davin resembles a mysterious sprite out of Celtic folklore, "a batlike soul waking to the consciousness of itself in darkness and secrecy and loneliness and, through the eyes and voice and gesture of a woman without guile, calling the stranger to her bed" (P 183). Similarly, when Emma shows interest in Father Moran and the Irish Renascence, she becomes a virginal Kathleen ni Houlihan, another "batlike soul . . . tarrying awhile, loveless and sinless" (P 221).

It is not enough to repudiate the female. The artist must usurp her procreative powers. Stephen seems to consider the aesthetic endeavor a kind of "couvade"—a rite of psychological compensation for the male's inability to give birth. He describes the act of aesthetic "postcreation" in metaphors of parturition, explaining to Lynch: "When we come to the phenomena of artistic conception, artistic gestation, and artistic reproduction I require a new terminology and a new personal experience" (P 209).

When Stephen awakens to "a tremulous morning knowledge, a

morning inspiration," his experience is oddly passive: "A spirit filled him, pure as the purest water, sweet as dew, moving as music. But how faintly it was inbreathed, how passionlessly, as if the seraphim themselves were breathing upon him!" (*P* 217). It soon becomes clear that it is not simply the seraphim who are breathing upon the artist, but the Holy Ghost, in an aesthetic drama that re-enacts the mystery of Christ's Incarnation. The poet welters in a confused haze of light and beauty, but the "instant of inspiration" is climactic: "O! In the virgin womb of the imagination the word was made flesh. Gabriel the seraph had come to the virgin's chamber" (*P* 217).[28]

In a strange instance of mental transsexuality, Stephen identifies with the Blessed Virgin Mary, to whom the angel Gabriel announced the conception of Christ. The virginal imagination becomes handmaid to the Lord, echoing Mary's words: "Be it done unto me according to thy word." Stephen here suggests a fleshly embodiment of the divine word through an "immaculate conception" in the mind of the poet. He assumes that the artist can engender "life out of life" through an exclusively spiritual process. The imagination is impregnated by the seminal lightning of the Holy Ghost. It then gives birth to the word incarnate in art—or perhaps, as Stephen fails to understand, to a stillbirth untouched by the vitalizing forces of physical reality. So long as the aesthetic consciousness remains virginal, it fails to conceive works of art that reflect the life of the outer world.[29]

Despite the apparent sophistication of Stephen's aesthetic theory in *A Portrait*, the virgin womb of his imagination has yet to be fertilized by external experience. The artist's talents are woefully incommensurate with his idealistic conceptions. Inspired by masturbatory fantasies after a wet dream, Stephen pens the "Villanelle of a Temptress," a mediocre poem that conflates profane and religious imagery in a hymn of praise to the seductive muse. Emma, his model, is once again transmuted by lyrical stasis. Stephen identifies the "rose and ardent light" of inspiration with her strange and "wilful heart, strange that no man had known or would know, wilful from before the beginning of the world" (*P* 217). Emma merges with all the sirens and beautiful women of religious history and myth—with the Virgin Mary, with Dante's Beatrice, and with the "secret rose" of Yeats's early poetry.

Stephen bitterly speculates that Emma has prostituted herself to the Irish Renascence and to a "church which was the scullerymaid of christendom" (*P* 220). "Rude brutal anger" fragments her image in a kaleidoscope of sordid memories. Emma, however, is never allowed to defend herself. Stephen sets himself up as all-seeing judge, surmising and speculating about Emma's change of heart, but contemptuous of direct communication with his putative betrayer. He feels angry that she will confess her sins to the vulgar Father Moran, a "priested peasant," rather than to Stephen, "a priest of eternal imagination, transmuting the daily bread of experience into the radiant body of everliving life" (*P* 221).

Stephen thinks of Emma with a curious mixture of homage and disdain. He mingles love with lust, religious worship with lascivious desire. In his sexual fantasies, Emma yields her warm, naked body to his amorous embrace. "Conscious of his desire she was waking from odorous sleep, the temptress of his villanelle. . . . Her nakedness yielded to him, radiant, warm, odorous and lavish-limbed, enfolded him like a shining cloud, enfolded him like water with a liquid life" (*P* 223). Emma is seductress and muse, Blessed Mother and aesthetic siren, whose "waters circumfluent in space" engender the "liquid letters" of poetic speech, "symbols of the element of mystery" (*P* 223). Here female fluidity becomes essential to art, and the eternal temptress baptizes the nascent poet with the gift of lyrical utterance.[30]

Does Emma fade out of the novel as the temptress of Stephen's villanelle? Does she "lure the seraphim" and have her will of man through *"languorous look and lavish limb"* (*P* 223)? This is hardly the Emma we recognize from the novel. The formal, highly-wrought verses of Stephen's poem reveal his perpetual obsession with the terrifying eroticism of the female. Art enables him temporarily to control the archetypal seductress, whose *"eyes have set man's heart ablaze"* (*P* 223) from the beginning of time. Against overwhelming enchantment, Stephen pits the forces of aesthetic transformation. As poet-priest, he transubstantiates the eternal feminine into a static, disembodied muse. Once out of nature, the Circean figure ceases to threaten. Consigned to the realm of Byzantium, she can no longer arouse animal lust or sensuous passion. The seductive female is safely embalmed and held suspended in the "everliving life" of art.

Throughout *A Portrait*, Stephen habitually makes use of poetry to sublimate personal emotions of rage, jealousy, and desire. Suspecting Emma of a liaison with Cranly, he imagines an illicit affair between the two, then calms himself by uttering some misremembered lines from Nash: *"Darkness falls from the air"* (*P* 232). Filled with excitement as

Emma passes, Stephen cannot decide whether his emotion is erotically or lyrically inspired: "A trembling joy, lambent as a faint light, played like a fairy host around him. But why? Her passage through the darkening air or the verse with its black vowels and its opening sound, rich and lutelike?" (P 232–33). After a scatological meditation on life in Stuart England, Stephen responds to Emma's presence like an animal scenting its prey: "Vaguely first and then more sharply he smelt her body. A conscious unrest seethed in his blood. Yes, it was her body he smelt: a wild and languid smell" (P 233). Aroused and unsatisfied, comforted neither by woman nor by verse, the louse-ridden poet abandons his pursuit: "Well, then, let her go and be damned to her. She could love some clean athlete who washed himself every morning to the waist and had black hair on his chest. Let her" (P 234). Stephen's rejection of Emma is not without a touch of self-pity. He thinks mournfully: "But him no woman's eyes had wooed" (P 238).

Even a servant girl singing "Rosie O'Grady" is transmuted in Stephen's mind into an ephemeral image of liturgical incantation: "The figure of woman as she appears in the liturgy of the church passed silently through the darkness: a whiterobed figure, small and slender as a boy and with a falling girdle" (P 244). The androgynous phantasm, with a voice "frail and high as a boy's," intones a passage out of the Bible. Stephen's mind is immersed in the aesthetic beauty of ecclesiastical rites. He protests that he cannot place his faith in the "real love" associated with "sweet Rosie O'Grady" until he first sees the enigmatic Rosie.[31] True love between man and woman may, indeed, be nothing but a chimera of the romantic imagination.

Toward the end of the novel, Stephen's Platonic musings give way to flippant remarks and lewd jokes. In the company of Lynch, he follows a "sizable hospital nurse" and comments on her cow-like proportions. The young men resemble two "lean hungry greyhounds walking after a heifer"(P 248). The "wild spring" brings Stephen's roving eye to rest on girls "demure and romping. All fair or auburn: no dark ones. They blush better" (P 250). The motif of shame and humiliation continues to inform his thoughts about women. He feels pity for Emma, "humbled and saddened by the dark shame of womanhood" (P 223), and equates menstruation with a fall from innocence. He remarks facetiously that, according to Lynch, statues of women "should always be fully draped, one hand of the woman feeling regretfully her own hinder parts" (P 251). In Stephen's mind, the female is "shame-wounded" by nature, bovine and buttocks-bound, chafing from the scatological burdens of bodily process.

In his final meeting with Emma, Stephen freezes her image in the guise of an idealized Beatrice by opening the "spiritual-heroic re-frigerating apparatus, invented and patented in all countries by Dante Alighieri" (P 252). He concedes in his diary: "Yes, I liked her today" (P 252). But the seeds of friendship or affection will not be allowed to ripen. Rejecting the arms of women, Stephen chooses "the white arms of roads, their promise of close embraces and the black arms of tall ships that stand against the moon, their tale of distant nations" (P 252).

Throughout A Portrait, Stephen has manifested a psychological hor-ror of the female as a figure of immanence, a symbol of physical temptation, and a perpetual reminder of mortality. At the end of the novel, he flees from all the women who have served as catalysts in his own growth. His journey into exile will release him from what he perceives as a cloying matriarchal authority. He must blot from his ears "his mother's sobs and reproaches" and strike from his eyes the insistent "image of his mother's face" (P 224). Alone and proud, isolated and free, Stephen proclaims joyful allegiance to the masculine fraternity of Daedalus, his priest and patron: "Welcome, O life! I go to encounter for the millionth time the reality of experience and to forge in the smithy of my soul the uncreated conscience of my race. . . . Old father, old artificer, stand me now and ever in good stead" (P 252–53). The hyperbolic resonance of Stephen's invocation leads us to suspect that his fate will be Icarian rather than Daedalian. Insofar as women are concerned, he goes to encounter the "reality of experience" not for the millionth time, but for the first.

Joyce's protagonist has constantly tried to achieve mastery over the outer world by adopting a male model of aesthetic creation. In the very act of "word-shaping," he can impose his will on a resistant environ-ment and reduce the chaotic fluidity of life to the controlled stasis of art. Much of the irony in A Portrait, however, results from Joyce's satire of Stephen's logocentric paradigm. The hero naively gathers phrases for his "word-hoard" without infusing his "capful of light odes" (U 415) with the spark of human sympathy.

Certainly, the reader may feel baffled or uneasy about the degree of irony implicit in Joyce's portrait of the artist as a young man. To what extent is the author gently mocking his character in a fictional exposure of adolescent narcissism? There is a great deal of evidence in A Portrait that Stephen's misogyny is, in fact, still another example of his youthful priggishness. The pervasive irony that tinges the hero's scrupulous devotions and gives his aesthetic theory that "true scholastic stink" surely informs his relations with women—from his mother and Dante Riordan to Emma and the unnamed bird-girl he idealizes on the beach. Joyce makes clear to his audience that Stephen's fear of woman and contempt for sensuous life are among the many inhibitions that stifle his creativity. Before he can become a priest of the eternal imagination, Stephen must first divest himself of the "spiritual-heroic refrigerating apparatus" that characterizes the egocentric aesthete. Misogyny is one of the adolescent traits he has to outgrow on the path to artistic maturity. Not until *Ulysses* will a new model begin to emerge—one that recognizes the need for the intellectual artist to "make his peace" with woman and to incorporate into his work the vital, semiotic flow of female life.

NOTES

1. Certain archetypal structures apparently determine infant psychology and influence human development. In *The Great Mother: An Analysis of the Archetype*, Erich Neumann explains that "in both sexes the active ego consciousness is characterized by a male symbolism, the unconscious as a whole by a female symbolism" ([1955; rpt. Princeton: Princeton University Press, 1972], p.28). Julia Kristeva emphasizes, throughout her work, the "semiotic" dimensions of maternal consciousness in contrast to the "logocentric" nature of male thought. (See, for instance, *Polylogue* [Paris: Editions du Seuil, 1977]). The inebriate Simon Dedalus, however, is hardly a model of rationality. One of Stephen's childhood disillusionments is the discovery that this "godlike" patriarch is socially and economically impotent.

2. Quoting Jung on "The Significance of the Father" (an essay found in Joyce's library), Jean Kimball observes that enuresis or bed-wetting may be seen, in Freudian terms, as "an infantile sexual substitute" ("Freud, Leonardo, and Joyce: The Dimensions of a Childhood Memory," *James Joyce Quarterly*, 17 [Winter, 1980], 169-70). Hence the importance of maternal ministrations after Stephen has wet the bed. If the horn is interpreted as a "phallic synonym," then the sailor's hornpipe suggests repressed erotic interest in the mother. Stephen unconsciously identifies his female parent as a "phallic mother" whom he sexually desires but simultaneously fears. Kimball points out that "as early as 1911 or 1912 Joyce owned Freud's essay on Leonardo, which highlights the artist's relationship with his mother," and that he probably read Freud's 1905 publication of *Three Essays on the Theory of Sexuality*, "which focused on the

crucial effect of infant sexuality on the psychological destiny of the adult" (p. 165). For a list of the psychology books in Joyce's library and a discussion of their possible influence, see Richard Ellmann, *The Consciousness of Joyce* (New York: Oxford University Press, 1977).

3. Chester Anderson argues that in this scene Stephen "is threatened with 'castration' in the most classic way: by having his eyes pulled out, as Oedipus himself pulled out his with Jocasta's brooch." Anderson identifies Dante as the "terrible mother" or castrator and feels "it is important that the threat comes from Dante, the 'bad' mother split from the 'nice'" ("Baby Tuckoo: Joyce's 'Features of Infancy,'" in *Approaches to Joyce's "Portrait": Ten Essays*, ed. Thomas F. Staley and Bernard Benstock [Pittsburgh: University of Pittsburgh Press, 1976], p. 149). Anderson's distinction, however, obscures the revelation of Mary Dedalus as a female authority figure.

4. Dorothy Dinnerstein, *The Mermaid and the Minotaur* (New York: Harper and Row, 1977), p. 28. As Erich Neumann points out, the figure of the Great Mother may be terrible or beneficent: "What Bachofen described as the death character of the material-maternal is an expression of this archetypal domination of nature and the unconscious over life, and likewise over the undeveloped childlike, or youthfully helpless, ego consciousness. In this phase the Archetypal Feminine not only bears and directs life as a whole, and the ego in particular, but also takes everything that is born of it back into its womb of origination and death" (*The Great Mother*, p. 30).

5. In "Unlocking the Word-Hoard: Madness, Identity and Creativity in James Joyce," Jeanne McKnight suggests that young Stephen may be suffering from what Philip Slater terms the "oral-narcissistic dilemma"—an "infantile conflict between the desire to remain an undifferentiated part of the mother and the developmental wish to be separate and free" (*James Joyce Quarterly*, 14 [Summer, 1977], 422).

6. Simone de Beauvoir, *The Second Sex*, trans. and ed. H. M. Parshley (1949; rpt. New York: Bantam, 1961), p. 136.

7. *Ibid.*, p. 129.

8. See Michel Foucault's discussion of the similarities among educational, penal, and military institutions. (Part 3, "Discipline," in *Discipline and Punish*, trans. Alan Sheridan [1975; rpt. New York: Random House, 1979]). Hugh Kenner also notes that "Stephen finds himself, like Simon Moonan, engaged in the rhythm of obedience to irrational authority, bending his activities to a meaningless act, the arithmetic contest. He is being, in other words, 'a good little boy': obedient" ("The *Portrait* in Perspective," in *James Joyce: Two Decades of Criticism*, ed. Seon Givens [1948; rpt. New York: Vanguard Press, 1963], p. 146).

9. In *Discipline and Punish*, Foucault interprets Jeremy Bentham's Panopticon as a utopian paradigm of institutional surveillance, "a mechanism of power reduced to its ideal form." By allowing the authority figure to "see all," this "pure architectural and optical system" insures complete psychological control over subjects. The Panopticon becomes a polyvalent symbol, "a way of defining power relations in terms of the everyday life of men" (pp. 205–206).

10. Philip E. Slater, *The Glory of Hera* (1968; rpt. Boston: Beacon Press, 1971), p. 416.

11. *Ibid.*, p. 439.

12. As Charles Rossman observes, Stephen perceives Emma "in a blend of falsifying images: first, as a vaguely religious figure, a nunlike innocent with a 'cowled head'; then, on the tram step below him, as a temptress trying to coax him out of his protective isolation, down from his height." The poem that he writes in her honor reduces their encounter to "a vague mood of longing, and a farewell between the disembodied lovers, who give the kiss that Stephen had withheld." This lyrical endeavor "substitutes for lived experience, refining the human actors out of existence. Here art, like religious grace in chapter three, signifies experiential death" ("Stephen Dedalus and the Spiritual-Heroic Refrigerating Apparatus: Art and Life in Joyce's *Portrait*," in *Forms of Modern British Fiction*, ed. Alan Warren Friedman [Austin: University of Texas Press, 1975], pp. 118–20).

13. In the language of the unconscious, Eros can be deflected from the life of the body into the excremental function. (See Norman O. Brown, *Life Against Death* [Middletown, Conn.: Wesleyan University Press, 1960].) Freud also talks about the "cloaca theory" of sexuality developed by young children, whose own coprophiliac inclinations lead them to believe that birth entails the expulsion of an infant "like excrement, like a movement" ("On the Sexual Theories of Children," in *The Sexual Enlightenment of Children*, ed. Philip Rieff [1908; rpt. New York: Collier Books, 1976], p. 34).

14. Erwin Steinberg makes a similar point about Stephen's encounter with the prostitute: "Stephen is 'beseiged' and 'penetrated'; and as the language mounts in intensity, it suggests both violation and orgasm" ("The Bird-Girl in *A Portrait* as Synthesis: The Sacred Assimilated to the Profane," *James Joyce Quarterly*, 17 [Winter, 1980], 155).

15. The language of this description is based on the murkier prose of a Nietzschean reverie that Joyce recorded as an "Epiphany" in 1903: "What moves upon me from the darkness subtle and murmurous as a flood, passionate and fierce with an indecent movement of the loins? What leaps, crying in answer, out of me, as eagle to eagle in mid air, crying to overcome, crying for an iniquitous abandonment?" (*The Workshop of Daedalus: James Joyce and the Raw Materials for "A Portrait of the Artist as a Young Man,"* ed. Robert Scholes and Richard M. Kain [Evanston, Ill.: Northwestern University Press, 1965], p. 41).

16. Jeanne McKnight observes that "Joyce's manuscript notes for *Stephen Hero* suggest that he had once intended Stephen's sexual initiation to have been oral. The plan was for Stephen to participate in *Soixante-neuf* (after a walk)" ("Unlocking the Word-Hoard," p. 427). See *The Workshop of Daedalus*, p. 71.

17. De Beauvoir, pp. 150–51. Sheldon Brivic feels that "sexual desire is linked in Stephen's mind to dread of being reduced to a woman" ("Joyce in Progress: A Freudian View," *James Joyce Quarterly*, 13 [Spring, 1976], 315).

18. Interpreting the Jungian anima, Erich Neumann suggests that the "hermaphroditic" quality of the psyche "makes possible an inner 'independent'

experience of the opposite sex. In other words, the man possesses an inner, though primarily unconscious, experience of the woman, and the woman of man" (*The Great Mother*, p. 24).

19. De Beauvoir, pp.166–67.

20. According to Willian York Tindall, the "wading girl near the Bull Wall, who embodies mortal beauty, unites all previous suggestions." Stephen associates her with "Emma, the Virgin, the rose, and the womb of the imagination, whose priest he becomes" (*The Literary Symbol* [1955; rpt. Bloomington: Indiana University Press, 1974], pp. 80–81).

21. Edmund Epstein identifies this woman as a prostitute; the text, however, seems to counterpoint her image with the Nighttown setting. For Epstein, the bird-girl "is the earth itself, the 'vegetable chaos' of earthly life" (*The Ordeal of Stephen Dedalus* [Carbondale: Southern Illinois University Press, 1971], p. 99). Charles Rossman feels that the wading girl "is the mirror of Stephen's emotional state, the self-serving projection of a doomed yearning. She is the natural descendant of the imagined 'harlots with gleaming jewel eyes,' who had previously stimulated Stephen's orgies of auto-eroticism" ("Art and Life in Joyce's *Portrait*," p. 121).

22. Florence Howe sees the delicate, crane-like figure as "land-bound." She feels that Stephen's "ambivalence towards the young girl is at once a combination of his earlier idealistic view of women and his experience with a prostitute as well as his way of moving past that to declaim himself a man and an artist. . . . The artist can fly and create, even in motion. We women are of the earth. . . . The male artist, whether he is Stephen or Joyce or someone else, must conceive his power, or his difference from women, must take his measure against them, must finally define the two sexes as different species" ("Feminism and Literature," in *Images of Women in Fiction: Feminist Perspectives*, ed. Susan Koppelman Cornillon [Bowling Green, Ohio: Bowling Green University Popular Press, 1972], pp. 263–64).

23. Stephen's epiphany is indeed "sacramental" insofar as it proves to be the "outward sign of an inward grace." Compare the fervid invocation in the narrative essay "A Portrait of the Artist": "Thou wert sacramental imprinting thine indelible mark, of very visible grace. A litany must honour thee: Lady of Apple Trees, Kind Wisdom, Sweet Flower of Dusk" (*P* 264). The protagonist of Joyce's 1904 essay turns away from "waders, into whose childish or girlish hair, girlish or childish dresses, the very wilfulness of the sea had entered" (*P* 262). The woman he praises seems to combine characteristics later ascribed to Emma, the bird-girl, and the eternal temptress. His prayer climaxes in a flood of romantic ecstasy: "A kiss: and they leap together, indivisible, upwards, radiant lips and eyes, their bodies sounding with triumph of harps!" (*P* 264).

24. See Barbara Seward, "The Artist and the Rose" (1947; rpt. *Twentieth Century Interpretations of "A Portrait of the Artist as a Young Man*," ed. William M. Schutte [Englewood Cliffs N.J.: Prentice-Hall, 1968], pp. 53–63). Seward illuminates Joyce's use of "symbolism strongly reminiscent of the *Paradiso*" (p. 58).

25. Bernard Benstock interprets images of "pervading dampness" in *A Portrait* as part of a "symbolic understructure." "The symbology derives from three areas of Clongowes, the urinal 'square,' . . . the square ditch, . . . and the communal baths. . . . The relatively innocent bathwater, which causes Stephen a 'vague fear' as he passes the baths on the way to the infirmary, eventually forms part of a larger concept in the work" ("A Light from Some Other World: Symbolic Structure in *A Portrait of the Artist*," in *Approaches to Joyce's "Portrait,"* p. 206).

26. James Naremore indicts Stephen for wallowing in "the literary atmosphere of the nineties, . . . rarefied nearly out of existence. Even in his later, 'artist' phase Stephen is continuing to react against what he regards as the 'common and insignificant' reality, continuing to pare his fingernails above what he no doubt feels are the base and dirty aspects of his life. He hopes to escape into the free, pure air of art; but until he recognizes that no life is completely isolate, until he learns to accept and properly criticize his actual experience, he cannot be a poet or even a mature individual" ("Consciousness and Society in *A Portrait of the Artist*," in *Approaches to Joyce's Portrait*," p. 127).

27. Jean Kimball, quoting from Freud's essay on Leonardo da Vinci, notes that dreams of flight frequently disguise "a longing to be capable of sexual performance." She connects Stephen's vision of the birds in *Portrait* with his own repressed and stifled sexuality ("Freud, Leonardo, and Joyce," p.176). For an analysis of the bat images associated with women, see Elaine Unkeless "Bats and Sanguivorous Bugaboos," *James Joyce Quarterly*, 15 (Winter, 1978), 128–33.

28. Ironically, Gabriel is not a seraph at all, but an archangel, belonging to an entirely different angelic species from the seraphim. Are we to assume that Stephen, in the groggy aftermath of a wet dream, is so muddled as to have conflated the choirs of angels? Or does he deliberately choose to recreate biblical history by offering an aesthetic embellishment on the Annunciation? For further discussion of art as couvade, see R. Barrie Walkley, "The Bloom of Motherhood: Couvade as a Structural Device in *Ulysses*," *James Joyce Quarterly*, 18 (Fall, 1980), 55–67.

29. Chester Anderson compares Stephen's villanelle to the poems of Joyce's *Chamber Music*, lyrics viewed as "epicleti"—"moments of transubstantiation in which the Holy Ghost again descended with his wind-fire-light-water and bird-talk to impregnate the virgin-mother-artist, who can then give birth to the god-child-work." Stephen's "watery speech gives him not only the poem, but also a self-authorized 'uterim' from which he can give birth again to himself as a man and artist" ("Baby Tuckoo," pp. 151–52).

30. James Naremore observes that "the temptress in the verse remains a highly sexual creature, masked, like the Virgin Mary before her, in a religious imagery. One reason the poem is so poor is that it is dishonest to the emotions that led to its creation" ("Consciousness and Society," p. 126). Robert Scholes, in contrast, defends the villanelle as a "muse-poem," the celebration of a "great poetical archetype." He argues that "Joyce intended the poem to be the product of genuine inspiration. . . . It is at this point that Stephen ceases to

be an esthete and becomes a poet" ("Stephen Dedalus, Poet or Esthete?" in *"A Portrait of the Artist as a Young Man": Text, Criticism, and Notes*, ed. Chester G. Anderson [New York: Viking Press, 1968], pp. 478–80).

31. It is interesting that the "voice of a servant . . . heard singing," along with Cranly's Latin phrase, evokes in Stephen's imagination the liturgy for Holy Week and the words of the servant who accused Peter: "Thou too wast with Jesus the Galilean" (Matthew, 26:29). Stephen evidently identifies with Christ in his Passion and associates Cranly with Peter, the disciple who would thrice deny his master. Joyce's young man is still luxuriating in the role of hero-martyr-artist.

William York Tindall argues that Stephen's encounter with "Rosie" adumbrates his artistic maturity: "Rosie in her kitchen, the last great image of woman in *A Portrait of the Artist*, unites the ideal with the actual. Neither the wading girl nor Mercedes, both ethereal, can present to Stephen the idea and feeling of a union which someday he will understand. Far from seeing Rosie first, he sees her last, but by her aid, of which he is not fully aware as yet, he comes nearer his vision of above and below, of heavenly roses to be sure but of roses in kitchens" (*The Literary Symbol*, pp. 81–82).

Bertha's Role in *Exiles*

"Do you think I am a stone?"

An unconventional play, *Exiles* has been conventionally read. Critics have viewed Richard Rowan, a Dedalian figure who has endured (and enjoyed) nine years of exile in Italy for the sake of art and freedom, as the dominating figure of the drama. The other characters—Bertha, Robert Hand, and Beatrice Justice—have seemed mere shadows of Rowan's larger personality.[1] The crux of the play has seemed to be Hand's attempted seduction of Bertha. To Rowan that seduction would constitute a double betrayal of the artist by his friend, Hand, and by his mistress, Bertha.

Such an interpretation, according Rowan a dominant but suffering position among the characters, has been linked with views that Rowan himself is an insufferable bore, an egoist, and a writer without modesty, humor, or compassion.[2] Critics have likewise dismissed *Exiles* as incomplete and a failure.[3] Some have seen the play as an interruption in the development of Joyce's art, because it lacks the complex mythopoeic elements characteristic of *A Portrait of the Artist as a Young Man*, *Ulysses*, and *Finnegans Wake*.[4]

A more reasonable view, however, is that *Exiles* is neither minor nor a failure but is worthy of its place between *A Portrait* and *Ulysses* in the canon of Joyce's major works. The play achieves this stature when we recognize Bertha's pivotal role in the drama. Her centrality can be demonstrated not merely from characteristics parallel to those of Nora Barnacle, who was so protean an influence on Joyce, but also from a whole body of folklore, easily available to Joyce, which imparts symbolic depth to the play. This folklore links *Exiles*, through Bertha, to recurrent themes and devices in Joyce's work: the concept of epiphany, the Christ-martyr figure, the union of epic materials with ordinary life. Bertha's significance is proved also within the play, where Bertha's life force effects change in Richard, Beatrice, and Robert, and Bertha's character and values dominate the outcome of the action. Finally, it is Bertha who is the bridge between Joyce's most famous heroes, the aloof, aristocratic aesthete, Stephen Dedalus, and the kindly, human Leopold Bloom.

I

The parallels between Nora and Bertha are so well known as to need only the briefest summary here. Nora, a young woman of little education, fell in love with James Joyce, already a university graduate and writer, and joined him in his self-imposed exile in 1904. Their relationship was threatened in 1909 during Joyce's trip to Dublin when Vincent Cosgrave, a mutual friend, briefly convinced Joyce that Nora had been Cosgrave's mistress in 1904 while she was also seeing Joyce. Jealousy drove Joyce to denounce Nora and even to doubt the paternity of his son Giorgio (*SL* 157–59).

Once persuaded of Cosgrave's lie, Joyce repeatedly affirmed his intensified sense of Nora's value to him and to his work. For the remaining month of his Dublin stay, Joyce's letters were full of devotion to Nora. When they parted again, from October, 1909 to the beginning of the new year, his letters were forthright, intense expressions of their deep sexual bond (*SL* 172–96).[5] True, in a contrite moment Joyce vowed that "no man, I believe, can ever be worthy of a woman's love" (*SL* 160). Within forty-eight hours, however, he begged Nora to confirm that living with him had made her "capable of deeper and finer feeling." She, in turn, had warmed and brightened his being. His soul, which had "the pale passionless beauty of a pearl" when they met, was changed by her love: "Now I feel my mind something like an opal, . . . full of strange uncertain hues and colours, of warm lights and quick shadows and of broken music" (*SL* 161).

Joyce also insisted that only through Nora would he "learn the secrets of life" and become "the poet of my race" (*SL* 169). It was Nora who was to be the source of his art, for Joyce declared to her: "I *know* and *feel* that if I am to write anything fine or noble in the future I shall do so only by listening at the doors of your heart" (*SL* 173). Even when he had begun to establish himself, through *Dubliners* and *A Portrait of the Artist as a Young Man*, as the poet of his race, Joyce still acknowledged Nora's influence. Honoring that Dublin summer day when he and Nora first walked out together and she "made me a man" (*SL* 159), he made June 16, 1904, the first Bloomsday. And as a tribute to the shared years when he learned from Nora to know and to feel, Joyce wrote *Exiles*.

II

Joyce, as we know, was selective and deliberate in naming his characters. Michael Furey, Stephen Dedalus, Leopold Bloom, Nosey Flynn, Zoe Higgins, Anna Livia Plurabelle: major or minor, they have significant names. Bertha's name, like the others, seems to have been chosen by Joyce for its symbolic import. In Joyce's cast of characters for *Exiles*, Bertha's is the only name stripped free of what Adrienne Rich calls "definition through relatedness." [6] Without family name, without profession or title, she is simply Bertha.

Richard Rowan, on the other hand, has an easily recognizable Irish family name which alludes to Hamilton Rowan, the Irish patriot who died in 1794. Though Richard disclaims any relationship (*E* 45), he yet gives his son the hero's less well-known first name, Archibald, as if to make the child a transubstantial heir to glory. "Rowan" also suggests the ancient magical tree of Irish druids, called variously the rowan, mountain ash, quicken tree, or tree of life. The rowan tree in turn recalls the song of that name by Lady Caroline Nairne, recounting how a beautiful rowan, with its succession of leaves, blossoms, and scarlet berries, had once stood at the center of happy family life, sheltering everyone.[7] In sum, "Rowan" is an important name for Joyce insofar as it suggests family connections and resonates with political and musical overtones. In the cast of characters, Rowan is further identified by his profession, "writer," so we know him at once as an artist, a man of professional standing.

Richard's counterpart in the play, Robert Hand, has also a symbolic surname. "Hand," according to Skeat's *Etymological Dictionary*, derives from the Gothic *hinthan*, meaning "to seize." It is an appropriate connotation for this forerunner of usurpers like Buck Mulligan and Blazes Boylan. Joyce reinforces it by having Richard associate Robert (perhaps by assonance) with "robber." [8] Like Rowan, Hand has a profession. He is a "journalist"—a less prestigious, though more lucrative, version of "writer."

Bertha's female counterpart in *Exiles* is Beatrice Justice, whose family name suggests an evenhanded, blindly legalistic perspective, so chill as to be "ice, Just ice." It also connotes, quite appropriately, the balance that Beatrice cautiously maintains between Irish residence and foreign exile, between Richard and Robert, between health and illness. Like the men, she has a profession from which she draws part of her identity. Her work also relates her to Hand, for the music teacher might be perceived as a failed musician in the same way the journalist might be regarded as a prostituted writer.

Even the minor characters in *Exiles* have family or occupational identities. The child Archie, though an illegitimate offspring of Richard's and Bertha's union, is nevertheless "their son." Brigid is identified as an "old servant of the Rowan family," a title giving her both occupation and family. The cry in the street comes from a fish-woman, who at least has a commercial trade, if no other identity.

Only Bertha stands alone, without surname or profession: to join Rowan in exile she has given up "religion, family, my own peace" (*E* 100). Yet she has not taken Rowan's name, nor been given it by law or by the church. She does not have the title of wife. Within the play others, but never Richard, call her "Mrs. Rowan." (He does, however, recall their early passion at the time when she was his "bride in exile" [*E* 111].) Bertha has entered into exile and into her union with Rowan more nakedly than has Rowan himself, though it is he who expresses the ideal of a "naked union" between a man and a woman in love.[9] Bertha's lack of employment or profession is also indicative of her nature. She is a natural, untutored being, with little formal education, a Joycean woman not concerned with a career but able and willing to follow Rowan's desires even if they should direct her to Hand's bed.

To be only "Bertha" is not to be insignificant, however, and the folklore surrounding her single name is enlightening. According to Charlotte M. Yonge, a nineteenth-century authority on origins of names, Twelfth Night was called in the Eastern church both *Epiphania* (from which we derived "Epiphany") and *Theophania* (meaning a showing forth of God). Joyce, of course, associated this sense of showing forth with the term "epiphany." In old German this feast of Theophania, the showing-forth, became translated as "*Giperahta Naht*, the brightened night," or "Bertha's night." Yonge goes on to say:

> By the analogy of saints' days, Perahta, or Bertha, was erected into an individual character, called in an Alsatian poem, the mild Berchte; in whose honour all the young farming men in the Salzburg mountains go dancing

about, ringing cattle bells, and blowing whistles all night. Sometimes she is a
gentle white lady, who steals softly to neglected cradles, and rocks them in
the absence of careless nurses. . . . Herrings and oat-bread are put outside
the door for her on her festival—a token of its Christian origin; but there is
something of heathenism connected with her. . . .

That Frau Bertha is an impersonation of the Epiphany there seems little
doubt, but it appears that there was an original mythical Bertha, who
absorbed the brightened night. . . . [10]

In the early centuries of the church the Epiphany, later personified
by Perchta, celebrated not only the Magi but also the marriage at Cana,
baptism, and the blessing of waters. In the latter cases it occasionally
merged with pagan fertility rites. The Basilidean sect in Egypt, for
instance, celebrated Christ's baptism on Tobi 11 (January 6, Epiphany),
a feastday when the Nile and other river water was believed purest.
Springs and rivers were believed to turn into wine, an event Christians
identified with Christ's miracle at Cana. Alexandrian feasts at the
Temple of Kore, a virgin, celebrated the new pure water. For the
Egyptians, then, January 6 marked a celebration of fertility brought by
pure water, and also the feast of a virgin.[11]

In the Teutonic world Perchta was linked to earth goddess Hertha,
as well as to the springtime worship of water, a festival absorbed into
the carnival season preceding Lent. Perchta/Hertha's fertility rites
became associated, too, with the Christian celebration of the Virgin
Mary at Candlemas on February 2 (Joyce's birthday).[12] Sir James
Frazer, in *The Golden Bough*, relates Perchta celebrations to Epiphany
and Shrove Tuesday.[13]

The association of Theophania with brightness also dates to pre-
Christian times, for the Greeks celebrated Epiphania as the birthday,
and Theophania as the day of the showing-forth of Apollo, the God of
light—"not only the light of the sun, but the light of the mind, the light
of reason, the light of insight." [14] At Delphi Theophania was marked
only every ninth year, when it was celebrated together with Epiphania
on 7th Busios, the first month of spring.

Through the earth goddess Perchta, then, Bertha emerges as queen
of "the brightened night," a saint identified with Epiphany, linked by
ancient folklore to fertility rites, to the cleansing powers of water, even
to Christ's transubstantial creation of wine from elemental water as,
honoring a marriage, he performed his first miracle. Her links to the
Greek Apollonia are reflected in her association with brightness, in the

summer setting of *Exiles*, and in the Rowans' return to Ireland in their ninth year of exile.

The character of Perchta, in folk belief, was sharply divided into good and evil aspects. In addition to her bright, maternal qualities, she could be a harsh disciplinarian of bad children or of lazy, inept spinners; but she was also responsible for making the ploughed land fruitful and for causing cattle to thrive.[15] In her cruel manifestations she slit open the bellies of the idle, or of those who had not eaten the magic oatcakes or herring.[16] She was usually accompanied by many little children, though a baptized child would lag behind the rest, blubbering.[17] On the Eve of Twelfth Night good people left the remains of supper on the table for Perchta. When she and the children came to partake of these leftovers, anyone of the household who peeked at her through the keyhole was blinded for a year.[18]

Like Perchta herself, her celebrants represented both good and evil, the two groups being called the Beautiful and the Ugly Perchten. Costumed and masked according to their roles, they leapt and danced about the countryside on Epiphany night, ringing bells and cracking whips, using sausage-shaped rolls to strike lightly at women and girls among the spectators. Others, in a self-evident fertility rite, threw the effigy of a baby toward women spectators. Still others used swords, masks, jingling bells, and loud din to drive away evil spirits and demons and to guarantee good harvests. The Perchten also carried a "stretching-shears," built of lath and used to hand bouquets to women and to remove hats from men in the crowds.[19]

Finally, Teutonic belief held that the souls of the dead departed as breath which formed breezes, winds, or even a storm termed "Perchta's host." Likewise a single breath or soul of a living person might go forth during sleep to torment another sleeper as a nightmare; this nightmare was personified, in central Germany, as "Alp."[20]

Nowhere in the notes Joyce made for *Exiles* or in his correspondence does he state directly that he had the Perchta myths in mind when he wrote the play. However, a number of correspondences between the details of the myths and those of Joyce's drama serve to deepen our understanding of the play; and considered as a group, they make his use of the Perchta material probable, if not certain. The earth goddess of "the brightened night" is reflected when Joyce's preparatory notes, for instance, describe Bertha as "the earth, dark, formless, mother, made beautiful by the moonlit night."[21] Joyce develops this relationship between her earth-like being and her brightness elsewhere in the notes and in the play. Thus her age, twenty-eight, "is the completion of a lunar rhythm" ("Notes" 113). The moon's brightness is also a part of Robert Hand's perception of Bertha: "You passed. The avenue was dim with dusky light. I could see the dark green masses of the trees. And you passed beyond them. You were like the moon. . . . In that dress, with your slim body, walking with little even steps. I saw the moon passing in the dusk till you passed and left my sight" (E 31). Hand returns to this description later, calling Bertha "something beautiful and distant—the moon or some deep music" (E 32). Robert also identifies Bertha with the earth, with obvious allusions to fertility, in act 2: "The rain falling. Summer rain on the earth. Night rain. The darkness and warmth and flood of passion. Tonight the earth is loved—loved and possessed. Her lover's arms around her; and she is silent. Speak, dearest!" (E 87).

Not only in this scene but throughout *Exiles*, Bertha is associated with water, as Sheldon Brivic has pointed out.[22] In the first act Bertha and Archie enter from the strand, where she has taken her son bathing. In the rainstorm of act 2, Richard enters carrying an umbrella and Robert seeks to shelter under an umbrella but fails. Bertha, however, enters from the storm with "neither umbrella nor waterproof" (E 72), though apparently undampened. In this way the play incorporates Perchta's association with Epiphany as a baptismal and river festival, as well as Perchta's link to earth made fruitful by rainfall.[23]

Joyce also associates Bertha with water in the form of mist, for he notes: "Her mind is a grey seamist amid which common objects— hillsides, the masts of ships, and barren islands—loom with strange and yet recognizable outlines" ("Notes" 125). This seems to draw into the play the peasants' assertion that a mist floating over the fields was Perchta "gliding along in a white mantle."[24]

Archie, too, unites Bertha to the mythic level of the play. Not only does he represent, in Joyce's understated way, the crowd of children accompanying Perchta, but also through his enthusiasm for the milkman's horses and cows he relates Bertha to Perchta's concern for cattle. And Archie is evidence, of course, that Bertha is herself fertile, unlike Beatrice or Robert. (Richard, sleeping alone in his study, is temporarily "sterile.")

In another understated parallel, Hand, though without Perchta's stretching-shears, offers Bertha a bouquet of roses (*E* 26), and later Bertha hangs up Richard's hat (*E* 37).

On a larger scale, the omnipresent dualities within *Exiles*, which have long puzzled and even confused readers and critics, are understood more easily in terms of the contending Perchten of tradition. Joyce was not a writer to include leaping hosts of Perchten, hung with bells and swords, on his stage—not, at least, before "Circe." But he incorporates the duality in small details as well as in large structural elements of the play. *R*ichard and *R*obert, the two males; *B*ertha and *B*eatrice, the two females; *Ric*hard and Beat*ric*e, the cerebrotonics; *Rob*ert and *Bert*ha, the viscerotonics: the characters are carefully paired in both name and nature. Moreover, the play is structured as a series of dialogues between these pairs, probably reflecting the contending Perchten.[25] Joyce also provides Bertha with a pair of suitors, Richard and Robert; and both men stay awake during the night's dark hours. If neither leaps about the countryside, Richard does precede Bertha to the Ranelagh cottage, return to Merrion to work in his study, and conclude the night pacing the strand with his "thin cane" sword and making the sign of the cross upside down—a Perchta-mask of Joyce's devising—to ward off demons. Robert, who is more of a clown, rushes about the cottage with a perfume pump and darts in from the garden to fetch an umbrella before Bertha's arrival. After her departure he "leaps" about the city from the vice-chancellor's dinner to the office, to a nightclub, to Donnybrook in a cab—surely a restless night, even without bells.

Perchta's host, the wind of dead souls, also enters the play. Richard has prayed (*E* 22, 25) for his dead mother's hardness of heart; and her cold, dead spirit sweeps through the cottage in act 2 as gusts of chill wind (*E* 82, 83–4), forcing Robert to turn down the lamps he has lit for Bertha. Bertha's explanation of the night to Robert—"Remember your dream of me. You dreamed that I was yours last night" (*E* 106)— recalls "Alp" invading sleeping minds and foretells Joyce's own ALP, as yet unborn.

As Richard and Robert confront each other in act 3, even the fish-woman's cries of "Fresh Dublin bay herrings!" (*E* 107) seem to reinforce the mythic overtones. For though her cries may be interpreted as only the impingement of reality upon the cerebral arguments of Richard and Robert, they also serve at the mythic level as a reminder of the herring-gift owed the earth goddess for the epiphanies she has revealed to Rowan and Hand.

Bertha, then, has a name which brings to *Exiles* the mythic echoes of warm, fertile earth and the brightness of the moon. Through her link to Perchta we may expect Bertha to combine nurturing concern for children, animals, and the neglected, with a vivid anger directed toward the slothful, the over-curious, or the unclean. Sighing through the darkness, Perchta calls up the spirits of the dead or rouses that Alp who stirs our dreams. Through folklore centuries old, she ties pagan earth goddess to Christian baptism, exorcises demons, and guards fertility. Bearing in mind this somewhat heavy load of myth and folklore, we turn to examine the character of Bertha within *Exiles* and the epiphanic revelations she brings to the play.

III

As viewed by the male characters in *Exiles*, Bertha is an object, not merely sexual, but one representing artistic achievement or political victory. In act 1, for instance, Richard asserts ownership, as he would own the winnings in a card game: "I played for her against all that you say or can say; and I won" (*E* 40). Having won Bertha, Richard feels he can use her as a lure, through much of the play, to test Robert's discipleship.

Even when Richard appears to be yielding Bertha to another, she remains his possession, and he gives her selfishly in order to keep her. Thus in act 1 when he explains "to give" for his son Archie, we sense that Richard is speaking not merely of "a thing" given, but also of a wife given to a lover: "While you have a thing it can be taken from you. . . . But when you give it, you have given it. No robber can take it from you. . . . It is yours then for ever when you have given it. It will be yours always. That is to give" (*E* 46–47). The same sense that Bertha is one of Richard's possessions, like the household furniture, recurs when he tells Robert in act 2, "Steal you could not in my house because the doors were open: nor take by violence if there were no resistance" (*E* 62). But *if* resistance, to possible rape for instance, is to be made, it will be made by Richard on behalf of Bertha, his chattel: "I thought he [Robert] was a common robber, prepared to use even violence against you. I had to protect you from that" (*E* 73).

Robert, who follows Richard's concepts of possession as he does most of Richard's ideas, expresses the same sense that a man owns any woman, including Bertha. She is to Robert like a stone he may hold and caress (*E* 41–42), and to own that stone, he challenges Richard, saying: "I love her and I will take her from you, however I can, because I love her" (*E* 62).

At the same time, Robert recognizes the woman he loves as an object created by Richard, asserting, "She is yours, your work" (*E* 62), and in the same scene, "You have made her all that she is" (*E* 67). Later he reverts to a "yours" of ownership more than of workmanship: "She is yours. Keep her and forgive me, both of you" (*E* 71). In a final concession of ownership, near the end of the play, Robert declares to Richard: "Bertha is yours now as she was nine years ago, when you—when we—met her first" (*E* 108–109).

In most of these exchanges, Rowan and Hand might be discussing a ship or a horse rather than a woman they profess to love. At first Bertha herself does little to contest this view. Having been told by Richard, "I have allowed you complete liberty" (*E* 52), she accepts that liberty as her husband's gift and repeats to Hand, "He leaves me free" (*E* 83).

That Bertha is regarded as an object by Richard and by Robert is partly a result of her moon-like passivity during segments of the play. In act 1 Robert begs to kiss her hand. She replies coolly, "If you wish" (*E* 34). When he demands a kiss, Bertha replies, "Take it," and she, in turn, "kisses him quickly" (*E* 35). Struggling briefly against passivity, she repels his embrace and "breaks from him" (*E* 36). Then she relapses as, pressed for an assignation, she says, "I promise nothing" (*E* 37). Bertha's report to Richard about Robert's advances is equally detached: "I let him" kiss my hand (*E* 48) and "He has not nice lips" (*E* 49). Clearly she shows no passion, no inclination toward Robert. Moonlike, she reflects toward Richard the love Robert shows her, and toward Robert the ethical attitudes she hears from Richard.

This passivity, which makes Bertha an object-victim for the male characters, derives in part from Joyce's conception of her as a Christ figure: "Bertha's state when abandoned spiritually by Richard must be expressed by the actress by a suggestion of hypnosis. Her state is like that of Jesus in the garden of olives. It is the soul of woman left naked and alone that it may come to an understanding of its own nature. She must appear also to *be carried forward* to the last point consistent with her immunity *by the current of the action*" ("Notes" 115, emphasis added). For Joyce there is no inconsistency in a heroine who is at once

Perchta, the Teutonic earth goddess, and Christ. Both represent fertility; both are mild and gentle. Christian myth adds, as Perchta's myth does not, the Joycean elements of wounding and betrayal.

Richard first reveals his betrayal of Bertha as he painfully admits to Hand his "carnal" infidelities and recalls how, in the dark of night, he returned home, wakened Bertha to recount his betrayals, and "pierced her heart" (*E* 66). Bertha's wounds come not merely from these "carnal" betrayals which Richard confesses, but from his spiritual betrayal of her through his correspondence and conversations about literature with Beatrice Justice. In the bitter exchange between Bertha and Richard in the first act (*E* 53–55), Bertha reveals her fear of Rowan's love for Beatrice, her awareness of her own intellectual deficiencies, her suspicion that Rowan grants Bertha freedom only to free himself to pursue Beatrice. It is this suspicion which transforms her from the Christlike "mild Berchte" to the passionate Perchta as the act ends (*E* 53–56). Bertha shows similar anger when she discovers Richard in Hand's cottage at Ranelagh in act 2, and once more when defending Beatrice against Richard in act 3. Thus in each act of the play she is both the mild, suffering Christ and the furious Perchta of myth.

Between her extreme passivity and her rage at betrayal, Bertha displays other elemental traits. Among these is the unaffected naturalness which links her to Perchta, the earth goddess, as revealed in her praise of Archie (who "had too much nature" not to love her), as well as in her criticism of Richard (who was unnatural in hating his own mother [*E* 52]).

Simple naturalness also leads Bertha to easy action. Richard goes into exile self-consciously, as an act of defiance against his homeland and race. Robert keeps a snuggery where he may meet women and indulge his little affairs, partly so he may enjoy a *reputation* as a free spirit. Bertha simply acts. She joins Richard unasked because being with Richard is what she wants of life. As she says to Richard, "You knew I would go, asked or not. I do things" (*E* 75).

At other times Bertha's naturalness means acceptance in quietude. Such natural acquiescence is particularly evident in her attitude toward language and establishes a major contrast between her and Robert. When he makes much over "one word which I have never dared say to you" (*E* 31), Bertha asks calmly, "What is the word?" Still hesitant, Robert replies not with one word but with an ambiguous phrase: "That I have a deep liking for you." This is hardly a daring utterance, particularly for a man proud of his passionate free living and free thinking. In thus encouraging Hand to speak out, Bertha is like Rowan, who in his writing must provide the words which Beatrice lacks courage to say for herself (*E* 20).

Although Bertha can say openly the words Hand fears to utter, she nevertheless disdains the inflated, unnatural language he so often uses. After Bertha's light, quick kiss, Robert sighs melodramatically, "My life is finished—over." Bertha, who has reminded him already of his numerous "admirers" and his reputation as a libertine, replies with a realistic "O, don't speak like that now, Robert" (*E* 35). As Robert continues planning their rendezvous in language as overblown as his flowers, Bertha offers a succinct, factual question: "Where?" (*E* 36). This Robert misinterprets as a query about where he would like to kiss Bertha. (This small comedy is reworked by Joyce, of course, in "Penelope," when Molly Bloom, asked in confession where she'd been touched, replies "On the canal bank." Both women are preoccupied with geography; both men, with physiology.)

Just as Bertha responds to Robert's advances with frank and natural language, she is able to recount them to Richard with the same naturalness, almost without reserve. She hesitates a little before saying she had kissed Robert, frowns before admitting that though Robert has "not nice lips. . . . Still, I was excited of course." (The "of course" is by itself the voice of nature in Bertha.) Then she adds in an almost clinical comparison, "But not like with you, Dick" (*E* 49). Rowan strives to maintain the same clinical detachment, appropriate for the artist gathering matter for his acts of creation. His avid requests for each detail, however, reveal his profound emotional involvement.

Bertha's natural responses are closely related to her honesty: she is the only character who, during the play's action, never lies on her own initiative. True, she allows Robert to believe that he is pursuing her without Richard's knowledge; but she allows this because, as she explains to Robert in the second act, "you never spoke or asked me" (*E* 80). Had he asked whether Richard knew, she would have told the truth. It is also part of Bertha's honesty to feel that she, not Richard, ought to have told Robert that his advances were being discussed by the Rowans (*E* 73); for she could have revealed the truth without hurting Robert's feelings or causing him to feel the betrayed fool. Yet she also registers some surprise that he had not realized her complete honesty with Richard. Not to have told everything would have been unfair and impractical: ". . . you see, I could not keep things secret from Dick. Besides, what is the good? They always come out in the end. Is it not better for people to know?" (*E* 80). Bertha believes in frankness, then, for both pragmatic and moral reasons.

Robert, the professed man of the world, is astonished by Bertha's frankness. "Were you not ashamed?" he asks.[26] Bertha, in equal astonishment, replies, "No. Why? Is that terrible?" (*E* 81). In this pair, artful duplicity and natural truth astound each other. Bertha is equally surprised later at Robert's reluctance to speak truthfully to Rowan about their own evening at the cottage:

> BERTHA: But, Robert, you must speak to him.
> ROBERT: What am I to say to him?
> BERTHA: The truth! Everything!
> ROBERT, *reflects:* No, Bertha. I am a man speaking to a man. I cannot tell him everything.
> BERTHA: He will believe that you are going away because you are afraid to face him after last night.
> ROBERT, *after a pause:* Well, I am not a coward, any more than he. I will see him [*E* 105–106].

Robert yields not for love of truth, but out of cowardice, to protect his own good name and reputation for courage. There is, to be sure, an essential difference between Bertha's disclosures to Rowan and those Robert is to make. Bertha is revealing that she is desirable to other men but faithful to Richard. Robert appears to be conveying the reverse, that he has been an unfaithful disciple, but has failed to seduce Bertha. As Joyce noted in his plans for *Exiles:* "All believe that Bertha is Robert's mistress. This *belief* rubs against his own *knowledge* of what has been, but he accepts the belief as a bitter food" ("Notes" 123). In a reversal of Bertha's earlier speech (*E* 75), Robert has the name but not the gains of bad conduct. When he tells Richard the truth—that nothing happened—he is disbelieved. His reputation as betrayer overpowers his failure as seducer.[27]

Not only does Bertha's honesty set her in contrast to Robert, who characteristically speaks in hyperbole and acts with a sense of shame, "craftily, secretly, meanly—in the dark, in the night" (*E* 69).[28] Her openness also distinguishes her from Robert's cousin, Beatrice Justice, a creature not of darkness, but of grey shadow. A self-conscious "lady," Beatrice is webbed round by convention and lacks Bertha's naturalness.

Beatrice resembles the educated, literate women of Joyce's own class in Dublin—women like Mary Sheehy, whom he admired in his student days, or like the fictional Miss Ivors of "The Dead" and Emma Clery of *Stephen Hero* and *A Portrait*. More than her predecessors in Joyce's earlier work, Beatrice is a subject of compassion, an emotion Joyce conveys to the audience of *Exiles* by a gesture: Beatrice bends, with ill-adjusted glasses, to read Hand's article on Rowan (*E* 98). Her eyes are myopic, like her conventional values; and the gesture which reveals her defective vision symbolically reflects her character ("Notes" 114). To borrow a phrase from Leopold Bloom, Beatrice Justice is the girl who has "almosted it." No truth is fully perceived, no experience is quite complete, no relationship fulfilled for this woman.

When she met Rowan, Beatrice was Robert Hand's fiancée, betrothed by a kiss and the gift of a garter. (As we have seen, a kiss from Robert has no such significance for the more natural Bertha.) Beatrice could have become Rowan's mistress, but sensing what this Eveline's answer would be, Richard never asked her to accompany him to Italy. Unlike Bertha, she had not the courage to go uninvited. After Rowan and Bertha left Ireland, Beatrice became deathly ill; yet she recovered and is now almost well.

For eight years Beatrice has corresponded with Rowan, who not only writes to her but also makes her the subject of his art.[29] The basis of their friendship is not merely Rowan's physical attraction for Beatrice, but his courage to speak what she can only feel:

> RICHARD, *with some vehemence:* . . . I expressed in those chapters and letters, and in my character and life as well, something in your soul which you could not—pride or scorn? . . . Could not because you dared not. Is that why?
> BEATRICE, *bends her head:* Yes.
> RICHARD: On account of others or for want of courage—which?
> BEATRICE, *softly:* Courage.
> RICHARD, *slowly:* And so you have followed me with pride and scorn in your heart?
> BEATRICE: And loneliness [*E* 20].

If Joyce perceives Beatrice compassionately, Rowan does not. Despite the letters which have linked the exile to Dublin and provided material for his art, Rowan makes no acknowledgment of debt to Beatrice and expresses no thanks for her devotion. Instead, his cross-examination, laying bare her lack of courage, her unspoken love, her loneliness, offers a brutal repayment of her patient, though timid, devotion for nearly a decade. It is no wonder that her "yes" is only half affirmative, compared to Molly Bloom's. It is, after all, affirmation of her own conventional weakness.

Timidity, of course, contrasts Beatrice with Bertha, from whom Rowan also tries to win acknowledgment of his primacy:

> RICHARD: Then you have come here and led [Robert] on in this way on account of me. Is that how it is? . . . If so you have indeed treated him badly and shamefully.
>
> BERTHA, *points at him:* Yes. But it was your fault. And I will end it now. I am simply a tool for you. You have no respect for me . . . [E 74].

Both women have been used by Rowan, but Bertha recognizes the fact openly, if resentfully. Her "yes" is, like that of Beatrice, an admission of personal error, but of error committed out of love for Rowan, rather than from fear of society. She has vision and courage to see that Rowan shares the blame, and to state his responsibility with her head upright, not bowed.

Beatrice, too, has manipulated Robert for Richard's sake. Unlike Bertha, however, Beatrice has taken the initiative in maneuvering her cousin, though scarcely admitting even to herself what she has done: ". . . it was my cousin who urged Mr. Rowan always to come back. I have that on my conscience. . . . Because—I spoke to my cousin about Mr. Rowan when he was away and to a certain extent, it was I . . ." (E 95–96). Her responsibility, like her voice, trails off into silence. Even in the small accountability she accepts, there is no hint that her letters urged Rowan to return, that she praised his work, commended his potential achievement, defended him against gossip. In her hesitant, unsure way she only "mentioned" his name.

There is a qualitative difference in the way the two women take advantage of Robert Hand. Bertha is making it possible for Rowan to study and react to Hand's behavior. Perhaps Richard can incorporate the material in his art, a noble end. Beatrice is interested not in Hand but in the power to which he has access, power which she wants to put at the disposal of Rowan for her personal benefit.[30] Beatrice uses a conventional feminine device in a traditional situation where the male has at his call the power of the press and the vice-chancellor's friendship—has, in short, the means the female lacks to realize her goals. It is a further mark of Beatrice's conventionality that her conscience is pricked not by using Robert, but by her recalling Richard to

Dublin. What shame, after all, should there be in her manipulating power in the way women have traditionally done—through a man?

The two women are further contrasted by Bertha's very direct response to the timid confession Beatrice makes:

> It looks as if it was you, Miss Justice, who brought my husband back to Ireland. . . . By your letters to him and then by speaking to your cousin as you said just now. Do you not think that you are the person who brought him back?
>
> BEATRICE, *blushing suddenly:* No, I could not think that [*E* 96].

Even when Bertha, like Rowan, supplies the words, Beatrice can take credit only "to a certain extent." She "could not think" her responsibility so large as Bertha suggests.

Unlike Bertha, Beatrice is intellectually almost Richard's peer. As Joyce makes clear in *Exiles*, however, intellect is not enough. One must know *and* feel. Beatrice remains a disappointed bridge to her own womanhood, to Rowan's manhood, and to freedom of spirit or of mind.

If Beatrice is doomed to an incomplete life by her overcivilized outlook, Bertha exhibits a fundamental integrity of character which brings fulfillment. She manifests not only honesty and truthfulness, but also a profound personal wholeness of being. Bertha accepts what she is and what she does. In this, too, she is set apart from the other characters. Beatrice, who knows her own mind but cannot speak it, is also afraid to acknowledge her own actions. Robert is full of contradictions, likewise unacknowledged. At one moment he asserts he will fight for Bertha; the next he declares she is Richard's inviolable property. He describes Bertha to Richard as "a young girl not exactly your equal" and hastens to add, "I am simply using the language of people whose opinions I don't share" (*E* 39).

Of all the characters, Richard is closest to Bertha's kind of integrity, for he strives to establish his integrity in the name of art even when he remains painfully aware of deep divisions in his personality and character. He fears betrayal (*E* 44) even when—or perhaps because—he knows himself to be a betrayer (*E* 66), even when he longs "passionately and ignobly, to be dishonoured for ever, in love and in lust" (*E* 70).

Bertha surpasses all three better-educated people in her acceptance of herself. Though she regrets that her lack of education prevents her from understanding the intellectual side of Rowan (*E* 54, 100), she distinguishes, for Beatrice, between having a humble background and being humbled: "Humble me! I am very proud of myself, if you want to know. What have they ever done for him? I made him a man. What are they all in his life? No more than the dirt under his boots! . . . He can despise me, too, like the rest of them—now. And you can despise me. But you will never humble me, any of you" (*E* 100). Earlier, we remember, Hand has described Bertha as Rowan's work (*E* 62, 67), and Rowan has not contradicted him. No one else gives her credit, but Bertha knows that she has helped form Richard; and Joyce allows her to express her achievement in almost the same words he had used to Nora. Even Rowan nearly acknowledges his debt to Bertha when he says, "There is something wiser than wisdom in your heart" (*E* 75).

Just as Bertha accepts herself, she accepts the past without letting it prevent her from moving forward. Hand lays claim to the faith of the disciple in the master. Rowan asserts a superior faith of the master in the disciple who will betray him. Bertha, exiled, lonely, and manipulated, shows the greatest faith of all, that of the mistress in the lover who has betrayed her and may do so again. To Rowan she says in the final moments of the play, "I am yours. *In a whisper.* If I died this moment, I am yours" (*E* 112).

From her integrated wholeness Bertha is able to radiate to those around her a tender and encompassing love. Toward Archie she shows a traditional maternal concern, as Joyce planned: " . . . the love of Bertha for her child must be brought out as strongly and as simply and as early as possible in the third act. It must, of course, be accentuated by the position of sadness in which she finds herself" ("Notes" 126). As Archie prepares for his adventure driving the milkman's horses, Bertha questions the warmth of his clothing, combs his hair, hugs him, and wets a handkerchief with her tongue to dab at some dirt (*E* 92). When Ottocaro Weiss questioned this gesture, Joyce replied, "Did you ever see a mother cat cleaning her kitten?" (*JJ* 476). This catlike, spontaneous gesture, then, reveals Bertha as "dark, formless, mother, . . . darkly conscious of her instincts" ("Notes" 118).

Her maternal care for Archie shows in still other ways of which Archie, if not Rowan, is aware. She is a disciplinarian who establishes rules for her child and attacks Richard's indulgence of Archie:

> The work of a devil . . . to turn my own child against me. Only you did not succeed. . . .
> Whenever I tried to correct him for the least thing you went on with your folly, speaking to him as if he were a grownup man. Ruining the poor child,

or trying to. Then, of course, I was the cruel mother and only you loved him [*E* 51–52].

When Archie wants to ride with the milkman, he asks his father to ask his mother: Archie realizes that it is Bertha, not Richard, who makes the decisions. Archie is, indeed, quite insistent on getting his mother's permission through the agency of the father. (This reverses Catholic practice, of course.) Hence the child repeats his request three times, always in terms of "Ask mamma" (*E* 46–47). At length Archie goes to wait in the garden, but at the end of the first act he returns to demand thrice more of his father, "Well, did you ask her? . . . Can I go? . . . She said yes?" [31] Richard, who has never mentioned the subject to Bertha, looks at his son fondly and, telling a white lie, gives consent in Bertha's name (*E* 56).

In her attack on Richard's poor discipline, Bertha also claims credit for teaching Archie to love his father, even dissembling to her son about Richard's fatherly concern when Richard was in fact heedless of the boy. She has lied so that her son may be a loving person.

Bertha shows her nurturing instincts not only toward Archie but also toward Robert Hand, perhaps because she holds the conventional view that all men are really little boys. When Hand enters from the garden in the second act (like Archie he hides in the greenery while Bertha talks with Richard), he is drenched with rain.[32] Bertha insists he must change his coat. With Robert, as with the child, she expects obedience: Archie is to put on an extra vest because "I said you were to put it on, didn't I?" (*E* 92). Robert is told "Please change your coat, Robert, when I ask you." She even, jokingly and teasingly, commands him to change (*E* 78). It is a mother's right, as well as her duty, to prevent boys from catching cold.

Bertha's tenderness toward Robert is more than maternal. It is born of guilt ("I have treated him badly, shamefully" [*E* 73]), of her false belief that he regards her with respect (*E* 74), and of her empathy for him as a human being ("Only I feel for him too" [*E* 75]). If Bertha yields to Robert's entreaties—and we, like Richard, are never to know with certitude—she does so partly from tenderness, rather than from any passion matching Robert's lust for her or for all women (*E* 41–42).

Bertha's tenderness engenders Robert's epiphany. He has been willing to betray his friends and himself. His passions have been, in his own word, "common." A woman has been no more for him than "a stone, a flower, or a bird": "After all, what is most attractive in even the most beautiful woman? . . . Not those qualities which she has and other women have not but the qualities which she has in common with them. I mean . . . the commonest. *Turning over the stone, he presses the other side to his forehead.* I mean how her body develops heat when it is pressed, the movement of her blood, how quickly she changes by digestion what she eats into—what shall be nameless. *Laughing.* I am very common today . . . '' (*E* 41–42).

Bertha's direct contradiction of Robert's view is made not to him but to Beatrice in the third act: "Do you think I am a stone?" (*E* 100). Though he does not hear that question, Robert learns his error from Bertha's open, natural tenderness and from her willingness to meet him in Ranelagh. She reveals to Robert not the dishonest, crafty person he has been, but the open, honest, genuine man he may yet become. This revelation, not a sexual consummation which may—or may not— have occurred, is Robert's epiphany. After his hours with Bertha, though Robert can still write a leading article of ambiguous praise, he has at least improved enough to face Richard honestly. The pomposity of his language has diminished. And the man who, nine years earlier, accompanied Bertha and Richard to the boat but himself stayed in Ireland is now venturing his own small exile to Surrey (*E* 105). It is futile to speculate on what happens beyond the limits of the play. Yet these small changes in his demeanor in act 3 suggest that Hand will re-order his life more honestly and less craftily in the future.

Bertha's encompassing tenderness extends even toward those she has seen as enemies. She has denounced Beatrice as "the diseased woman" in whom Richard has a more than literary interest (*E* 54). She has confronted Beatrice, in act 3, with complaints that Richard now sleeps alone in his study and writes much "about something which has come into his life lately—since we came back to Ireland" (*E* 96). Then she softens her tone:

> Excuse me if I was rude. I want us to be friends.
> *She holds out her hands.* Will you?
> BEATRICE, *taking her hands:* Gladly.
> BERTHA, *looking at her:* What lovely long eyelashes you have! And your eyes have such a sad expression!
> BEATRICE, *smiling:* I see very little with them. They are weak.
> BERTHA, *warmly:* But beautiful. *She embraces her quietly and kisses her* [*E* 101].

This epiphanous moment marks the only time in *Exiles* that Beatrice, confessedly lonely, finds hands waiting when hers reach out. At last someone says a kind word to her. Timidly, she sent for Rowan; but it is Bertha who returns to Ireland to be her friend.

Bertha brings the most important epiphany of *Exiles* to Richard Rowan. It is born of their great love for one another and of the corresponding anguish each experiences during the drama. For her part, Bertha has joined her life to Richard's, even though, as she cries out to Beatrice, "I do not understand anything that he writes, . . . I cannot help him in any way, . . . I don't even understand half of what he says to me sometimes!" (*E* 98). She used to wait on the terrace of their house in Rome where "I was so sad. I was alone, Dick, forgotten by you and by all. I felt my life was ended" (*E* 111). She has borne Rowan a child who has "the nice name they give those children" (*E* 100), and returned with Rowan to face a hostile Dublin and malicious rumors. Through all the pain she has remained faithful to the vision of "ourselves, you and me, as we were when we met first" (*E* 111).

Rowan is also anguished—by his guilty conscience, by Hand's betrayal, but most of all by his doubt of Bertha's love. For nine years his light has come selfishly from the "luminous certitude" that his is "the brain in contact with which [Bertha] must think and understand," that his is "the body in contact with which her body must feel" (*E* 63). Now Richard fears that if Bertha chooses Hand, his own certitude will vanish in the darkness of night.

Facing such a prospect, Rowan is demonic. Bertha accuses him of deviltry (*E* 51), and he complains to Beatrice (*E* 98) and to Robert (*E* 109) of hearing the voices of demons on the strand, urging him to despair. Within the home he has shared with Bertha, where "beauty in its visible and invisible being is present" ("Notes" 115), Richard resists the demons. "It is too soon yet to despair" (*E* 112). Instead, dawn begins in Richard's spirit as on the strand: "It is not in the darkness of belief that I desire you. But in restless living wounding doubt" (*E* 112). He has learned one of the "secrets of life" from Bertha: doubt, not certitude, is luminous. By a Joycean reversal, Bertha's life force has made Rowan fertile again, and he has begun to be the artist great enough to conceive, in the womb of his imagination, a new kind of artist/hero.

In her frank naturalness of speech, her willingness to follow her physical and emotional instincts, Bertha has often been viewed by critics as the forerunner of Molly Bloom. She is more. She is herself the precursor of Joyce's new hero, the humane and lovable Leopold

Bloom. As the Odyssean Bloom will do in "Scylla and Charybdis," she has this night steered her difficult passage between arrogant intellect and coarse sensuality. Like Bloom, she has nurtured the young, shown compassion for the narrow lives of others, faced an antagonistic world with courage, and moved forward even when assailed by doubt. In the darkness of night she has shone like the moon, revealing to Hand courage and honor; to Beatrice, friendship; and to Rowan, compassion and the knowledge that he cannot, finally, know. Having once made Rowan a man, she now makes him human. It has been Bertha's night.

NOTES

1. It is not my purpose to trace critical interpretations of *Exiles*, but a brief summary of some critics' views of Rowan may be useful. Richard Ellmann (*JJ* 366) describes Rowan as "a figure through whom Joyce could keep his own matured persona as the center" of the play. In *A Short History of Irish Literature: A Backward Look* (New York: G. P. Putnam's Sons, 1967), Frank O'Connor calls Rowan a "somewhat flattering self-portrait" of Joyce (p. 207). Hugh Kenner, in *Dublin's Joyce* (Bloomington: Indiana University Press, 1956), labels Richard "the ape of God" and asserts "Richard swamps the other characters for reasons that are thematic . . . because the other three characters are . . . creatures of Richard's" (pp. 83, 85). Earl J. Clark rather paradoxically concludes that Rowan "completely dominates the action, such as there is, until his defeat" ("James Joyce's *Exiles*," *James Joyce Quarterly* 6 [Fall, 1968], 69). William York Tindall, in *A Reader's Guide to James Joyce* (New York: Farrar, Straus and Giroux, 1959; 1968) sees Rowan as a "failure" (p. 104), loveless and alone. James W. Douglas ("James Joyce's *Exiles*: A Portrait of the Artist," *Renascence* 15 [Winter, 1963], 82) calls Rowan "the character who controls . . . actions by the amoral strength of the emancipated artist."

2. James T. Farrell, for instance, repeatedly describes Richard as "chill." ("*Exiles* and Ibsen" in *James Joyce: Two Decades of Criticism*, ed. Seon Givens [New York: Vanguard Press, 1948], pp. 95–131). Tindall asserts that, for the reader, Richard seems to have masochism complicated by sadism (*A Reader's Guide to JJ*, p. 115). Hugh Kenner remarks that "contemplation of Richard Rowan's unequivocally joyless arrogance makes Stephen-worshippers feel they've been had" (*Dublin's Joyce*, p. 69). Darcy O'Brien charges in *The Conscience of James Joyce* (Princeton: Princeton University Press, 1968) that Rowan's motives include, "least nobly of all, . . . a desire to involve the innocent Bertha in guilt, thereby humbling and degrading her" (p. 56). Richard is "aristocratically arrogant in temperament" according to R. A. Maher ("James Joyce's *Exiles*: The Comedy of Discontinuity," *James Joyce Quarterly* 9 [Summer, 1972], 465). And Frank R. Cunningham claims that Richard is a "character who asks

that we should forsake our very humanity" ("Joyce's *Exiles*: A Problem of Dramatic Stasis," *Modern Drama* 12 [February, 1970], 405.

3. There was, for instance, no study of the play in *James Joyce Today: Essays on the Major Works*, ed. Thomas Staley (Bloomington: Indiana University Press, 1966), and *Exiles* is the last major work by Joyce to have a concordance, published in February, 1981. Again reviewing the criticism briefly, we note that Tindall complains of "general heaviness and solemnity" and calls *Exiles* a "nasty" play of "confusion" (*A Reader's Guide to JJ*, pp. 107, 111, 117). Harry Levin, classifying the drama among Joyce's opuscula, views it, with *Chamber Music* and *Dubliners*, as "merely the offshoots of a larger work," i.e., of *A Portrait* (*James Joyce: A Critical Introduction* [1941; rpt. New York: New Directions Books, 1960], p. 17). Herbert Gorman terms *Exiles* a "sombre interlude" between *A Portrait* and *Ulysses* (*James Joyce* [London: Geoffrey Bles, 1926], p. 103). Adaline Glasheen referred to Joyce's "terribly boring play" (*A Second Census of "Finnegans Wake*," s.v. "Hamilton Rowan" [Evanston: Northwestern University Press, 1963]). Eliott M. Simon argues that as far as the drama is concerned, Joyce had not finished the play. Simon asserts: "Joyce's 'theatre of ideas' dehumanizes the dramatic presentation to the point where even the actors become abstractions . . ." ("Joyce's *Exiles* and the Edwardian Problem-Play," *Modern Drama* 20 [March, 1977], 33).

4. Ellmann, for example, points out references to biblical characters, to Isolde, and to Sacher-Masoch and Sade in Joyce's "Notes" as a prelude to the extensive "counterpoint of myth and fact" in *Ulysses* (*JJ* 369).

5. See Mary T. Reynolds, "Joyce and Nora: The Indispensable Countersign," *Sewanee Review* 72 (Winter, 1964), 29–64, for an admirable analysis of the relationship between Joyce and Nora.

6. Adrienne Rich, "A Challenge to All Your Ideas about Motherhood and Daughterhood," *Ms.* (October, 1976), p. 100.

7. My articles, "Two Unnoted Musical Allusions," *James Joyce Quarterly* 9 (Fall, 1971), 140–42, and "Some *Mots* on a Quickbeam in Joyce's Eye," *James Joyce Quarterly* 10 (Spring, 1973), 346–48, discuss the origins of Rowan's name in Lady Nairne's song and in Irish history and folklore. Tindall identifies the fruit of the rowan as "pomes" and suggests an association with Joyce's *Pomes Penyeach* (*A Reader's Guide to JJ*, p. 106). Bernard Benstock and John Garvin have also discussed the symbolism of the rowan tree in Joyce's work.

8. See *E* 47, 51, 69, 70, 73.

9. Rowan, of course, is a writer, as Bertha is not. Through his letter-writing he has kept ties with at least one Irish friend, Beatrice Justice. Bertha, as she points out, knows no one in Dublin, after nine years away, except her husband's friends (*E* 111).

10. Charlotte M. Yonge, *History of Christian Names*, new ed., rev. (London: Macmillan, 1884; rpt. Detroit: Gale Research Company, 1966), pp. 213, 214. Folklore sources variously refer to this heroine as Bertha, Berchte, Perchta, or Perahta, and to her followers as the Perchten. To avoid confusion, I shall hereafter refer to Joyce's character as Bertha, and to the mythical goddess as Perchta.

11. "Epiphany, Feast of," *Encyclopaedia Britannica*, 11th ed. Also Kirsopp Lake, "Epiphany," *Encyclopaedia of Religion and Ethics*, ed. James Hastings, vol. 5, 1912. I want to thank Hilda Wick, who first directed me to Hastings's work.

12. Carl Rademacher, "Carnival," *Encyclopaedia of Religion and Ethics*, vol. 3, 1911. Rademacher also associates Hertha (mentioned in Tacitus) with the Roman *Bona Dea* and with the Dionysian festivals of Greece.

13. Sir James G. Frazer, *The Golden Bough*, 3rd ed., 6 (1913; rpt. London: Macmillan and Company, 1919), 240. John B. Vickery, in *The Literary Impact of the Golden Bough* (Princeton: Princeton University Press, 1973), devotes nearly two hundred pages to Joyce's handling of the mythic materials incorporated in Frazer's mighty work; yet Vickery makes no mention of *Exiles*, though including all Joyce's other works.

The locale of the Perchta celebrations, according to Frazer, was Alsace, Swabia, Bavaria, Austria, and Switzerland, but particularly Salzburg and the Tirol (p. 240). In 1913, Trieste, where Joyce wrote *Exiles*, was, like Salzburg and the Tirol, part of the Austro-Hungarian Empire.

14. Rollo May, *The Courage to Create* (New York: W. W. Norton, 1975), p. 98. See also W. J. Woodhouse, "Apollonia," *Encyclopaedia of Religion and Ethics*, vol. 1, 1908.

15. Cf. *FW* 330.28, "He goat a berth."

16. Cf. *FW* 514.24, "of a Tartar (Birtha)."

17. Joyce refused to allow the baptism of his own children, and his grandson, Stephen Joyce, was baptized secretly, against the wishes of his grandfather (*JJ* 660–61). Joyce's attitude is perhaps reflected in *Exiles*, where Archie bursts on stage in act 1 well *ahead* of Bertha (*E* 26–28).

18. Frazer, *The Golden Bough*, 6, 240–41.

19. *Ibid.*, 240–46. Rademacher, "Carnival," *Encyclopaedia of Religion and Ethics*.

20. Eugen Mogk, "Demons and Spirits," *Encyclopaedia of Religion and Ethics*, vol. 12, 1912. Of course *Finnegans Wake* still lay in the future in 1913–15. Yet the parallel between this manifestation of Perchta and the dream-disturbing quality of Joyce's later heroine, Anna Livia Plurabelle, is remarkable. See also Glasheen, *A Second Census of Finnegans Wake*, s.v. "Anna Livia Plurabelle."

21. James Joyce, "Notes by the Author," in Joyce, *Exiles*, pp. 113–27. Hereafter references will be cited in the text as "Notes."

22. Sheldon Brivic, "Structure and Meaning in Joyce's *Exiles*," *James Joyce Quarterly* 6 (Fall, 1968), 36–37. He includes Robert and Robert's cottage at Ranelagh ("rain-lake") in this watery element; but the cottage was also, and originally, Richard's, though Brivic terms Richard a "hydrophobe."

23. This of course continues the symbolism of "The Dead," where Gretta, the natural girl from Galway, laughs at galoshes, since she, like Michael Furey, is open to the elements. Molly Bloom had a similar aversion to umbrellas (*U* 687.15–.18), as did Nora Barnacle (Ole Vinding, "James Joyce in Copenhagen," *James Joyce Quarterly* 14 [Winter, 1977], 176). See also GJ 16, "Envoy: Love me, love my umbrella."

24. Frazer, *The Golden Bough*, 6, p. 241.

25. With four exceptions (pp. 28–30, 45, 92, 99–100), only two persons are on stage at the same time in *E*. (This does not include transitions allowing one of a pair to leave when a third person enters.)

26. Cf. Joyce's comment in the "Notes" 116: "Robert has risen from a lower world and so far is he from indignation that it surprises him that men and women are not baser and more ignoble."

27. Robert's sense of his failure with Bertha probably accounts for his tale—possibly false—of the conquest of a weeping divorcée in the car en route to Donnybrook. It may, as he suggests, disgust Rowan; but Hand values a disgusting success more than a noble failure. Consequently, he is a prominent journalist whose leading articles, phrased in clichés, are widely read; Richard, holding to artistic integrity, has sold thirty-seven copies of his book in Dublin (*E* 38).

28. Richard thus describes Robert's pursuit of Bertha. It proves an accurate description of Robert in other ways, too: Hand's newspaper article describing Richard as a "distinguished Irishman" but associating him by inference with those who have deserted Ireland in her hour of need is also written in dark of night (*E* 99) with enough craft to mislead the myopic Beatrice into thinking it praises Rowan.

29. Some critics have viewed Beatrice as the source of Rowan's inspiration. Certainly Bertha shares this view (*E* 53–4, 74). Joyce himself seemed to regard her not as a muse for the artist, but, like Eveline, Maria, or Mrs. Sinico, as flesh which might become word. As he comments ("Notes" 114), "It will be difficult to recommend Beatrice to the interest of the audience, every man of which is Robert and would like to be Richard—in any case Bertha's."

30. Beatrice seems to bring Rowan back to Ireland, as she visits his home, because "otherwise I could not see you" (*E* 19).

31. Joycean males learn young to value the affirmative "yes."

32. The parallel between Robert's stay in the garden and that of Michael Furey in "The Dead" is clear. This is doubtless one of the elements of conscious Joycean comedy in *Exiles:* a self-parody for a brief instant. But though Furey and Hand are both drenched, Furey is drenched for love, Hand in order to hide from the woman he loves. Hand is also a parallel to Gabriel Conroy here: Gabriel is constantly busy brushing snow off his own garments and urging galoshes upon his wife, to keep out the wetness of the snow; Hand seeks an umbrella but is forced by Bertha's arrival to go into the rain unprotected. Hand also resembles Gabriel in the superficiality of his actions. Michael comes in from the rain to die, Robert to change his coat to one of green velvet, suggestive, like the faded green plush of the Rowans' furniture and curtains, of Irish decay.

Gerty MacDowell: Joyce's Sentimental Heroine

The figure of Gerty MacDowell takes shape, like a "smiling soubrette," from the fashion pages of the *Lady's Pictorial*, the heated prose of Victorian sentimental novels, and the advertising columns of the *Irish Times*. Gerty's embarrassing proximity to the heroines of popular literature may account for her surprising lack of popularity as a subject of critical attention among Joyce scholars. Although Gerty is the second most prominent female in *Ulysses*, she has generally been ignored by traditional critics, who see her either as a virgin-temptress or as a pale shadow of the more flamboyant Molly Bloom.[1]

Gerty's portrait is complicated by the enigmatic tone of "Nausicaa." Does Joyce intend to ridicule his character for playing the seductive nymph? Or is he presenting her as the pathetic victim of social and religious enculturation—as a naive young woman trying to fend off the pressures of adult sexuality by adopting the mental pose of a chaste and virginal nun? Gerty often conflates her principal role model, the Catholic Virgin Mary, with the pagan goddesses of fashion worshipped in the popular press. She seems to have internalized the sweet illusions and the sweeter lies of Victorian sexual mythology, and she confuses both with the puritanical teachings of Irish Catholicism.

Mark Shechner insists that Gerty represents "the narcissistic phase of Irish Catholic adolescence whose primary role in Joyce's life and fantasies was to provoke desire and deny fulfillment. . . . If Gerty is a joke, she is nevertheless the *reductio ad absurdum* of a long line of virginal villains who are implied in her portrait."[2] Fritz Senn labels Gerty an "avatar of the temptress," but he also observes that Joyce may have created her as an autobiographical persona filtered through a parodic sex-role reversal.[3] Joyce seems to endow his ingénue with all the sentimental, languishing, romantic tendencies that he himself exhibited in his epistolary affair with Marthe Fleischmann. According to Heinrich Straumann, the author once sent Marthe a postcard addressed from "Odysseus" to "Nausicaa" (*Letters* II, 428). Does Joyce want us to sympathize with his fictional Nausicaa? Or is he using her satirically to exorcise what he sees as the ludicrous traits of his own personality?

The answer to such speculation must necessarily remain ambivalent. Gerty is a highly elusive character. Joyce parodies her adolescent narcissism, vanity, and willful self-deception. But he understands Gerty's foibles, and he respects her relentless compulsion to fictionalize experience. Like Leopold Bloom and like Stephen's Shakespeare, Gerty MacDowell is an "artist of life" who creates from the pain of loss. She imaginatively interprets her existence in the mode of sentimental romance, using art to mitigate a reality that otherwise might prove intolerable.

Gerty MacDowell is James Joyce's Emma Bovary. Her mind is thoroughly imbued with the orts, scraps, and fragments of Victorian popular culture. She religiously believes in all the illusions propagated by nineteenth-century fiction. And, to a large extent, she fashions her own self-image on the model of her literary namesake, Gerty Flint, the central character of Maria Cummins's 1854 novel *The Lamplighter*. On this "balmy summer eve," Gerty muses that "soon the lamplighter would be going his rounds . . . like she read in that book *The Lamplighter* by Miss Cummins" (*U* 363).

Like Cummins's protagonist, Gerty MacDowell feels emotionally orphaned and socially ostracized. She rationalizes her alienation by fantasizing a myth of secret aristocratic origins: "There was an innate refinement, a languid queenly *hauteur* about Gerty which was unmistakably evidenced in her delicate hands and higharched instep. Had kind fate but willed her to be born a gentlewoman of high degree in her own right and had she only received the benefit of a good education Gerty MacDowell might easily have held her own beside any lady in the land and have seen herself exquisitely gowned with jewels on her brow and patrician suitors at her feet vying with one another to pay their devoirs to her" (*U* 348). The archaic language of Gerty's meditation heightens the fairy-tale quality of her fantasies. She dreams of wealth and nobility, jewels and patrician suitors, the "devoirs" of chivalric courtship, and "the love that might have been" (*U* 348). Surely some wicked spell has condemned Gerty to an Irish household characterized by indigence, alcoholism, and domestic violence. Like

Sleeping Beauty, Gerty waits for the prince charming or "dreamhusband" whose magical kiss will waken her from adolescent isolation. She dreams that eventually, like Gerty Flint, she will be saved from her present fate by a father who will protect her, a lover who will worship her, or a father-lover who will "love her, his ownest girlie, for herself alone" (U 358).

Cummins's heroine in The Lamplighter, "by long and patient continuance in well-doing," earns "so full a recompense, so all-sufficient a reward" as marriage to her childhood beau, Willie Sullivan—a suitor who offers her love, money, and a life of bourgeois respectability. Willie yields to the "sweet and loving devotion, the saintly patience, and the deep and fervent piety" of his "own true Gertrude" and rejoices "to see the little playmate whose image I cherished so fondly matured into the lovely and graceful woman, her sweet attractions crowned by so much beauty as almost to place her beyond recognition." [4] At the end of the novel, Gerty Flint is fortuitously reunited with her true parent, Philip Amory, a gentleman who recognizes his daughter in a melodramatic and highly passionate reunion scene: " 'Yes, my child, thank God!' said Mr. Amory, reverently; 'restored, at last, to her unworthy father, and . . . gladly bestowed by him upon her faithful and far more deserving lover.' " [5]

In "Nausicaa," Joyce parodies Cummins's saccharine style and makes fun of the pious religiosity of her protagonist. Gerty MacDowell longs to write herself into a work of romantic fiction, but her "one shortcoming" disqualifies her from playing the traditional heroine. She ends up, instead, as one of the dramatis personae in a modernist novel. Like Emma Bovary, Gerty interprets the scenario of her life according to the directives of Victorian literature. Her fantasies may be pathetic and futile, but they appear to be crucial to her mental well-being. To shield her wounded sensibilities, Gerty has withdrawn to the comforting shelter of romantic myth. She is desperately trying to like herself; and in an effort to mold a positive self-image, she compensates for bodily deformity by heightened pride in physical attractiveness. What initially appears to be narcissism may also be interpreted as a bold defiance of isolation. Once we learn of Gerty's lameness, we have to admire the bravado of her self-assertion in the competitive sexual market of 1904.

The poignant, satirical jest of "Nausicaa" is directed less against Gerty than against the manipulative society of which she is a product.

The episode offers a striking parody of female socialization in the modern world. Joyce's portrait of Gerty MacDowell, composed over fifty years ago, provides an incisive criticism of a media-controlled self-image.

Gerty has been reared on sentimental journalese, and her mind has been shaped by the clichéd rhetoric of fashion magazines: "It was Madame Vera Verity, directress of the Woman Beautiful page of the Princess novelette, who had first advised her to try eyebrowleine which gave that haunting expression to the eyes, so becoming in leaders of fashion, and she had never regretted it" (U 349). The aim of Madame Verity's cosmetic art is not truth, as her name would imply, but a simpering obfuscation of reality. Gerty has been sucked into a whirlpool of commercial fantasy that promises instant panacea. Relief is just a swallow (or a touch) away.

Had Gerty consulted the *Irish Times* on June 16, 1904, she would have been offered the wonders of "Beecham's Pills," a medicine "specially suitable for females of all ages" and a mandatory prescription for "every woman who values health." She might have been allured by the more dazzling advertisement for "Carter's Little Liver Pills," guaranteed to cure "biliousness, sick headaches, torpid liver, indigestion, constipation, sallow skin, dizziness, and furred tongue." Or she could have been seduced by a simple panacea such as "Mother Seigel's Syrup," a mixture promising relief from any troubling symptom.[6] It is ironically appropriate that Gerty should be attracted to Leopold Bloom, whose career as an advertisement canvasser depends on public gullibility. The twentieth-century media provide opiates for the masses. Commerical art deceives, manipulates, and ultimately paralyzes.

Subjected to a daily bombardment by coutless promises of feminine fulfillment, Gerty longs for the miracle drug or elixir that will transform her into Cinderella. The young girl feels convinced that if she conscientiously makes use of all the products offered by Madame Verity and Woman Beautiful, she will surely attract the man of her dreams.

Needless to say, Gerty MacDowell is male-identified. And the paucity of masculine affirmation in her life intensifies her alienation. Her father is an alcoholic; Father Conroy, a celibate; and Reggy Wylie has exhibited little affection since his days in short pants. In a society where males are enervated, impotent, or simply uninterested, male-identification may be disastrous.

Gerty's monologue springs from the "Romeo and Juliet" notion of

love parodied in "Cyclops." If the earlier chapter satirized manly
virtues of brutality and aggression, "Nausicaa" mocks traditional notions of feminine passivity. "Cyclops" depicts a boisterous world
dominated by a male power drive and characterized by political
myopia. "Nausicaa" portrays an inverted image of disembodied spir-
ituality, an idealized realm of fantasy painted over with sentimental
cosmetics. Gerty MacDowell "loves to love love" and is convinced that
"this person loves that other person because everybody loves some-
body but God loves everybody" (U 333).

Joyce described "Nausicaa" to Frank Budgen as an episode "written
in a namby-pamby jammy marmalady drawersy (alto la!) style with
effects of incense, mariolatry, masturbation, stewed cockles, painters'
palette, chitchat, circumlocutions, etc., etc." (Letters I, 135). We are
not, of course, inside Gerty's consciousness. Joyce employs what
Hugh Kenner has labeled the "Uncle Charles Principle," whereby the
"normally neutral narrative vocabulary" of the author is "pervaded by
a little cloud of idioms which a character might use if he [or she] were
managing the narrative." [7] "Nausicaa" mimics the "marmalady
drawersy" style of Gerty's thoughts by using the voice, linguistic
patterns, and syntax appropriate to her speech.

Gerty's fantasies combine the rhetoric of advertising with the language of popular fiction, and her perceptions are filtered through the
pallid world of contemporary women's magazines. Gerty sees herself
as a "fair specimen of winsome Irish girlhood. . . . Her figure was
slight and graceful, inclining even to fragility. . . . The waxen pallor of
her face was almost spiritual in its ivory-like purity" (U 348). The
young woman identifies with the stereotyped nineteenth-century fictional heroine. She cultivates a "strained look on her face" and a
"gnawing sorrow" in her heart. Gerty's "pentup feelings" are paradoxically deflated by a desire to "cry nicely before the mirror" (U 351).
Romantic anguish becomes a function of vanity, emotional expression
a narcissistic exercise. Colorless and anemic, Gerty exhibits the waxen
pallor of a Greek nymph, a plaster saint, or the Catholic Virgin, "Tower
of Ivory." She dresses in electric blue reminiscent of Mary and of the
gods who "drink electric light." Weeping coyly before the mirror,
Gerty prefigures Issy, the tender temptress of Finnegans Wake.

Gerty disdains eating in public and would prefer a more lyrical diet:
"She didn't like the eating part when there were any people that made
her shy and often she wondered why you couldn't eat something

poetical like violets or roses" (*U* 352). Gerty bears a striking resemblance to the spiritualized nymph of "Calypso," who protests in "Circe": "We immortals, as you saw today, have not such a place and no hair there either. We are stonecold and pure" (*U* 551). The nymph promises Bloom a respite from desire: "Only the ethereal. Where dreamy creamy gull waves o'er the waters dull" (*U* 552). Such languid virtue is contingent on sexual repression. Once threatened, the nymph draws a poniard and tries to dispatch Bloom. The plaster saint cracks, emitting a cloud of stench from her private parts. She proves to be the Janus-image of Bella Cohen, "mutton dressed as lamb" (*U* 554). Similarly, the lamb-like Gerty can break out of her reverie to express envy, cattiness, or sheer ill temper. Erotic desire smolders just beneath the surface of her romantic musings and finally explodes in pyrotechnic fury. Like Leopold Bloom, Gerty sustains herself through the copious creations of a fertile imagination. Bloom dreams of erotic titillation; Gerty yearns for spiritual passion. Both share a pathetic isolation from consummated physical love.

Caught in a trap of self-deception, Gerty MacDowell places naive faith in all the opiates her society has to offer: religion and poetry, eyebrowleine and romantic myth. In a toilettable drawer, she has stashed "her girlish treasures trove, the tortoiseshell combs, her child of Mary badge, the whiterose scent, the eyebrowleine, her alabaster pouncetbox" and her confession album with "some beautiful thoughts written in it in violet ink that she bought in Hely's of Dame Street" (*U* 364). Like Mary Dedalus, the young girl collects trinkets and relics of a paralyzed past. She regards religion as a kind of cosmetic that mitigates the harshness of reality. Her "child of Mary" sodality badge recalls the communion ritual earlier observed by Leopold Bloom in All Hallows' Church: "Something going on: some sodality. Pity so empty. Nice discreet place to be next some girl. . . . Good idea the Latin. Stupefies them first" (*U* 80). Popular culture and popular religion both offer "one way out" for a society that demands narcotic forgetfulness. Myth consumes the spirit and lays the weary heart to rest in a heavenly ideal. "It would be like heaven. For such a one she yearns this balmy summer eve" (*U* 352). The metaphysical power of that final, consummating kiss can never be described in words. The ecstasy of love, like divine beatitude, is ineffable. As the media assure Gerty, romance ought to be the "one great goal" of every young girl's existence.

Brainwashed by popular literature, the ingénue is convinced that love should be "a woman's birthright," her chief preoccupation, and her final happiness. Hence Gerty's frustration at the difficulty of claiming a matrimonial heritage. She feels like a disinherited female, but she continues "hoping against hope" (*U* 351). She pathetically snatches at the least sign of interest or affection to fire her romantic dreams: "Yes, she had known from the first that her daydream of a marriage . . . was not to be. He was too young to understand. He would not believe in love, a woman's birthright. The night of the party long ago in Stoers' (he was still in short trousers) when they were alone and he stole an arm round her waist . . . and snatched a half kiss (the first!) but it was only the end of her nose" (*U* 351). Hence the source of Gerty's elaborate dreams of "weddingbells ringing for Mrs. Reggy Wylie T. C. D."; of "expensive blue fox"; of love and marriage; of husband, home, and morning "brekky." That memory of Reggy's juvenile kiss seems to be one of the few treasures in Gerty's barren hope-chest. She constructs "worlds" from words, gestures, a peck on the nose, and a vacation postcard. As Bloom later remarks: "She must have been thinking of someone else all the time. What harm? Must since she came to the use of reason, he, he and he. First kiss does the trick. The propitious moment. Something inside them goes pop. Mushy like, tell by their eye, on the sly. First thoughts are best. Remember that till their dying day" (*U* 371).

Rejected by Reggy, the child-lover who has ceased to ride his bicycle in front of her window, Gerty yearns for an older man who will offer her both passion and compassionate understanding: "No prince charming is her beau ideal to lay a rare and wondrous love at her feet but rather a manly man with a strong quiet face who had not found his ideal, perhaps his hair slightly flecked with grey, and who would understand, take her in his sheltering arms, strain her to him in all the strength of his deep passionate nature and comfort her with a long long kiss" (*U* 351–52).[8]

Like Stephen Dedalus, Gerty MacDowell has been deserted by an alcoholic "consubstantial" father. God, Leopold Bloom, and Father Conroy ("tree of forbidden priest" [*U* 375]) all seem promising surrogates. She considers, but rejects, the carbuncly gentleman strolling along the beach: "She would not like him for a father because he was too old or something or on account of his face (it was a palpable case of doctor Fell) or his carbuncly nose with the pimples on it" (*U* 354). Out of her own sense of isolation, Gerty turns to the dark stranger roaming the strand: "He was in deep mourning, she could see that, and the story of a haunting sorrow was written on his face" (U 357).

With surprising accuracy, Gerty identifies Bloom as a grass widower. She intuits more about his mental state than even he will acknowledge. Gerty sympathizes with Bloom's melancholy because she feels his pain. She is "heartbroken about her best boy throwing her over. . . . She had loved him better than he knew. Lighthearted deceiver and fickle like all his sex he would never understand what he had meant to her" (U 362). Gerty insists that she is "not a one to be lightly trifled with. As for Mr. Reggy with his swank and his bit of money she could just chuck him aside as if he was so much filth and never again would she cast as much as a second thought on him and tear his silly postcard into a dozen pieces" (U 362). Gerty unwittingly projects her own sense of rejection onto Bloom: "Perhaps it was an old flame he was in mourning for from the days beyond recall. She thought she understood" (U 364). The young girl does, in fact, understand the pathos of Bloom's state of mind, though she misinterprets the circumstances of his suffering. She apparently attributes to the mysterious stranger a fictional history similar to the plight of Philip Amory in Cummins's The Lamplighter.[9] Gerty perceives Bloom through sentimental, tear-stained glasses: "The face that met her gaze there in the twilight, wan and strangely drawn, seemed to her the saddest she had ever seen" (U 356).

Idealizing Bloom as her fantasy lover, Gerty fits him into the stereotypical role of "manly man." Ironically, she remains oblivious both of Bloom's Jewishness and of his womanliness. Gerty speculates about his nose, "aquiline" or "slightly retroussé." But she does not associate it with the "bottlenosed fraternity" scorned by the Citizen, and Bloom is glad that she never sees him in profile. Gerty elevates Bloom to the sublime status of "her dreamhusband, because she knew on the instant it was him. . . . She was a womanly woman . . . and she just yearned to know all, to forgive all if she could make him fall in love with her, make him forget the memory of the past. Then mayhap he would embrace her gently, like a real man, crushing her soft body to him, and love her, his ownest girlie, for herself alone" (U 358).

Gerty turns to Bloom for both amorous approval and paternal solicitude. Safe in the "sheltering arms" (U 351) of her father-love, she no longer need fear rejection for "that one shortcoming" (U 364). Intuitively, Gerty knows that no cosmetic will ever sufficiently compensate for her lameness or give her an equal chance on the marriage market. Physical deformity has jeopardized her amorous birthright. As she struggles to emulate the ideal "womanly woman," Gerty must assure herself that "love laughs at locksmiths" (U 364). Nothing is impossible in the realm of true romance. Surely a magical dreamhusband will unbind her from the chastity belt of lameness.

Gerty MacDowell takes refuge in the "dreamy, creamy" Platonic sphere of adolescent fantasy. Joyce tempts us to think of her as a virginal nymphette, a sweet young Lolita barely out of undies: "As for undies they were Gerty's chief care and who that knows the fluttering hopes and fears of sweet seventeen . . . " (U 350). But Gerty is no longer an adolescent. We are prepared to accept her as a starry-eyed teenager. Joyce teases us, then deflates our expectations by adding, "though Gerty would never see seventeen again" (U 350). She will be "twenty-two in November" (U 352), the same age as Stephen Dedalus. Gerty has reached her majority. She should be "womanly wise" but is not. In Dublin of 1904, Gerty MacDowell is fast on the decline toward old maidenhood. Despite elaborate dreams of matrimony, she is still unkissed (or half so), unwedded, and unbedded.

Occasionally, grouchy and vindictive "spinster-like" traits break through Gerty's romantic façade and reveal another side of her personality. The young woman thinks of the "exasperating little brats of twins" as "little monkeys common as ditchwater. Someone ought to take them and give them a good hiding for themselves to keep them in their places" (U 359). She envies Cissy, who runs with "long gandery strides": "It would have served her just right if she had tripped up over something accidentally on purpose with her high crooked French heels on her to make her look tall and got a fine tumble" (U 359). And Gerty dismisses Edy Boardman as an "irritable little gnat . . . poking her nose into what was no concern of hers" (U 360), "like the confounded little cat she was" (U 362). "Sister souls showing their teeth at one another" (U 369), Bloom observes.

With intermittent sadistic lapses, Gerty retreats to a spiritualized notion of her "beau ideal." "Art thou real, my ideal?" asks "that poem that appealed to her so deeply that she had copied out of the newspaper she found one evening round the potherbs" (U 364).[10] The reader is led to suspect that very few of Gerty's romantic ideals approach reality. Considering the paucity of her amorous experiences in the past, one can assume that June 16, 1904, will be a landmark in her imagination. She has proved, perhaps for the first time, that she can attract and arouse male sexual interest: "And while she gazed her heart went pitapat. Yes, it was her he was looking at and there was meaning in his look. His eyes burned into her" (*U* 357). Gerty's heightened emotion corresponds to Bloom's tumescence. She palpitates with excitement, then imaginatively elaborates on the scene. Gerty is so starved for love that several fantasies crowd in at once. She regards the stranger as a devil whose eyes burn into her: he spiritually seduces and scorches her with his gaze. He resembles a matinée idol and a foreigner. And his "pale intellectual face" (*U* 357) may suggest the conquering "pale Galilean" of Swinburne's verse. Like Christ, "he had suffered, more sinned against than sinning" (*U* 358). Gerty, the Blessed Virgin Nausicaa, star of the sea and refuge of sinners, longs to take him to her bosom in a sympathetic embrace. She recalls Father Conroy's confessional forgiveness, and she wants to forgive Bloom "even, if he had been himself a sinner, a wicked man" (*U* 358); but she cannot pardon the "exasperating little brats of twins" for noisily quarreling.

Gerty has so confused religious and erotic sentiment that choir music from the Catholic benediction service provides a fitting background for her titillating striptease: "The choir began to sing *Tantum ergo* and she just swung her foot in and out in time as the music rose and fell" (*U* 360). As the music rises, so does Bloom; and so do Gerty's skirts. Her foot simulates the piston and cylinder movement of the sexual act, and the young "seductress" takes vicarious pleasure in Bloom's agitation. The two reenact the primal temptation between Eve and the serpent in the Garden of Eden: "He was eyeing her as a snake eyes its prey. Her woman's instinct told her that she had raised the devil in him" (*U* 360). Gerty innocently blushes at the euphemistic reference to Bloom's erection. But she quickly sublimates physiological fact to allegorical interpretation: "His dark eyes fixed themselves on her again drinking in her every contour, literally worshipping at her shrine" (*U* 361). In her mind, she is not Eve but the Virgin Mary receiving adoration.

Gerty, however, is less innocent than she will admit:

> . . . because she knew about the passion of men like that, hot-blooded, because Bertha Supple told her once in dead secret and made her swear she'd never about the gentleman lodger that was staying with them out of the Congested Districts Board that had pictures cut out of papers of those

skirtdancers and highkickers and she said he used to do something not very
nice that you could imagine sometimes in the bed. But this was altogether
different from a thing like that because there was all the difference because
she could almost feel him draw her face to his and the first quick hot touch of
his handsome lips [*U* 365–66].

The ingénue deliberately exposes herself and takes pleasure in
Bloom's arousal. Good Catholic that she is, Gerty recognizes her "sin"
and absolves herself in advance: "Besides there was absolution so long
as you didn't do the other thing before being married . . . and besides
it was on account of that other thing coming on" (*U* 366). With a voice
sounding suspiciously like Molly Bloom's, Gerty argues that all sins
can be forgiven in confession; and besides, it is "only natural" to feel
sexual desire at the time of menstruation. Bloom seems to share Gerty's opinion: "Near her monthlies, I expect, makes them feel ticklish"
(*U* 368). "Devils they are when that's coming on them. Dark devilish
appearance" (*U* 369). He realizes that Gerty is fully aware of his
excitation: "Did she know what I? Course. Like a cat sitting beyond a
dog's jump" (*U* 371).

Gerty is determined to preserve her chastity and not to "do the other
thing before being married." She feels nothing but contempt for prostitutes and "fallen women": "From everything in the least indelicate her
finebred nature instinctively recoiled. She loathed that sort of person,
the fallen women off the accommodation walk beside the Dodder that
went with the soldiers and coarse men, with no respect for a girl's
honor, degrading the sex" (*U* 364). Gerty wants a Platonic relationship,
free of physical contact, and her wishes are granted. This "fair, unsullied soul" shares Bloom's passion, but she preserves her virginity
intact. Spiritual masturbation may be as close as Gerty ever comes to
sexual expression. Beneath her romantic dream of matrimony lies a
virginal terror of the sexual act: "No, no: not that. They would be just
good friends like a big brother and sister without all that other in spite
of the conventions of Society with a big ess" (*U* 364).

Leopold Bloom is still an "unconquered hero," "a sterling man, a
man of inflexible honour to his fingertips" (*U* 365). He has proved to be
Gerty's ideal, "her all in all, the only man in all the world for her for
love was the master guide" (*U* 365). Bloom assures the young girl of
her sexual attraction, but he makes no physical demands. He "knows
what a woman is" and respects the privacy of her sentimental dream
world.

Bloom is the perfect Platonic lover: like a chaste courtier, he pierces his lady with nothing more dangerous than a burning gaze. In fact, he resembles the suitor depicted in an almanac picture that Gerty has tacked on the wall of her water-closet: "the picture of halcyon days where a young gentleman in the costume they used to wear then with a three-cornered hat was offering a bunch of flowers to his ladylove with oldtime chivalry through her lattice window. You could see there was a story behind it" (U 355). Gerty's image of perfect devotion is "oldtime chivalry," a gesture of sacerdotal obeisance that sublimates erotic aggression. The "ladylove" is tucked safely behind a lattice window: she symbolically accepts flowers, but not defloration. The courtier submits to the spiritual reign of his beloved, to whom he offers the ideal praise of asexual devotion.

In actuality, Gerty's dreams of feminine power and masculine docility are controverted everywhere in the Dublin environment of 1904. Irish society assures power to males from infancy to old age. In a culture that tacitly approves of masculine aggression, "boys will be boys" (U 347). The golden rule of male permissiveness forces girls and women to be "feminine" and constantly to mollify incipient violence. Tommy and Jacky Caffrey mimic war games and play raucously on the shore. Whether the "apple of discord" be a sand castle or a rubber ball, females must arbitrate disputes and minimize the destructive effects of anger. The woman's role is to smooth over "life's tiny troubles," to kiss away "the hurtness" (U 347), and to assuage the unpleasantness of castor oil with a placating gift of syrup and brown bread. When male violence is sanctioned, the female must assume the complementary role of eternal placebo. ("Of course," thinks Bloom, "they understand birds, animals, babies. In their line" [U 371].) Tommy Caffrey displays his burgeoning manhood by throwing a temper tantrum and appropriating a rubber ball: "The temper of him! O, he was a man already was little Tommy Caffrey since he was out of pinnies" (U 353). Like a miniature war general, Tommy wins the day by bullying Cissy into snatching the toy from baby Boardman. "Anything for a quiet life" (U 353), Cissy explains. She tries to restore halcyon days at whatever price.

Even the "young heathen," baby Boardman, has already learned the power of intimidation. His "infant majesty" is most obstreperous and will be appeased only by a surrogate female teat from a suckingbottle. This "perfect little bunch of love . . . would certainly turn out to be something great, they said" (*U* 357). But no such promises of grandeur await Cissy Caffrey, Edy Boardman, or Gerty MacDowell. Cissy sometimes rebels against her female role by acting the part of a tomboy or playing transvestite games. The only alternative she can envision is that of a masculine woman who usurps phallic power, complete with burned cork moustache, cigarette, and the sadistic right to flagellate the effeminate. Prefiguring Bella Cohen, "Madcap Ciss" expresses a desire to spank the gentleman opposite on the "beetoteetom": "Give it to him too on the same place as quick as I'd look at him" (*U* 353).

Gerty, in contrast, would never be sufficiently brazen to challenge male authority. She sees herself as a "sterling good daughter" and "ministering angel" (*U* 355). Only once does the source of her "pentup feelings" reveal itself. Conscious of the men's temperance retreat concluding nearby, Gerty muses that her home life might have been different: "had her father only avoided the clutches of the demon drink, by taking the pledge or those powders the drink habit cured in Pearson's Weekly" (*U* 354). Gerty sublimates the hostility she feels toward her father by lamenting the ravages of alcohol, "that vile decoction which has ruined so many hearths and homes. . . . Nay, she had even witnessed in the home circle deeds of violence caused by intemperance and had seen her own father, a prey to the fumes of intoxication, forget himself completely for if there was one thing of all things that Gerty knew it was the man who lifts his hand to a woman save in the way of kindness deserves to be branded as the lowest of the low" (*U* 354). The young girl witnesses her father's acts of household violence and recoils at the spectacle of masculine brutality. She retreats into the sentimental rhetoric of domestic virtue: "Poor father! With all his faults she loved him still" (*U* 354). But she has few compunctions about looking elsewhere for a surrogate to replace her inebriate Oedipal figure.

Scornful and defiant of her lifelong religious training, Gerty offers herself on the altar of amorous devotion to her new father-lover, Leopold Bloom. "She would make the great sacrifice. . . . Come what might she would be wild, untrammelled, free" (*U* 364–65). Gerty suppresses shame and modesty in order to share a moment of erotic intimacy with Bloom: "Whitehot passion was in that face, passion silent as the grave, and it had made her his. . . . His hands and face were working and a tremor went over her. She leaned back far to look up where the fireworks were and she caught her knee in her hands so as not to fall back looking up and there was no one to see only him and her when she revealed all her graceful beautifully shaped legs . . . and she seemed to hear the panting of his heart" (*U* 365). The young girl feels herself "trembling in every limb from being bent so far back he had a full view high up above her knee no-one not even on the swing or wading and she wasn't ashamed and he wasn't either to look in that immodest way like that because he couldn't resist the sight of the wondrous revealment half offered" (*U* 366).

Both Bloom and Gerty experience some kind of amorous gratification, though Gerty's "little strangled cry" may be an unwitting moan of erotic frustration. Gerty seems to linger in tumescent ecstasy, passionately aroused and tortured by the sweet pain of unconsummated desire: "She would fain have cried to him chokingly, held out her snowy slender arms to him to come, to feel his lips laid on her white brow the cry of a young girl's love, a little strangled cry, wrung from her, that cry that has rung through the ages. And then a rocket sprang and bang shot blind and O! then the Roman candle burst and it was like a sigh of O! and everyone cried O! O! in raptures and it gushed out of it a stream of rain gold hair threads" (*U* 366–67). The young woman encourages her lover to come, but she fails to share the fruits of physical release.[11] "My fireworks," thinks Bloom. "Up like a rocket, down like a stick" (*U* 371).

Joyce is obviously satirizing the disjunction between Bloom's highly physical response to the scene and Gerty's romantic fantasy. As "Nausicaa" shifts its parallactic perspective, Bloom is chided by an inflated narrative voice attuned to the parodic excesses of "Cyclops": "What a brute he had been! At it again? A fair unsullied soul had called to him and, wretch that he was, how had he answered? An utter cad he had been. He of all men!" (*U* 367). Such outworn, sentimental ethics are no longer appropriate to the mores of contemporary society. Bloom's reaction to Gerty's deformity may be self-indulgent, but it is emotionally honest and far from callous: "Glad I didn't know it when she was on show. Hot little devil all the same. . . . Anyhow I got the best of that" (*U* 368). Bloom's thoughts correspond to physical detumescence, and they expose uncensored layers of postorgasmic reflection. Unlike Gerty, Bloom does not confuse compassion with passion. He knows that the two are separate, discrete emotions, conflated in popular "soap opera" journalism but distinct in real life. "See her as she is spoil all. Must have the stage setting, the rouge, costume, position, music" (*U* 370).

Masturbation may be a "Mulligan" solution to sexual frustration.

Yet Bloom's "bird in hand" has harmed no one; nor has he violated his own humanitarian ethic of love, the "opposite of hatred." Bloom pities Gerty as she limps away: "Poor girl! That's why she's left on the shelf and the others did a sprint" (*U* 367-68). And he realizes that some kind of personal communication has taken place in their encounter: "Still it was a kind of language between us" (*U* 372). Like Gerty, Bloom perceives a redemptive mutuality in the experience, despite his smug feeling that he has gotten the best of the bargain: "Cheap too. Yours for the asking. Because they want it themselves. Their natural craving" (*U* 368). Both Bloom the "seducer" and Gerty the "temptress" have shared a moment of intimacy that allows temporary escape from individual isolation.

In the "Circe" episode, the phantasm of Gerty limps forward onto the stage, displaying *"coyly her bloodied clout."* She accuses Bloom of a perverse act of psychological defloration: "You did that. . . . When you saw all the secrets of my bottom drawer. . . . Dirty married man!" (*U* 442). The assertion involves a pun on Gerty's underwear and reminds us of her sacramental "toilettable drawer" stuffed with adolescent mementoes. But Gerty adds candidly: "I love you for doing that to me" (*U* 442). The young girl's unconscious admits what her waking mind would never acknowledge.

Both participants in the afternoon drama are "thankful for small mercies" (*U* 368). Bloom feels flattered that Gerty "saw something in him," though he cannot imagine what. "Sooner have me as I am than some poet chap with bearsgrease, plastery hair lovelock over his dexter optic" (*U* 369). He senses the young woman's need for tenderness and privacy: "Gently does it. Dislike rough and tumble. Kiss in the dark and never tell" (*U* 369). Gerty is attracted to Bloom for much the same reason that Molly found him handsome years earlier: "Why me? Because you were so foreign from the others" (*U* 380).

In *Joyce in Nighttown*, Mark Shechner culls from "a number of sly, circumstantial hints" that Gerty's cameo appearance in "Circe" might label her a professional prostitute.[12] The theory is playful but unfounded in the text. Gerty MacDowell is no more (and no less) a whore than Molly Bloom, Josie Breen, or the Princess Selene — all of whom arise as spectres in Nighttown. Leopold Bloom has mentally deflowered the nymph of his fantasy, and his psyche registers the impact. Gerty accuses him of voyeuristic rape, but she delights in her erotic victory over the dark, enchanting stranger. Bloom's id may label Gerty a prostitute and Lipoti Virag a pimp, but one is a technical virgin and the other is dead. Neither phantasm has a "real" identity in the Dublin night world.

Gerty MacDowell is far more than a pornographic pin-up for Leopold Bloom. In "Nausicaa," Gerty soars to ecstasy with the rockets and with Bloom. She proves that she can arouse, titillate, and satisfy masculine desire, and the incident constitutes an erotic victory. As the new "blessed virgin" and votary of Dame Fashion, "a beacon ever to the storm-tossed heart of man" (U 346), Gerty shows mercy to a sex-starved gentleman who worships at her shrine. She is paid the final tribute of Bloom's unspoken ejaculation: "For this relief much thanks" (U 372).

At the end of the episode, Bloom is still uncertain about his male ego, and he fails to go beyond the vapid assertion of "I. . . . AM. A" (U 381) to an affirmation of personal identity. Once again, Joyce challenges us to fill in the blank: "I am a man?" "A lover?" A human being?" "A fool?" Fritz Senn points out that there is "a faint adumbration of a Jehovean I AM WHAT I AM" and reminds us that AMA is one form of the Latin verb "to love." [13] As we later learn in "Ithaca," Bloom, like Ulysses, is "everyman" and "noman." In the role of "everyman," he can be every ghost lover that has haunted the dreams of Gerty Mac-Dowell. Because he is "noman," Bloom offers an erotic *tabula rasa* on which fantasies of love and romance can be etched by Gerty's fictional imagination.

Gerty may be a pawn of social self-definition, but so is Bloom. And Joyce may be suggesting that, in some way, we all are conditioned by the popular culture that surrounds us. In a world that worships sexual power, Gerty serves as a herald of the twentieth-century goddesses staring from the covers of *Cosmopolitan*, *Woman's Day*, and *Playboy*. She may be guilty of committing mental adultery with Bloom. But in a society that glorifies seduction, sexuality, and erotic satisfaction, who would be willing to cast the first stone?

NOTES

1. This essay appeared in an earlier form as part of my discussion in *Joyce's Moraculous Sindbook: A Study of "Ulysses,"* Chapter 8, " 'Nausicaa': Romantic Fantasy / 'Oxen of the Sun': Procreative Reality," (Columbus: Ohio State University Press, 1978), pp. 153–69.

2. Mark Shechner, *Joyce in Nighttown: A Psychoanalytic Inquiry into "Ulysses"* (Berkeley: University of California Press, 1974), pp. 161–62.

3. Fritz Senn, "Nausicaa," in *James Joyce's "Ulysses,"* ed. Clive Hart and David Hayman (Berkeley: University of California Press, 1974), pp. 284, 290.

4. Maria Susanna Cummins, *The Lamplighter* (Leipzig: Bernhard Tauchnitz, 1854), p. 495. Gerty Flint's character has undergone a dramatic reversal since the beginning of the novel, when she was known for threatening fits of temper: "spirited, sudden and violent, she had made herself feared, as well as disliked" among the "rude herd" of orphan children (p. 10).

5. *Ibid.*, p. 505.

6. *Irish Times*, June 16, 1904, p. 1, col. 6; p. 3, col. 9.

7. Hugh Kenner, *Joyce's Voices* (Berkeley: University of California Press, 1978), p.17.

8. At this point, Gerty begins to fashion Bloom in the image of Philip Amory, Gerty Flint's long-lost father in Cummins's *The Lamplighter*. Her thoughts unconsciously echo the language of Cummins's sentimental reunion scene. When Gerty Flint recognizes Amory as her father, she throws herself "upon his bosom, and, her whole frame trembling with the vehemence of long-suppressed and now uncontrolled agitation, she bursts into a torrent of passionate tears" (Cummins, pp. 473–74).

9. The tale of Amory's past is a masterpiece of convolution, coincidence, melodrama, and improbability. Amory is falsely accused of forgery by Mr. Graham, his step-father and employer. In a confrontation scene with Graham, Amory accidentally manages to blind Emily, his true love, by throwing a chemical in her face to revive her from a fainting fit. "I know not what the exact character of the mixture could have been; but it matters not,—its effect was too awfully evident. The deed was done,—the fatal deed,—and mine was the hand that did it!" (Cummins, p. 449). Banished from Boston and wracked by guilt, the distraught exile sets sail for South America, marries on board a ship to Rio, engenders Gerty, and later becomes separated from his wife and child during a malaria epidemic. By the end of the novel, Amory, now a widower, is happily reunited both with Gerty Flint, his daughter, and with the blind and saintly Emily Graham, who has become a foster mother to Gerty. Emily goes "to live on the hill-side with Philip." "And is the long-wandering, much-suffering, and deeply-sorrowing exile happy now? He is" (Cummins, p. 509). It is no wonder that Gerty MacDowell, whose mind is imbued with the romantic story of *The Lamplighter*, thinks that Bloom, the "dark stranger" she encounters on the beach, is in deep mourning for "an old flame . . . from the days beyond recall" (*U* 364).

10. In *Stephen Hero*, Madden shows Stephen a poem entitled "My Ideal," written by the teacher Mr. Hughes. The final stanza is meant to offer "a certain consolatory, hypothetical alternative to the poet in his woes":

> Art thou real, my Ideal?
> Wilt thou ever come to me
> In the soft and gentle twilight
> With your baby on your knee?
> (*SH* 83)

Stephen is roused to aesthetic horror by these "tawdry lines" and disdains the "ludicrous waddling approach of Hughes's 'Ideal.' " The "inexplicable infant" and gratuitous image of the madonna "cause him a sharp agony in the sensitive region" (SH 83). Joyce must have delighted in the private authorial joke of having Gerty MacDowell express admiration for sentimental verses recorded in an earlier, unpublished manuscript. One can see how the poem, with its evocation of an ideal madonna shrouded in the "soft and gentle twilight," would appeal to Gerty's romantic sensibilities.

11. Charles Peake declares that the tumescent style of the chapter culminates in "her [Gerty's] self-induced orgasm and his [Bloom's] masturbation." There is little evidence, however, to support the theory that Gerty and Bloom achieve simultaneous orgasm. Although Joyce may have believed that the friction of Gerty's swinging legs could be sexually stimulating, it seems more likely that he is figuratively describing her erotic agitation and vicarious excitement at witnessing Bloom's "dewy wet" climax. Peake goes on to suggest that "for Gerty, the self-deception and auto-eroticism are enough" (James Joyce: The Citizen and the Artist [Stanford: Stanford University Press, 1977], p. 245). Yet the pathos of the chapter lies precisely in the impoverishment of Gerty's situation. She remains persistently optimistic in the face of emotional bankruptcy.

12. Shechner, Joyce in Nighttown, p. 165.

13. Senn, "Nausicaa," pp. 281, 294–95.

ELAINE UNKELESS

The Conventional Molly Bloom

If Molly Bloom is the elusive and multifaceted character that so many readers have found her to be, how can one think of her as conventional? She is always judged a memorable creation, no matter what perspective critics adopt. It is Joyce's language that makes Molly so alive, but the traits with which he endows her stem from conventional notions of the way a woman acts and thinks.

Most of Molly's actions are associated directly or indirectly with sex, and non-sexual activities are scarcely mentioned. We read little of the Molly who runs a household: she does the laundry, makes the bed, and cleans the house along with Mrs. Fleming, who cannot do the job herself. Joyce does not encourage the reader to observe these activities. He describes Molly as a middle-class housewife who would like to be a queen. There are hints that Molly has stayed in bed until late in the morning. To be sure, Molly has prepared the house for Boylan's visit,[1] but Joyce emphasizes Molly's laziness and suggests that she has spent much of the day beautifying herself ("my hours dressing and perfuming and combing" [U 742]). To Joyce, Molly's lethargy is typically female. He tells Valery Larbaud: "Autour de cette parole ["yes"] et de trois autres également femelles l'episode tourne lourdement sur son axe." The episode turns ponderously around four "female" words ("because," "bottom," "woman," "yes" [Letters I, 169, 170]), the heaviness too becoming female by implication.

Critics condemning Molly for begrudging what "little housework" she has to do have implied that she is not fulfilling her feminine role.[2] Indeed, Joyce emphasizes Bloom's work in the kitchen, explicitly describing Bloom's preparation of breakfast for two and later cocoa for two. As Stephen watches Bloom light the hearthfire, the young man is reminded of his mother and his godmother as well as of his father and Brother Michael at Clongowes Wood (U 670). It is Bloom, not Molly, who represents the feminine warmth of the hearth.

Molly, however, performs most of the drudgery. Although critics delight in pointing out the implications of the fact that Mr. Bloom buys his own breakfast, cooks the kidney, and serves his wife tea, few readers note that Molly does most of the shopping, prepares dinner, and in general is responsible for maintaining order. We picture her accusing Mary Driscoll of stealing oysters, slapping her daughter for talking back when Milly does not want to buy potatoes, skimping on the tea (compared to Bloom's seemingly generous serving in the morning), and looking "just after dinner all flushed and tossed with boiling old stew" (U 747).[3] Molly is not neglecting her "womanly role." Joyce's dismissal of her duties as housewife in only a few sentences or phrases manifests his assumption that the responsibility of executing household chores rests on the female. True, on the night of June 16 Molly has more interesting events to contemplate, but the one sphere in which she regularly acts is hardly touched upon in the novel. Typically, Molly performs, without much comment, the unsavory duties traditionally considered womanly. That Bloom's fewer and more palatable tasks are described extensively by Joyce does not preclude Molly's conventionally feminine role.

If one of Molly's major employments is hardly mentioned, another, her singing, is stressed. A professional singer, Molly is endowed with a talent that had special meaning for Joyce. Ellmann writes that the high point of Joyce's musical career was the night he "shared the platform" with John McCormack and J. C. Doyle (JJ 173). Like Joyce, Molly is scheduled to sing with these "topnobbers" on her proposed tour. Apparently, she has a fine soprano voice, although there are suggestions that the quality has deteriorated: "The wife has a fine voice. Or had. What? Lidwell asked" (U 288). William Empson has written that music is "one of the few serious positive arts" in *Ulysses*, and "everybody takes singing extremely seriously." [4]

Yet Joyce also disparages it. In *Ulysses*, Stephen Dedalus resists encouragement to become a singer. As Ruth von Phul notes, one of the reasons that Joyce rejected a musical career (a career that Shaun in *Finnegans Wake* adopts) is that to him, "the interpreter of another man's music has a role inferior to the creative role Joyce—and Shem—elected."[5] Songs, Joyce often suggests, are merely airs—the flatulence of Simon Dedalus or the "winds" of Molly Bloom:

> yes Ill sing Winds that blow from the south . . . give us room even to let a
> fart God or do the least thing better yes hold them like that a bit on my side

piano quietly sweeeee theres that train far away pianissimo eeeeeeee one
more song
   that was a relief wherever you be let your wind go free" [U 763].[6]

Throughout *Ulysses*, music is frequently linked with sex. The war-
bling sirens lure with song and body, the rebound of garter their most
enchanting music. Stephen talks about the theory of music and plays
the piano in Bella Cohen's "musicroom." Molly's singing is almost
always connected with her sexuality—in the way she envisions herself
on stage ("close my eyes breath my lips forward kiss sad look
eyes . . . my eyes flash my bust that they havent" [U 762]), and in its
association with men. Invariably, when Molly sings with someone,
flirtation accompanies the performance. Simon Dedalus "was always
on for flirtyfying too when I sang Maritana with him . . . he had a
delicious glorious voice" (U 774). Bartell d'Arcy "commenced kissing
me on the choir stairs after I sang Gounods *Ave Maria* what are we
waiting for O my heart kiss me straight on the brow and part which is
my brown part . . . my low notes he was always raving about . . . I
liked the way he used his mouth singing" (U 745).

   About Molly's tour with Boylan, Bloom tells M'Coy, "She's going to
sing at a swagger affair." (An affair with Boylan, the swaggerer.) "That
so? M'Coy said. . . . Who's getting it up?" (U 75). Nosey Flynn asks
the same question while Bloom is thinking of Plumtree's potted meat
and a limerick about a *"royal old nigger"* who ate *"the somethings of the
reverend Mr MacTrigger. . . . His five hundred wives. Had the time of their
lives. . . . It grew bigger and bigger and bigger."*

> Getting it up? [Bloom] said. . . .
> Ay, now I remember, Nosey Flynn said. . . . Isn't Blazes Boylan mixed up
> in it?
>   . . .
> Yes, he said. He's the organiser in point of fact [U 171, 172, 173].

"That's the bucko that'll organise her," declares the narrator in
"Cyclops" (U 319).

   To Molly too, of course, singing with Boylan means making love
with him. Sometimes she connects the two unconsciously: "he must
have eaten oysters I think a few dozen he was in great singing voice no
I never in all my life felt anyone had one the size of that to make you
feel full up" (U 742). When she contemplates their forthcoming tour to
Belfast, not once does she concern herself about the way they will

perform. Instead, she imagines "doing it" on the train, shopping with Boylan for a present for her "after what I gave," and perhaps eloping with him: "that gets you on on the stage" (*U* 748, 749). Molly, who has not given a concert for over a year, is not concerned about her musical career. For Madame Bloom singing is a talent which helps to create her identity not as a singer or as an independent person but as a lover.

Molly's other activities have been minimal; for instance, she has played piano in a coffee shop, "has left off clothes of all descriptions" (*U* 269), has pleaded with Mr. Cuffe to save her husband's job, and has thrown a coin to a sailor. However, the first three examples occur in the past, and for the last, a single event, her commitment is slight. Recently Molly has had little to do with her daughter. Molly's energies, then, are diverted to housework, which is for the most part boring and which is minimally described in the novel; singing, which can hardly be considered independent of her sexual activities; and sex. On June 16, Molly Bloom's one significant act is to have an affair with Blazes Boylan. Delineating Molly mainly as a sexual being, Joyce confines her character to a conventional mold. Molly recognizes that she can attract a man exclusively by her physicality, and, like the Wife of Bath or Madame Bovary, Molly Bloom believes that she can be fulfilled only by engaging a man's attention: "A wys womman wol besye hire evere in oon / To gete hire love, ye, ther as she hath noon."[7] Molly adheres to the counsel that a wise woman will busy herself to get a lover if she has none. Though Molly complains that men reap the pleasure of intercourse while women satisfy themselves through masturbation, she clearly finds gratifying physical relief—if not satiation[8]—from lovemaking with Boylan. Molly looks forward to Blazes's return for her own sexual pleasure as well as for the feeling of importance she gains from the affair—a confidence which she can win only by having a romantic life. At the same time that her love-making represents a kind of freedom for Molly, it is indicative of her limitations: although she is rebellious against Bloom and social mores, in her affair she is still dependent on Boylan's approval. Even her adultery is part of the prescribed pattern in her society for the way a woman might escape the boundaries of her marriage.

Not only are Molly's actions stereotyped, but so is the fact that she does so little. In the "Penelope" episode her only act is to take care of her bodily needs. Since Molly is confined to her house, or even to her bed, her perspective remains narrow. When Mary Ellmann talks about the woman as formless being, she says: "Beds, as the most amorphous articles of furniture in the house, are favored in the stereotype."[9] In bed, waiting alone for her husband-lover to return, the woman day-dreams about her pleasures and anxieties, her formless fantasy world becoming her only reality. Simone de Beauvoir analyzes the conse-quences of the passive woman's inaction:

> In the world of men, her [woman's] thought, not flowing into any project, since she *does* nothing, is indistinguishable from daydreaming. She has no sense of factual truth, for lack of effectiveness; she never comes to grips with anything but words and mental pictures, and that is why the most contradic-tory assertions give her no uneasiness; she takes little trouble to elucidate the mysteries of a sphere that is in every way beyond her reach. She is content, for her purposes, with extremely vague conceptions, confusing parties, opinions, places, people, events; her head is filled with a strange jumble.[10]

Though Molly may be content just to lie in bed, her outpouring of words is in part a manifestation of her frustration at not participating in the world outside 7 Eccles Street.

Some readers might contend that action or inaction in *Ulysses* is not a significant issue. T. S. Eliot, in "*Ulysses*, Order and Myth," argues that Joyce uses a mythical method, not a narrative one; therefore, Eliot implies, discussions of plot and characterization are more suitable for nineteenth-century novels than for modern works like Joyce's. On the other hand, there are readers, like Stanley Sultan, who think that growth of character through action is a focal point of the book; they sometimes analyze *Ulysses* with reference to what they would call Bloom's assertiveness in bringing Stephen home with him. I agree with critics like S. L. Goldberg, John Bayley, Mark Shechner, or Marilyn French, who, keeping in mind the functions of myth and style, find relevant the study of a character's method of dealing with a given situation.[11] *Ulysses*, as a twentieth-century novel, encourages analysis of words and form rather than of plot. But, using the modern *monologue intérieur* to examine the conscious mind and the uncon-scious, Joyce takes from the nineteenth century the emphasis on characters' feelings, their subtle moral decisions, and the resulting rational or irrational behavior. This behavior, while it forms the plot of *Ulysses*, more importantly helps to reveal the attributes of a character. It is noteworthy that Molly's one major action of the day is one of the foundations for the novel's plot, but that Bloom's many mundane acts develop his personality for the reader. Joyce's portrayal of Molly as a lethargic and passive woman is significant in that it indicates Joyce's assumption about one of his major female creations: the woman character can be successfully described not by chronicling her interaction with others on a daily basis but, almost exclusively, by revealing her fantasy world and her emotions.

Examining this world to discover Molly's characteristics and her opinions, I see Molly as a comic figure whose unraveling thoughts, composed of illogical juxtapositions and conclusions, reveal her naiveté. Both David Hayman and James Van Dyck Card have discussed Molly's "contradictions," Hayman writing that these "make her so intriguing: her bold earthiness and curious reticence; her tendency to be by turns masterful and submissive, unsentimentally frank and lyrically sentimental. . . ." [12] Whereas Hayman focuses on Molly's character in general, Card points out, in an insightful and amusing paper, some of Molly's contradictory statements. For instance, when she wants to be Stephen's lover, she thinks, "I suppose hes 20 or more Im not too old for him if hes 23 or 24" (*U* 775), and when she feels maternal, "I suppose he was as shy as a boy he being so young hardly 20" (*U* 779).[13] There are, of course, many other funny inconsistencies: for her own singing performance, "Ill change that lace on my black dress to show off my bubs" (*U* 763), but when Mrs. M'Coy does the same, "and her old green dress with the lowneck as she cant attract them any other way" (*U* 773). Thinking about the musician Kathleen Kearney "and her lot of squealers," "lot of sparrowfarts," Molly says, "let them get a husband first thats fit to be looked at"; and four lines later, "I could have been a prima donna only I married him" (*U* 763).

Card says accurately that "Molly can have it both ways because she's mindless." But one must question whether "Joyce is laughing with her as well as at her" since Molly, unaware of the incongruities, does not laugh at herself. Joyce's derision of Molly is not predominantly bitter; however, his comedy is based on a supposition that a woman's method of thinking is irrational and disconnected. Even if Molly's sentences can be punctuated, even if each statement follows the one before it "realistically" within the stream of consciousness technique, and even if scholars can find patterns in Molly's thoughts, Joyce intends the sentences to be flowing and elusive, and the statements to be illogical.[14]

Molly's opinions about sex, the most prevalent subject in her musings, are examples of her inconsistent thought. (Although Molly's frankness and her use of four-letter words were of course revolutionary, the fact that she thinks so much about sex—as well as the fact that she is a sex object—is part of a traditional convention.) Believing that sex is "only nature" (*U* 776), Molly denounces Mrs. Riordan and bishops who don't want women to wear bloomers or ride bicycles: "that old Bishop that spoke off the altar his long preach about womans higher functions about girls now riding the bicycle and wearing peak caps and the new woman bloomers God send him sense and me more money" (*U* 761). But to Molly, unlike the Wife of Bath, these licenses, which seem to concern all women, are meant for her alone. When other women do the same, they are indecorous. Bloom is "always skeezing at those brazenfaced things on the bicycles with their skirts blowing up to their navels . . ." (*U* 746). Molly is also severe about Milly's conduct: "riding Harry Devans bicycle at night its as well he sent her where she is she was just getting out of bounds wanting to go on the skatingrink and smoking their cigarettes" (*U* 766). That Molly's jealousy dominates her statements here does not negate her variable standards and narrowness.

Some of Molly's strictures on sexual activity apply to herself as well. "Why cant you kiss a man without going and marrying him first" she asks (*U* 740). Her question is not unusual or shocking. Molly does kiss other men and has sexual intercourse with Bloom before they are married (*U* 736), but she believes that a woman should be a virgin for the man who will be her husband. Mulvey said he would come back to her "and if I was married hed do it to me and I promised him yes faithfully Id let him block me now" (*U* 761).

Even when Molly desires sex, her language sometimes reveals her prudery. Boylan, she thinks, probably did not notice how heavy she is because "he was so busy where he *oughtnt* to be" (*U* 770; emphasis added). When describing Bloom's sexual advances towards her, she says three times that she tried to keep him from doing "worse" (*U* 740.28, 746.2, 746.38), and she calls her masturbation a "natural weakness" (*U* 771). Molly's guilt about her affair is obvious in her reaction to the thunder which woke her at ten o'clock that night: "God be merciful to us I thought the heavens were coming down about us to punish when I blessed myself and said a Hail Mary" (*U* 741). Molly's double standards (adultery is permissible—almost natural—but she feels guilty about committing the "sin") show that her ideas are formulaic. On one hand, she holds the traditional belief that women are naturally and predominantly physical beings. She advocates sexual freedom, sounding like "the new woman" whom the bishop admonishes. On the other hand, her statements often conform to the standard that women be "proper." Her inconsistent notions are based on convention, not on her own ethical decisions.

Molly's conceptions of the way a man or a woman should look and act correspond to customary viewpoints: "Of course a woman is so sensitive about everything" (*U* 742), "the woman is beauty of course" (*U* 753), Bloom "was very handsome at that time trying to look like lord Byron I said I liked though he was too beautiful for a man" (*U* 743). When Bloom was sick at one time, "he looked more like a man with his beard a bit grown" (*U* 738); and Molly wishes he would smoke a pipe "to get the smell of a man" (*U* 752). And it "of course must be terrible when a man cries" (*U* 741).

In what seems to be a daring thought, Molly, twice in the monologue, expresses the desire to be a man: "its well for men all the amount of pleasure they get off a womans body were so round and white for them always I wished I was one myself for a change just to try with that thing they have swelling upon you so hard and at the same time so soft" (*U* 776). David Hayman, probably expressing Joyce's intentions accurately, writes that in Molly's wish " 'penis envy,' disgust with woman's functions, and narcissistic delight are mixed. . . . such attitudes are the perfect complement to Bloom's sexual disposition." [15] For several reasons, then, Molly says that she would want to be a man. One is that she believes that men experience more enjoyment than women during intercourse: "Nice invention they made for women for him to get all the pleasure" (*U* 742).

In addition, there are implications that Molly likes to take an active role in love-making. Hayman is suggesting that as a complement to Bloom's disposition as a "womanly man," Molly is a "manly woman." Hayman does caution: "The Blooms' tendencies should not be overstated, despite the evidence in Circe and Penelope that each covets the other's role. The progress of Bloom's day is toward . . . mastery and assertiveness. . . . What he needs is a role which does not strip him of his pride just as Molly needs one that does not blot her femininity, a delicate balance in fact." [16] Yet Hayman's implication, reflecting Joyce's, is that when a woman is "active," she is taking over the "masculine" role. A "feminine" person, he intimates, is one who lies back and says "yes," a role which Molly "needs" and toward which she is "progressing." But if Joyce, in fact, wants to create the impression here that Molly is a manly woman, he does not succeed. I do not mean only that Molly is not androgynous, but that, despite her predilection for activity in intercourse (perhaps, to Joyce, "masculine"), the predominating tone of her thoughts is not even "masculine" in the conventional sense.

Molly does not project herself into the consciousness of a man. She thinks of "that thing *they* have swelling upon *you*" (emphasis added). "You," of course, means "me" — Molly's imaginings are from her own point of view. What is most impressive in the two passages in which Molly says explicitly that she would like to be a man is her narcissism, a tendency which Hayman notes. Molly's love for her own body is more obvious, perhaps, in the second passage. Sitting on her chamberpot, she contemplates: "I bet he never saw a better pair of thighs than that look how white they are the smoothest place is right there between this bit here how soft like a peach easy God I wouldnt mind being a man and get up on a lovely woman" (*U* 770).

According to Freud, narcissism, which is "normal" in the sexual development of a child, remains a characteristic in women more than in men. Therefore, to him narcissism is "feminine": "We attribute a larger amount of narcissism to femininity, which also affects women's choice of object, so that to be loved is a stronger need for them than to love. The effect of penis-envy has a share, further, in the physical vanity of women, since they are bound to value their charms more highly as a late compensation for their original sexual inferiority." [17] Since women naturally feel inferior to men, Freud says, they try to counteract that feeling by loving their external selves excessively. Simone de Beauvoir, however, believes that social conditions "lead woman more than man to turn toward herself and devote her love to herself." Since as a "subject," she is forbidden "masculine activities," and since her "aggressive sexuality remains unsatisfied," woman sees herself only as a "thing" who "is forced to find her reality in the immanence of her person."

> If she can thus offer *herself* to her own desires, it is because she has felt herself an object since childhood. Her education has prompted her to identify herself with her whole body, puberty has revealed this body as being passive and desirable; it is something she can touch, like satin or velvet [or a

peach], and can contemplate with a lover's eye. In solitary pleasure, woman may divide herself into male subject and female object; thus Irene, a patient of Dalbiez, would say to herself: "I am going to love myself," or more passionately: "I am going to have intercourse with myself. . . ." [18]

Whether or not Joyce considers Molly's narcissism to be natural or learned, he depicts a woman whose love for herself seems an intrinsic part of her character. Throughout her monologue, Molly is concerned about her body — her figure, her skin, her hair. When she was a girl, she liked looking at her breasts (U 761), and she declares, "I used to love myself then" (U 763). Breasts are the most obvious feature of Molly's sexuality to people other than herself, and for that reason, her bosom is important to her — from reflecting about singing, to pleading with Mr. Cuffe for Bloom's job ("I know my chest was out that way" [U 753]), to Boylan's "sucking them" (U 753). "They excite myself sometimes," she says (U 776).

Whereas Stephen Dedalus is in love with his mind, Molly loves her body. Joyce treats Stephen's egocentricity ironically but at the same time indicates that Stephen's narcissism is a necessary characteristic if he is to achieve intellectual superiority in the Dublin of 1904. Molly's preoccupation, however, serves no positive purpose, except, perhaps, to alleviate temporarily her insecurities about her sexuality. Nor is the preoccupation seen as an unusual female attribute.[19] Bloom too is narcissistic. But physical and "womanly" though he is, though he thinks of his genitals floating like a flower (Narcissus) in the bath and masturbates once during the day, he is not preoccupied or in love with his body. To use Beauvoir's vocabulary, Bloom, a man, can transcend his immanence by means of actions directed outside of himself. Joyce does not give Molly the same freedom. Molly's wish to be a man during intercourse does not mean that she is masculine. Rather, her momentary desire for "flight from womanhood," as Karen Horney phrases it, is due both to her sexual insecurity and to her inability to find some freedom of action. In portraying a woman who fantasizes becoming a man, Joyce, ironically, describes this desire in such a way that it becomes a reflection of her narcissism, which is conventionally feminine.

Another one of Molly's traits which makes her appear to be masculine is her domineering tone. Hence, critics, assuming along with Joyce that dominance belongs to the male, have said that Molly "wears the pants" in the house, that she is "master."[20] However, critics have confused this domineering tone with dominance. A re-examination of Molly's overbearing attitude reveals that it is a weak trait traditionally labeled "feminine."

Some of Molly's strongest assertions of independence are couched in her complaints and her commands:

—Hurry up with that tea, she said, I'm parched.

                                         . . .

—Poldy!
—What?
—Scald the teapot [U 62].

From this first view of Molly in Ulysses, the reader sees Molly's haughty manner and Bloom's reaction to it. When Bloom tries to explain the word "metempsychosis," he is uxorious and shy, "glancing askance at her mocking eye" (U 64). As Bloom worries about Molly throughout the day, he reminds himself that he has to pick up Molly's face lotion, which he sometimes associates with Molly's affair. He runs into the museum gates to escape a meeting with Boylan, and then remembers: "lotion have to call" (U 183). Later, at the Ormond Bar, after he has watched Boylan jaunt off to Molly, Bloom is again reminded of the lotion (U 281).

In the "Circe" episode, when Bloom envisions Molly, he thinks of the lotion once more:

A voice: (Sharply.) Poldy!
Bloom: Who? (He ducks and wards off a blow clumsily.) At your service [U 439].

Appropriately, Molly wears trousers, orders Bloom to call her "Mrs Marion," and has a "friendly mockery in her eyes." Bloom tries to exonerate himself for forgetting Molly's cosmetic: "I was just going back for that lotion whitewax, orangeflower water. Shop closes early on Thursday. But the first thing in the morning" (U 440). Though Molly "softens," her seeming friendliness is misleading, like that of the stereotyped fickle temptress. "In disdain [Marion] saunters away, plump as a pampered pouter pigeon, humming the duet from Don Giovanni" (U 441).

The reader continues to note Molly's obstinance about the lotion in the final monologue. Molly thinks of the presents Bloom has given her this month — violet garters and the face lotion (like the husband in Sweets of Sin who buys his wife gifts — for Raoul). Then: "I told him over and over again get that made up in the same place and dont forget it God only knows whether he did after all I said to him Ill know by the bottle anyway if not I suppose Ill only have to wash in my piss like beeftea or chickensoup with some of that opoponax and violet" (*U* 751).

Interestingly, at the end of the day when Bloom enumerates the "imperfections" of June 16, he does not remember that he has forgotten Molly's lotion. Perhaps Bloom is so fearful about the matter that he is trying to repress this failure;[21] however, it is also possible that the lotion (or the forgetting of it) is no longer so important to the man who has survived an attack on his senses and who has assisted another human being. (Joyce himself, of course, may have forgotten to list this "imperfection.")

While Bloom at times appears to be ruled by Molly, he is, in reality, only henpecked by her. He will open the blinds for her in the morning or get her breakfast or worry about her lotion, feeling humble when with her and having doubts about himself throughout the novel. But the only time Bloom is totally dominated by Molly is in Nighttown, where his fantasies greatly magnify Molly's power. His exaggeration does not make his fears less real; however, ultimately, Bloom is in control of his life. He is not governed by Molly. If he thinks about her often, if his major "development" is in relation to his attitudes toward her, still he has made his own decisions and acted independently.

Molly is channeling her suppressed sexual aggression in attempting to control Leopold. Having little influence over the major or many of the minor events which affect her life with Bloom, Molly tries to manipulate certain situations. Her "plots and plans," unlike Bloom's, are not schemes for projects to better the house, Ireland, or mankind. Farfetched and funny though some of Bloom's ideas are, they often concern the world outside of himself. Molly plots almost exclusively to manipulate men for her own interests. Her methods as well as her goals have customarily been labeled feminine, not masculine.

Yet even with the potential power manipulation offers, Molly does not usually succeed. In the significant aspects of the Blooms' marriage, Leopold's decisions are, if anything, more influential than Molly's. That Molly feels resentment rather than appreciation for her husband's gift of face lotion is understandable: it is he who makes the money, he who gets out of the house to buy the lotion, and he who encourages his wife to look young and beautiful—for Raoul. Molly's definitive statements reveal her annoyance that, in fact, she cannot force her husband to act according to her will and to tell her what she wants to know. Molly's domineering tone is a sign of frustration, not strength. Simone de Beauvoir explains that "the tyranny exercised by woman only goes to show her dependence; . . . if she seeks desperately to bend [her husband] to her will, it is because she is alienated in him—that is, her interests as an individual lie in him. She makes a weapon of her weakness; but the fact remains that she is weak." [22] Molly's brusqueness in the morning is a reflection of her nervousness about Boylan's imminent visit and her resentment both of Bloom's sexual impotence and of his social independence in a "man's world" ("they have friends they can talk to weve none" [U 778]). In addition, she feels she has to exercise dominion in her own small sphere. In the evening, Molly rants about seducing and manipulating Bloom: "then if he wants to kiss my bottom Ill drag open my drawers and bulge it right out in his face as large as life he can stick his tongue 7 miles up my hole . . . then Ill tell him I want £1 or perhaps 30/- . . . yes O wait now sonny my turn is coming . . . O but I was forgetting this bloody pest of a thing pfooh you wouldnt know which to laugh or cry were such a mixture of plum and apple" (U 780, 781). Despite Molly's rage, she will not carry out the threats she makes. .

Ironically, in the "Penelope" chapter, which consists only of thoughts, Molly belittles the importance of words. For to Molly, words used by men "leave us as wise as we were before" (U 744). Critics often find amusing Molly's poor use of language ("It must have fell down" [U 64]), and lack of intellect. Although one laughs at Molly's curious juxtapositions and naive statements (as one does with a child), one must also recognize that Molly, a stereotype of the simpleminded woman, is being ridiculed. When she visits Dr. Collins: "your vagina he called it . . . asking me had I frequent omissions where do those old fellows get all the words they have omissions" (U 770). Masculine logic, having no significance in her narrow world, is threatening. Molly responds to life with her emotions, with the immediacy of her own feelings. Even when she muses on situations outside of her direct experience—politics or the kinds of names people have in Gibraltar— Molly sees them subjectively: "Pisimbo and Mrs Opisso in Governor street O what a name Id go and drown myself" (U 779).[23]

"Pen — stupid," writes Joyce in his notes on the "Penelope" chapter.[24] A series of sentences Joyce used to teach English at a Berlitz school reads: "A husband is usually an ox with horns. His wife is brainless. Together they make a four-legged animal" (*JJ* 224). Molly asks Bloom about the word "met him pike hoses" not because she is curious but because she suspects that there might be something tantalizing about "meeting him." Once Bloom mentions transmigration of souls, Molly loses interest and becomes frustrated at her inability to comprehend: "O, rocks! she said. Tell us in plain words" (*U* 64); "he can never explain a thing simply the way a body can understand" (*U* 754).

Stanley Sultan believes that "what is taken to be stupidity is a lack of education in a rather perceptive mind." Molly, he says, has an "ingenuous *Weltanschauung*." [25] Sultan's statements may be more valid for Gretta Conroy and Bertha Rowan than for Molly Bloom. For Molly, who is uneducated, is also unable to learn. We remember that Bloom has little success in teaching Molly objective information: "She followed not all, a part of the whole, gave attention with interest, comprehended with surprise, with care repeated, with greater difficulty remembered, forgot with ease, with misgiving reremembered, rerepeated with error" (*U* 687). Yet Sultan is probably correct in assessing Joyce's intentions if the critic means that Molly's perceptiveness is based on intuition. Even though she is stupid, Molly can "sense" certain things about Bloom, his friends, men and women in general. However, when we look closely at these "perceptions," we see that they are unoriginal or they are guesses which happen to be correct. (Molly suspects, for instance, that Bloom had an orgasm on June 16.) Molly declares that women should govern the world: "you wouldnt see women going and killing one another and slaughtering." Several lines following, she complains that there is always "some woman ready to stick her knife in you I hate that in women" (*U* 778–79). Even though her statements seem contradictory, in fact, Molly "perceives" an established stereotype: that men are aggressive directly and women indirectly. Such "feminine intuition," as Mary Ellmann reminds us, is an unsubstantial basis for thought: "In the end, the only intuitive perceptions which can be wholly endorsed, and even these perhaps leave a tiny residue of uneasiness, are those which directly and practically benefit the recipient. In that event, the faculty, like fire for a savage, seems no more mysterious than serviceable." [26]

Molly's anti-intellectuality is sometimes viewed as a positive attribute. She derides Bloom's political activities and his attempts to understand religious and philosophical ideas, though she acknowledges that he "knows a lot of mixed up things." Mocking men's creations, Molly, according to William York Tindall, represents "reality,"[27] and most critics seem to take for granted that Molly is "natural life" in contrast to Stephen, who represents "mind." Perhaps, giving Molly the "last word," Joyce is humbling himself—men's words are shallow compared to the experience of life which Molly supposedly represents. Yet Molly herself thinks words are unimportant because she lacks comprehension of them, not because she adopts the critical attitude that words can never fully express human experience. She is not ironic, only negative. If Molly as a symbol is Joyce's vehicle for showing deference to the natural, as an individual her lack of knowledge limits her to the stereotyped role of the ignorant female. Thinking of Molly's anti-intellectuality as praiseworthy for her sake, as some critics do, saying that she is the wisest character in *Ulysses* and that she represents a world superior to Joyce's, is at best fallacious.

From chaos Gea-Tellus sprang, and from the dullness and triviality of her existence, Molly, in the last two pages of her monologue, is transfigured into someone who is more accepting than the character portrayed previously. With the chaotic jumble of Molly's words modulating into a rhythmical throb, the reader is carried joyously to the Hill of Howth. Joyce is more romantic here, using fewer ironic deflations than before in the monologue. By his magnificent language, he transforms Molly into the rolling earth, amoral, indifferent. Yet Joyce does not reclaim stereotypes. If Molly transcends her daily existence, she does so as a symbol, not as an individual. In magnifying her significance, Joyce dehumanizes her. Bloom and Stephen also, Joyce suggests, become abstractions in "Ithaca," in which they are "heavenly bodies, wanderers like the stars at which they gaze" (*Letters* I, 160). However, Bloom's significance as the symbol of a cosmic body is less predominant in the novel than his importance as an ironic parallel of mythical heroes—Christ, Ulysses, Sinbad the Sailor—and as such he retains his human form. Joyce depicts Molly's transcendence more by making her become a life force or woman's essence than by creating her to be analogous to Mary, Eve, or Penelope. She is not a hero, but a power beyond the realm of human experience.

In the final pages Molly is also the sensual woman on the rolling hills of Howth. Longingly, Molly recalls Bloom's proposal. Her remembrances of Bloom, Mulvey, and Gibraltar, suffused with the feelings of

an escape from reality, give her added dimension as a literary character. Yet far from a Proustian recognition, Molly's recollections, consist-
ing of sense impressions, do not reveal the growth of her mind or help
her make a decision about her present situation. Frustrated in her life
with Bloom, Molly muses upon the man who once called her "flower
of the mountain." Again, Joyce's exquisite language, not Molly's
understanding, makes this passage so powerful.

This essay has described Molly as a realistic character. Marilyn
French, in *The Book as World*, asserts that Joyce intended the character
of Molly Bloom to be archetypal rather than realistic, that discussion of
her on a naturalistic level leads to distortion or exasperation. But
Richard Ellmann is correct when he suggests that Joyce delights in
mythologizing and then demythologizing Molly, in turn or at the same
time.[28] A feminist interpretation of Molly's role as archetype will be a
welcome contribution to Joyce studies; the analysis in this essay focuses exclusively on Molly as a realistic figure in order to help define
Joyce's attitudes toward her as a woman.

Robert Adams writes that "Joyce seems to have given Mrs. Bloom
the first name of 'Marion,' which can be either masculine or feminine,
to suggest that she is a manly woman, as Bloom is a womanly man."[29]
But if her name is epicene, her character is not. Carolyn Heilbrun
defines androgyny as a "condition under which the characteristics of
the sexes, and the human impulses expressed by men and women, are
not rigidly assigned. Androgyny seeks to liberate the individual from
the confines of the appropriate."[30] As Joyce himself says in his letters,
Molly is limited, and she is so in large part because she is confined to
preconceived ideas of the way a woman thinks and behaves. Her
supposedly "masculine" traits—the domineering tone, the attempts to
control others, the aggressive sexuality—are actually aspects of her
"femininity." Resulting from the frustration of passivity, they represent only indirect means toward action, and her ideas and resolutions
finally remain unexecuted.

NOTES

1. In "Molly's Mistresstroke" (*James Joyce Quarterly* 14 [Fall, 1976], 25–30),
Margaret Honton shows convincingly that Molly not only cleans up the house
and puts new linen on the bed but also moves the furniture in the front room.

2. See, *e.g.*, Stanley Sultan, *The Argument of "Ulysses"* (Columbus: Ohio State University Press, 1964); Darcy O'Brien, *The Conscience of James Joyce* (Princeton: Princeton University Press, 1968).

3. The only pleasant description of Molly in the kitchen is her fantasy of getting delicacies for breakfast to take up to Stephen's bedroom (*U* 779).

4. William Empson, "The Theme of *Ulysses*," *The Kenyon Review*, 18 (Winter, 1956), 31.

5. Ruth von Phul, "Joyce and the Strabismal Apologia," in *A James Joyce Miscellany*, 2nd ser., ed. Marvin Magalaner (Carbondale: Southern Illinois University Press, 1959), p. 131.

6. As William York Tindall has pointed out in his introduction to *Chamber Music* (New York: Columbia University Press, 1954), urination is part of the music in Joyce's poems.

7. Geoffrey Chaucer, "The Wife of Bath's Prologue" in *Canterbury Tales*, in *The Works of Geoffrey Chaucer*, ed. F. N. Robinson (Boston: Houghton Mifflin, 1957), ll. 209–10.

8. An interesting article on women's satiation-in-insatiation in coitus is Mary Jane Sherfey's "On the Nature of Female Sexuality" in *Psychoanalysis and Women*, ed. Jean Baker Miller (Harmondsworth, Middlesex, England: Penguin Books, 1973).

9. Mary Ellmann, *Thinking About Women* (New York: Harcourt Brace Jovanovich, 1968), p. 76.

10. Simone de Beauvoir, *The Second Sex*, trans. and ed. H. M. Parshley (1949; rpt. New York: Bantam, 1961), p. 564.

11. T. S. Eliot, "*Ulysses*, Order and Myth," in *James Joyce: Two Decades of Criticism*, ed. Seon Givens (1948; rpt. New York: Vanguard Press, 1963); Sultan; S. L. Goldberg, *The Classical Temper: A Study of James Joyce's "Ulysses"* (London: Chatto and Windus, 1963); John Bayley, *The Character of Love: A Study in the Literature of Personality* (New York: Collier Books, 1960); Mark Shechner, *Joyce in Nighttown: A Psychoanalytic Inquiry into "Ulysses"* (Berkeley: University of California Press, 1974); Marilyn French, *The Book as World: James Joyce's "Ulysses"* (Cambridge: Harvard University Press, 1976).

12. David Hayman, "The Empirical Molly," in *Approaches to "Ulysses": Ten Essays*, ed. Thomas F. Staley and Bernard Benstock (Pittsburgh: University of Pittsburgh Press, 1970), p. 120.

13. James Van Dyck Card, " 'Contradicting': The Word for 'Penelope,' " *James Joyce Quarterly* 11 (Fall, 1973), 19.

14. To Harriet Shaw Weaver, Joyce wrote, ". . . *Penelope* has no beginning, middle or end" (*Letters* I, 172). Yet some critics have found patterns. In "The Final Octagon of *Ulysses*" (*James Joyce Quarterly* 10 [Summer, 1973], 439–54), Diane Tolomeo states: "In deliberate writing such as we find in *Ulysses*, it is difficult to believe that any chapter of the book does not possess a tight organic structure of its own. . . . Attending to structure and number in 'Penelope' proves more fruitful than emphasizing the episode's flux and uncertainty" (p. 441). Tolomeo's interpretation that Molly's eight sentences suggest a Viconian patterning is convincing. Indeed, if in revising the text, Joyce added words to

form a specific pattern of descent and then ascent in Molly's soliloquy, the pairing of images is concealed in such a way that Joyce's intentions seem to be to make the pattern illustrative of the mysterious interweavings of a woman's mind. (The cyclical aspects of Molly's monologue are often pointed out. See *e.g.* William York Tindall, *A Reader's Guide to James Joyce* [New York: Farrar, Straus & Giroux, 1959], pp. 234–35).

15. Hayman, p. 121. Whether or not Freud's notion of "penis-envy" is valid, it is not unlikely that Joyce's intention is to have Molly express such envy.

16. *Ibid.*, pp. 134–35.

17. Sigmund Freud, "Femininity," in *New Introductory Lectures on Psychoanalysis*, trans. and ed. James Strachey (New York: W. W. Norton, 1965), p. 132.

18. De Beauvoir, pp. 592–93. In a footnote on the same page, de Beauvoir points out "Havelock Ellis's ideas on the relationship between narcissism and what he calls 'undinism'—that is, a kind of urinary eroticism. (See *The Psychology of Sex*, vol. 3, part 2)." Molly is on her chamberpot urinating when she feels her thighs.

19. Narcissism has been described in various ways. Popularly, its primary meaning is an excessive love for the self. Sometimes the word is used to suggest a valuable, positive self-concept; on the other hand, "negative narcissism" is defined as exaggerated self-deprecation. To Freud, who first used the word to describe a neurosis, narcissism is sexual arousal stimulated by oneself rather than by a different person. As it is associated with the female, the term usually means a preoccupation with examining, beautifying, and valuing one's body. I believe that Molly's narcissism in the context of the present discussion fits into this last category. For a recent discussion of narcissistic characters in novels, see Patricia Meyer Spacks's *The Female Imagination* (New York: Alfred A. Knopf, 1975).

20. See, *e.g.*, William York Tindall, *James Joyce: His Way of Interpreting the Modern World* (New York: Charles Scribner's Sons, 1950); O'Brien; Hayman.

21. Margaret McBride, "At Four She Said," *James Joyce Quarterly* 17 (Fall, 1979), 31.

22. De Beauvoir, p. 454. I would like to make two points here. One is that while Bloom's having to buy the lotion might be a chore, he is the one who strolls around town. It has been reported that the duty housewives mind least is shopping since they can leave home and interact with various people. Molly, however, does not intimate that if Bloom does not get the lotion, she will. Second, Bloom's impotence with Molly and what Molly sees as his unusual sexual desires are obviously baffling and disconcerting for her and are among the reasons for Molly's general frustration. Further analysis of this issue, which I shall not attempt here, would not change the discussion of the resultant trait—Molly's domineering tone.

23. Molly makes this comment after she reflects: "Dedalus I wonder its like those names in Gibraltar." When Stephen ponders the meaning of his name in *A Portrait of the Artist as a Young Man*, he recognizes the connection between himself and the great artificer. Stephen, like Molly, thinks about the name in

relation to himself, but, a man, he is inspired to use the Greek hero as a model for his own creativity. Molly's thoughts are funny, but they reveal her lack of experience and education.

24. James Joyce, "Notesheets for 'Penelope,'" *British Museum Additional MSS. # 49975*. See Phillip F. Herring, *Joyce's "Ulysses" Notesheets in the British Museum* (Charlottesville: University Press of Virginia, 1972), p. 504.

25. Sultan, p. 426.

26. Mary Ellmann, p. 113.

27. William York Tindall, "Dante and Mrs. Bloom," *Accent* 11, no. 2 (Spring, 1951), 89.

28. French, pp. 258–59; Richard Ellmann, *Ulysses on the Liffey* (New York: Oxford University Press, 1972), p. 164.

29. Robert Martin Adams, *Surface and Symbol: The Consistency of James Joyce's "Ulysses"* (New York: Oxford University Press, 1967), p. 68.

30. Carolyn G. Heilbrun, *Toward a Recognition of Androgyny* (New York: Alfred A. Knopf, 1973), p. x.

SHARI BENSTOCK

The Genuine Christine: Psychodynamics of Issy

Clive Hart's assertion that "duality of being is perhaps the most important of all the basic structural concepts in *Finnegans Wake*"[1] underscores a significant principle in Joyce's *Wake* universe: whatever other more complex numerological systems Joyce experiments with in the *Wake*, the most fundamental and pervasive structure is rooted in the concept of duality. Such an assumption has particular relevance for characterization in the *Wake* since, as Hart explains, "everything in the book exists in two versions, one exalted and one debased." Numerous examples of this phenomenon are readily available, but one easily identified is Issy, daughter of HCE and ALP, the young nubile who is both the saccharine sweet "nuvoletta in her lightdress, spunn of sisteen shimmers" (157.8), and the sexually precocious writer of obscene footnotes to the children's lessons in II,2. The contrasting aspects of Issy's personality predominate in any discussion of her role in the *Wake*, and she is often referred to as the "lookingglass girl," a reference to the mirror image with which she is narcissistically involved.

Interest in this dual Issy led Adaline Glasheen to investigate her psychology further, in search of evidence that Issy "is one of those girls with a multiple personality,"[2] a counterpart to the young lady described by Dr. Morton Prince in his study, *The Dissociation of a Personality* (Boston, 1905, 1908).[3] Finding that references to "Christine L. Beauchamp" (Dr. Prince's patient) and to "Sally" (Miss Beauchamp's alter ego) abound in the Issy sections of *Finnegans Wake*, Glasheen sees similarities between the two women: the Christine/Sally split is reflected most obviously in Issy's uneasy amalgam of the sacred and profane, one side of the split ego characterized by the virginal Nuvoletta, the other by the sexually provocative and enticing temptress. Carrying the argument further, Glasheen suggests that the "Maggies," Earwicker's temptresses in Phoenix Park, are another extension of Issy and "her grateful sister reflection in a mirror" (220.9) and that the famous letter from Boston, Mass., is written from one Maggy "selfpenned" to her "other" (489.33–34). This interpretation suggests that Issy-as-temptress is her father's downfall, but Issy-as-letterwriter is her father's salvation, the letter itself constituting the defense which can resurrect him. In short, the argument rests on the implicit assumption that a psychologically unstable daughter—the disintegrated Issy—serves both as her father's destroyer and as the agent of his redemption.

The supposition that Issy's unfocused and flighty personality results from a mental aberration, fragmenting her personality into secondary selves (the antithetical "twinstreams" and "twinestraines" of her identity [528.17]), reduces Issy's role to the realm of psychological disorder and confines Hart's duality principle to the narrower region of psychotic behavior. Apart from the uncomfortable suspicion that Joyce's inability to accept his own daughter's mental illness might obviate such an easy correlation between biographical fact and artistic creation,[4] Glasheen's theory rests on the assumption that character delineation in *Finnegans Wake* functions much as it does in more traditional frameworks—i.e., that we can talk about Issy's psychological motivations in the same terms we might use when discussing a character like Gerty MacDowell. Indeed, there are certain similarities between the two. The vignette constituting the first half of "Nausicaa" provides an illuminating portrait of Gerty employing feminine wiles not unlike those being cultivated by the juvenile Issy. But even the gooey narrative describing her techniques cannot disguise Gerty's singular lack of success in her efforts to attract a husband. Beyond her prime, she buffers the reality of her situation by explaining away the younger Reggy Wylie ("that was far away") and replacing him with middle-aged Bloom: "Here was that of which she had so often dreamed" (*U* 358). Her expectations have dwindled from marriage to an illicit affair (but one which stops short of that "other thing," confining itself to "hot" kisses [*U* 366]). What she settles for, as we observe, is something far less. When the final piece of evidence sealing Gerty's fated spinsterhood is revealed ("She's lame! O!" [*U* 367]), her portrait is complete, and all her subterfuges prove illusory. Much of Gerty's behavior can be explained by her physical affliction, and Christine Beauchamp's by her mental illness, but Issy's complexities elude such straightforward answers: there is simply not enough evidence to justify any single theory of Issy's personality structure.

Missing as elements of portraiture in the *Wake* are the definable surface reality, plot development, psychological motivators, consistent tone, and precise diction found in traditional narrative structures. The distortion of the dream language, blending incident and landscape, blurs objectivity and conceals the narrative stance. All events are filtered through the guiltridden perspective of the dream, a process that denies character "development" or autonomous action on the part of the dreamer's cast.[5] Each family member is complex and contradictory, for each subsumes archetypes (Issy is virgin/whore; Anna Livia is mother/muse), allusive frames (HCE is Finn MacCool, Tim Finnegan, Adam, Noah, and Humpty Dumpty), and historic models (Shem and Shaun serve as Cassius and Brutus or Napoleon and Wellington). Ultimately, these characters blend into the primary categories of male and female, sexual distinctions marking the lines of demarcation between individuals. All males are subsumed in HCE; all females are contained in ALP. These parent figures become the male and female principles of the novel.

So Anna Livia transcends the human level to assume status as woman. The surface reality that confines a Molly Bloom to 7 Eccles Street does not contain ALP. Such constraints calcify Molly's already contrary nature as she strains against prevailing decorum, striving to satisfy her sexual needs. Imbued with idiosyncratic tastes and all too human personal prejudices, she is characterized by the equivocal "Yes because" of her monologue. By comparison, Anna Livia represents the unifying principle of the *Wake*, even as she carries in her wake the "twinstreams" that the younger Issy now embodies. The antinomies demonstrated by the multiple brother battles between Shem and Shaun and captured in the inconsistent behavior of sister Issy are never erased nor ultimately merged, but are finally subsumed by the male and female principles. Entwined, but never resolved, these opposing elements compose a structural net supporting the basic tensions of the novel, analogous to the plot frame of more conventional fictions.

The collapse of linear time into the ever-whirling modes of the dream cycle further emphasizes the interweave of disparate elements while eliminating any possibility that characters will be seen in the hard light of day. There is no need to speculate on the "morning after" of the Porters as there has been with the Blooms, precisely because the dream replaces reality by constantly retelling the same tale—Earwicker's fall in Phoenix Park. The story of Earwicker's rise and fall not only provides the psychological highs and lows of this tale, but it also accounts for the appearance and disappearance of conflicting personality characteristics in the *Wake* cast. In his less guilty moments, Earwicker sees his daughter, for instance, as an innocent child; at his most culpable, he thinks of her as his compatriot in lust. In short, such abstract principles as "innocence" or "guilt" are allowed to surface in various ways throughout the dream, providing the warp and woof of its fabric.

Impossible as it is to narrow the focus of sexual guilt enclosing the *Wake* (everyone is guilty at some stage), even more risky is the attempt to pinpoint Joyce's private attitudes about sex or sexual roles by analyzing persons present at the *Wake*. One might speculate, for example, that Joyce preferred to cast women in traditional roles, as bearers of children, protectresses of the male ego, nurturers of the racial consciousness, and symbols of passive domesticity. (Daughters continue the cycle by imitating their mothers and ultimately replacing them.) But such attitudes are confirmed by the traditions of the civilization described by the *Wake* and may be less the product of Joyce's own view than embodiments of the myth, fable, history, and literature from which *Finnegans Wake* is shaped. That ALP is the culmination of or the successor to other Joycean women like Gretta Conroy, May Goulding, Molly Bloom, or that Issy supplants Emma, Gerty, or Milly, may point us toward Joyce's abstract conception of the female principle. But all of this speculation is mitigated by the vision of the *Wake*, a vision that belongs to Earwicker, whose dream is fashioned from his own guilty desires, a dream in which females play interchangeable roles, but where each is—ultimately—woman. How Earwicker sees Issy, or his wife, is the only "vision" analyzed in the *Wake*. Thus, Glasheen's emphasis is perhaps misplaced: it may not be Issy who is "split," but rather her father's image of her which divides itself.

Dr. Prince's Patient

Following Adaline Glasheen's lead, I shall re-examine Issy's situation. "*Finnegans Wake* and the Girls from Boston, Mass." makes a careful accounting of the Morton Prince–Christine L./Sally Beauchamp material in the *Wake*, and clearly the references and echoes of *The Dissociation of a Personality* appear interwoven with the Issy material. That Joyce knew this work (or knew of it) seems rather certain; that he "used

Miss Beauchamp as a model for Issy" is much less definite.[6] Morton Prince's portrait of Christine Beauchamp confines itself to a case history aimed at an accurate rendering of the diagnostic process, and significantly, the appearance of Christine's "double" is occasioned by the rape attempt made by her friend, Mr. Jones.[7] Such a psychic trauma leads to Christine's abnormal mental processes, characterized at their earliest stages by Sally's special "language" which "implied a concomitant existence for herself, a double mental life for Miss Beauchamp. She always spoke as if she had her own thoughts, perceptions, and will *during the time while Miss Beauchamp was in existence.*" [8] Prince concludes finally that "Chris [later called Sally] was not simply a hypnotic self, but she was a distinctly pathological condition, both as an alternating and as a subconscious self." [9] A cured Christine is achieved only by "killing off" the second self, thereby reintegrating the dichotomous personality strains.

Issy's behavior falls short of this kind of death struggle. She exhibits none of the telltale signs of psychopathology which lead Prince to his theory of Miss Beauchamp's dissociated personality (e.g., altered speech patterns, distorted handwriting, or modifications in physiological processes apparent through changes in body weight, facial coloring, taste in food, or predisposition to physical illness). Yet there is the nagging suspicion that Issy's personality is remarkably diffuse and disintegrated. Such inconstancy, however, is not equivalent to mental illness, as the choice of Christine Beauchamp as the "model" for Issy's behavior implies. If Issy's character is drawn in distinctly different terms from the general pattern of characterization in the *Wake*, having the source of its multiplicity in a psychopathology, then the reasons for her aberrant behavior remain obscured, and the cause of the dissociation is markedly absent from the diagnosis.[10]

Issy is not Joyce's patient, nor is her portrait limited to a textbook definition of personality deviance. Within the family structure, she remains in her role as daughter, her "dadad's lottiest daughterpearl and brooder's cissiest auntybride" (561.15–16), assumed by ALP to be her replacement ("What will be is. Is is" [620.32]). At the level of cosmic correspondence, Issy's role as her mother's past and future provides a correlative to her familial role: as the little cloud, she catches up the moisture from the river-mother and brings it back to the Wicklow hills as rain. This process is described by ALP in her closing monologue: "what wouldn't you give to have a girl! Your wish was mewill. And, lo, out of a sky! The way I too" (620.26–28). While Issy's role in the future may be cast as the unifying principle now apparent in Anna Liffey, in the *Wake* Issy is a temperamental and unsettled adolescent whose personality is not yet structured or coherent. Primping at her dressing table, she is enthralled with her own image, her "double." From the cradle she has contented herself with this playmate: "Her shellback thimblecasket mirror only can show her dearest friendeen" (561.16–17). Issy's "double" is not a recent apparition brought about by some mental shock (as was Christine's), but rather a consistent feature of her otherwise inconsistent character: "Alone? Alone what? I mean, our strifestirrer, does she do fleurty winkies with herself. Pussy is never alone, as records her chambrette, for she can always look at Biddles and talk petnames with her little playfilly when she is sitting downy on the ploshmat" (561.33–562.1).[11]

From this initial mirror duplication of the daughter arises Issy's dual existence in Earwicker's dream when she appears as the "Maggies," as Glasheen suggests, "after Magdalene and the Magazine wall."[12] The two "sides" of Issy are represented then by the Virgin Mary (under whose aspect the "sweet" Issy is cast [561.27]) and her counterpart, the fallen Mary Magdalene. Issy's double role as the two Marys is not without psychological implications, since the virgin and whore images serve as models for the kind of "split" personality that some have seen in Issy's character, a split which is certainly apparent in the Christine/Sally syndrome. The story of Mary Magdalene's "conversion" is germane: before her call to Christ, she was possessed by seven devils (the number associating itself with Issy as the seven rainbow girls); her whoring was "proof" of the possessed state. When Christ exorcised the devils, Mary followed a chaste life (Luke, 8:1). The belief that illicit sexual behavior is a manifestation of possession by a devil persists throughout Western literature, re-appearing in Puritan thought and writing in New England and maintaining a firm hold in popular belief in America into the late 1800s.[13] Christine's Boston upbringing, completely sunk in its Puritan roots, is evidenced in her horror at the behavior of Sally, who is eager for Jones's attentions and who causes Christine to suffer for her strong religious beliefs by making her say and do un-Christian things. Christine's cure is brought by forcing her to recognize the validity of her sexual drives, thus eliminating the cause of this psychological split.

Similarly, the "good" Issy is described as "sister Isobel," a bride of

Christ, who at twenty is "the beautiful presentation nun" (556.4–5) and also "nurse Saintette Isabelle with stiffstarched cuffs" (556.7), another association allying her with prim Nurse Beauchamp. On the other side, Issy is the harlot of the "Mime" and, in her role as the "Maggies," tries to seduce her brothers and her father. In her role as a young schoolgirl, Issy attends "brigidschool" (562.13), named for St. Brigid, also known as "Mary of the Gael." The female patron saint of Ireland, St. Brigid is the two-faced woman, with half of her face radiating beauty, the other half distorted and ugly. Brigid is yet another one of the "split" females in *Finnegans Wake*, and her role parallels that of Mary Magdalene. Brigid's conversion to Christianity also marked her turning away from pagan whoredom and entering the "chaste" life.

Issy's duality may be seen as another extension of the virgin/whore complex already evident in Western literature and prevalent in religious thought, but especially familiar to readers of Joyce as it dominates descriptions of females from *Chamber Music* through *Ulysses*. Most apparent, perhaps, is Stephen Dedalus's ambivalence in *A Portrait* toward Emma Clery, the girl who is both the fantasy object of a wet dream (*P* 217), and the refined, ethereal spirit pervading his villanelle. Another incident involving confused sexual responses occurs in *Ulysses* when Leopold Bloom, under Bello's spell in the Circean nightmare, assumes the role of Rip Van Winkle and dreams of a woman:

Bloom

(*In tattered moccasins with a rusty fowlingpiece, tiptoeing, fingertipping, his haggard bony bearded face peering through the diamond panes, cries out.*) I see her! It's she! The first night at Mat Dillon's! But that dress, the green! And her hair is dyed gold and he . . .

Bello

(*Laughs mockingly.*) That's your daughter, you owl, with a Mullingar student.
   (*Milly Bloom, fairhaired, greenvested, slimsandalled, her blue scarf in the seawind simply swirling, breaks from the arms of her lover and calls, her young eyes wonderwide.*)

Milly

My! It's Papli! But. O Papli, how old you've grown! [*U* 542].

Here in microcosm is the central subject of Earwicker's dream: the aging sleeper (the father) dreams of his first love, who is young/ beautiful/tempting, only to discover that the girl of his dreams is his daughter (a younger version of his wife) and that the man in her arms is not himself but her young lover. The confusion of mother and daughter, father and lover, perhaps accounts for the divided vision portraying woman as both innocent (Issy and Milly in their roles as daughter) and enticing (Issy-ALP/Milly-Molly as temptresses).

From Earwicker's point of view, Issy is "the queenly pearl you prize, because of the way the night that first we met she is bound to be, methinks, and not in vain, the darling of my heart, sleeping in her april cot, within her singachamer, with her greengageflavoured candy-whistle duetted to the crazy-quilt, Isobel, she is so pretty" (556.12–16). As the object of her father's devoted affection, Issy appears in his dream on the night in question, as do his wife, Anna Livia, and Kate, the symbolic mother figure. In the most innocent version of this dream, HCE accidentally comes upon a young maiden micturating in the park, "her waters of her sillying waters of and there now brown peater arripple" (76.27–30). The "sillying waters" hint at Issy's presence as ALP's diminutive, and Earwicker's titillation at this scene is the result of his transferring sexual desire for his wife when she was young to his enticing teenage daughter. This incestuous possibility is carefully disguised from Earwicker by a transference: one Dublin daughter becomes two Dublin maidens in the dream (they are waitresses, servant girls, maids, young "fillies," or the "jinnies," and go by various names); the possibility that the girls are really Earwicker's own daughter is carefully hidden, especially from the dreamer himself, most frequently by making Earwicker the uncle ("dear dutchy deep-linns" [76.25–26]) and the girls his young nieces: "Uncle Arth, your two cozes from Niece" (608.7–8). Father and daughter are present— but at a double remove from each other.

Earwicker's Vision

The "sin" in the park, involving Earwicker and two young mistresses, becomes the central mystery of the novel. And, in good Joycean fashion, all possible combinations of motive and method are left open. But the basic variations seem to include the following: either the two girls in the park are harmlessly urinating while Earwicker accidentally and innocently watches (34.12–29, 178.26–30, 348.21–25); or the two girls are temptresses willingly titillating their aging observer, who in turn is either a casual bystander or a participant responding by urinating, defecating, or possibly masturbating (52.1–3, 107.1–7, 366.22–25). The evolving dream offers numerous versions of the basic incident, many of them elevating the micturition-voyeurism theme to the level of incest coupled with heterosexual or homosexual perversion.[14] But one constant remains, despite hundreds of consequential revisions of the incident: whatever the two maidens are doing (whether it be incidental urination or deliberate self-exposure), they are doing the same thing and doing it *together*. They are either both temptresses or both innocents, but nowhere in *Finnegans Wake* is there any indication that one plays the innocent and the other the temptress. The vision of the maidens is not contemporaneously "split"; rather, the alternations in behavior occur over time as Earwicker's dream exposes his ambivalence toward his wife, daughter, and mother. Where his daughter is concerned, his motivations are antithetical: he wants to see her as the "sweet nuvoletta," even though he is tempted by her beauty and charm, but he never sees her simultaneously as virgin and vamp. Her mother's view of her, which is decidedly different from her father's in its consistency, is not offered until the final pages of the book and acts as an alternative vision against which Earwicker's dream vision can be measured.

Before we get Anna Livia's final word, Joyce offers several analogues to the park incident, all of which bear on Earwicker's guilty attraction to his daughter: the old man/young girl theme is carried through numerous revisions, each offering a different possibility as to the guilty party and the degree of his/her responsibility. These corresponding motifs also produce some interesting variations on the number of participants needed to play this game. The multiple participants intrude as Joyce recasts various mythic and legendary figures, incorporating them into the dream scenario. The park setting itself is allegorically Eden, and Earwicker plays Adam while the twin Eves stand for both daughter ("Ishah"—Adam's name for Eve)[15] and wife, a situation which offers a corollary to the suspicion that Earwicker's lust for his daughter is really love for his wife. The designation "Milton's Park" (96.10) gives a clue as to which version of Adam and Eve's fall Joyce is rewriting: it seems fairly clear that the sin is a sexual one and that Eve tempted Adam (the twin maidens are later called "apple harlottes"

[113.16]). Here the primary relationship includes one man and one woman in a single temptation. But even on this point there is little certainty, as Lilith (the precursor of Eve in traditional Hebrew literature) seems to be present as "lilithe maidenettes" (241.4) threatening Earwicker's easy sleep: "the besieged bedreamt him stil and solely of those lililiths undeveiled which had undone him, gone for age" (75.5–6). Perhaps there are two women, one man, and multiple temptations.[16]

The Finn MacCool/Grania/Dermot romance as well as the Mark of Cornwall/Iseult/Tristram trio offer other variations on this same theme. In Joyce's renderings of these tales, the young girls are portrayed as naughty temptresses who first seduce the old lover, leading him to a sexual fall, and then leave him for a younger paramour. Grania, for instance, is described as serving up "that same hot coney *a la Zingara* . . . to the greatsire of Oscar, that son of a Coole" (68.9–11) as does her counterpart, the "nautchy girly" Luperca Latouche. Luperca is a prostitute "selling her spare favours in the haymow or in lumber closets or in the greenawn . . . or in the sweet churchyard close" (68.5–8). These last two settings hint at the bower/park scene of Earwicker's dream. The Grania/Finn duo appear in one version of ALP's letter, her rendition emphasizing Grania's efforts to play coy: "He cawls to me Granny-stream-Auborne when I am hiding under my hair from him and I cool him my Finnyking he's so joyant a bounder" (495.18–20). But even as Grania plays the temptress to old Finn, her heart has been captured by the young Dermot to whom she pleads, "I have soreunder from to him now, dearmate ashore, so, so compleasely till I can get redressed, which means the end of my stays in the languish of Tintangle" (232.19–21). In this variation, the triangle of "Tintangle" (two men and one girl) forms the basic structure for this love-sex relationship. In the Mark of Cornwall/Iseult/Tristram version, the possibilities multiply, offering at various stages two men and one girl, two girls and one man, two girls and two men. HCE, Finn MacCool, and Mark come to represent declining sexual prowess that forces men to voyeurism and other perversions; young Tristram and Dermot are linked with Shem and Shaun as the new generation, supplanting and surpassing their aging counterparts.

Book II is dominated by the viewpoint of the four elders (who take their names from the evangelists but are the historians of the novel as well), here subsuming the voyeurism of HCE and Mark of Cornwall.

These four multiply the number of participants on the loveship of Tristram and Iseult, but the four serve as judges rather than as mere observers and are particularly disgusting because they lack humanity and offer a jaundiced point of view. As the four bedposts, these old codgers gaze lustfully at Tristram and Iseult making love. The "strapping modern old ancient Irish prisscess" (Iseult/Issy) has a "firstclass pair of bedroom eyes, of most unhomy blue" (396.7–8, 11–12), but the "ladies' foursome" have "green eyes" as they peer and leer at the young lovers.

The interrelationships examined in this sequence become complex as Mark and Tristram vie for the attentions of Iseult of Ireland. For Mark, of course, there is only one Iseult (the one he marries), but for Tristram there are two: Iseult of the White Hands (whom he marries in lieu of his first love, Iseult of the Fair Hair) and Iseult of Ireland, with whom he eventually escapes on the loveship. In Joyce's version of this story, there is only one Iseult who serves any important function, that is, Iseult of Ireland as temptress for old Mark and lover to young Tristram. While Issy's mirror reflection may be Iseult of the White Hands (145.1–2), this latter figure seems to be absent in the *Wake* as an active participant in the Mark/Iseult/Tristram love story, presumably because she is merely the wife and is eventually replaced in Tristram's affections by his first love and the real temptress in the tale, Iseult of Ireland. This "old story, the tale of a Treestone with one Ysold" (113.18–19), is retold hundreds of times in the *Wake* with variations that include Arthur/Guinevere/Lancelot as well as Shakespeare/Dark Lady/ Fair Man. Although the basic triangle expands to include multiples of the primary configuration, and the major characters constantly intersect, the principal actors remain HCE and Issy.

From legendary heroes Joyce moves to the theater of historical personages for his models, choosing as examples of the old men such disparate figures as Dante and Daddy Browning, Swift and Charles Dodgson. Playing as free with real persons as he did with mythic characters, Joyce pursues this complex game of who-does-what-with-which-to-whom. We find in ALP's "untitled mamafesta memorialising the Mosthighest" (104.4) a reference to "Nopper" (Earwicker) and his "Notylytl Dantsigirls" (105.10). The "dancing girls" are the two ladies from the park, but "Dantsigirls" incriminates Dante Alighieri and by extension Beatrice Portinari, who becomes his poetic muse and spiritual guide in the *Divine Comedy*. Beatrice, of course, exists in two versions, one exalted (as the sainted guide who leads him to *Paradiso*) and the other debased (in Joyce's version) who becomes "waxen" in the hands of her tutor, Denti Alligator himself (440.6). It is not at all clear what these two are doing together, but it involves "turning up and fingering over the most dantellising peaches in the lingerous longerous book of the dark" (251.23–24). Issy's name is a clue to her role as a "peach,"[17] and if "peaches" in this context refers to her, then Denti is nibbling away at her firmly shaped and tantalizing breasts. But the syntax is not easily parsed, and it is possible that young Beatrice/Issy is fingering old Dante's testicles. Purposefully ambiguous, this passage mirrors HCE's dream; it points toward guilt, but never with any certainty as to who is responsible. Allusions to HCE abound in this passage ("when your *goche* I go dead") as well as to ALP (" 'twas ever so in monitorology since Headmaster Adam became Eva Harte's toucher") and he has "man's mischief in his mind whilst her pupils swimmed two heavenlies" (251.27–30). The book they are reading—that "book of the dark"—is Dante's *Inferno*. Like Paola and Francesca (*Inferno*, v. 137), who have been brought together in their reading of Lancelot and Guinevere by "Galilleotto," these two—tutor and student—are brought together by reading the *Inferno*. Therefore, Joyce's charge of pandering (251.25) is attributed to Dante, and this moment of "man's mischief" constitutes a debt owed to Dante: "I is a femaline person. O, of provocative gender. U unisingular case" (251.31–32). The combination of Anna Livia, the "femaline," HCE, the "provocative" male, and Issy, the "unisingular" case, seems to identify the participants in this trio. But even here there is an essential ambiguity: while Issy is present in the un*is*ingular case, a strong hint that at the surface level—and outside Earwicker's dream—she is not the "split" character personified by her father's guilt, she is also present in the "I" femaline person and in the "O," symbol of the female sexual organ, associated with ALP and representing the "provocative gender." The ambiguity which surrounds the *provocateur*, both as to gender and as to responsibility, remains central to the mystery that is Earwicker's dream.

The Dante/Beatrice liaison has its complement in the Daddy Browning and Peaches affair. While Dante's interest in the young Miss Portinari was quite probably platonically pristine, despite Joyce's speculations, Daddy Browning's interest in "Peaches" was thoroughly prurient. As sugar daddy to his young mistress, he was the center of a sex scandal which ended in a court trial, widely publicized in American newspapers. Joyce's version is not a newspaper account but a script for a "newsyreel" depicting a "guaranteed happy lovenest" (65.9), an ironic correspondent to the loveship of Tristram and Iseult:

> Take an old geeser who calls on his skirt. . . . He vows her to be his own honeylamb, swears they will be papa pals, by Sam, and share good times way down west in a guaranteed happy lovenest when May moon she shines and they twit twinkle all the night, combing the comet's tail up right and shooting popguns at the stars. Creampuffs all to dime! Every nice, missymackenzies! For dear old grumpapar, he's gone on the razzledar, through gazing and crazing and blazing at the stars. Compree! She wants her wardrobe to hear from above by return with cash so as she can buy her Peter Robinson trousseau and cut a dash with Arty, Bert or possibly Charley Chance (who knows?) so tolloll Mr Hunker you're too dada for me to dance (so off she goes!) and that's how half the gels in town has got their bottom drars while grumpapar he's trying to hitch his braces on to his trars [65.5–20].

This story, basically, is about an "old geeser" with a young girlfriend who loves him for his money. The suspicion is that "grumpapar" has been buying "bottom drars" for half the girls in town; while he is "downright fond" of his "number one" girl, "he's fair mashed on peaches number two so that if he could only canoodle the two, chivee chivoo, all three would feel genuinely happy, it's as simple as A. B. C." (65.25–28). But Peaches finds the old man "too dada for me to dance" (a hint that grumpapar is getting senile), and she is showing interest in A. B. C.—"Arty, Bert or possibly Charley Chance." The numerical combinations add up to five beyond the original duo (grandpa has selected two peaches while the young mistress is interested in three men) even though the primary configuration seems to be based on the familiar triangle. This version of the old story rests on mutual exploitation: Peaches is interested in her clothing allotment while grandpa is "gone on the razzledar," perhaps finding young love an antidote to old age.

There is at least one other important model for this motif, one that offered Joyce the important image of mirror reflection and personality reversal incorporated by Issy's characterization. The association of Issy with Lewis Carroll's Alice provides a specifically literary context for the Issy/Maggy duplicate and for the aging pervert with sexual designs on precocious young females. The literary Alice (of *Wonderland*) is based on the real-life figure of Alice Liddell, photographic subject of Charles

Dodgson, whose pseudonym was Lewis Carroll.[18] Dodgson, peering through his camera at the pre-pubescent Miss Liddell, represents an interesting psychological reversal of Earwicker (as well as of Mark of Cornwall and the four Elders), since the "lookingglass" of his camera allows him a socially acceptable method of "peeping." And Joyce couldn't wait to expose this "Lewd's carol" (501.36), hinting that Carroll's peeping—like that of HCE and the Elders—had onanistic implications as well (361.18–25, 396.34–397.2). Alice Liddell was neither the first nor the last of Dodgson's young female friends and was followed in his affections by Isa Bowman, an actress who played Alice in Wonderland on stage (curiously, Miss Liddell made it a practice to call Dodgson "Uncle"—a fact that Joyce incorporated into the *Wake*).[19] The numerical configurations here seem to compound the possibilities to include one man (with two "identities") and two girls, in some sort of sequential order, with a third (literary) female operating as a kind of pivotal force—fictional Alice, based on the real Miss Liddell, is reproduced on stage by the actress, Isa Bowman. Here Joyce has a noteworthy corollary to the pattern of reversal and transference offered by the dream structure of the novel itself.

The Real Missisliffi

As Joyce's correspondence indicates, the Alice material came late in the progress of the *Wake*, after both writing technique and his major motifs were already defined (*Letters* I, 255).[20] The question of timing—when certain materials were incorporated into the texture of "Work in Progress"—becomes an important one in positing "models" for the five figures comprising the Earwicker family. While the textual references to Christine L. Beauchamp and Morton Prince are not corroborated by Joyce's correspondence (as is the *Alice in Wonderland* material), the *Finnegans Wake* manuscripts and David Hayman's *First Draft Version of "Finnegans Wake"* offer some interesting textual evidence. There are only two references in the *Wake* which seem to point clearly to the Christine Beauchamp/Morton Prince coupling: "With best from cinder Christinette if prints chumming" (280.21–22) and "My prince of the courts who'll beat me to love!" . . . (but don't tell him or I'll be the mort of him!)" (460.12–13, 22).[21] In the first-draft versions of both these passages, no reference to Beauchamp/Prince occurs. Further, the sections in which these passages appear comprise two of the most reworked sections of the *Wake*;[22] pages 278–82 (including Issy's "practice" letter to her teacher) went through at least seven drafts and were not completed until 1933, and pages 459–60 (Issy's amorous letter to Jaun including her confession that she plays tricks on "nurse Madge, my linkingclass girl," as she sleeps) were subjected to "an extravagant number of revisions." [23] The earliest appearance of the second, and more direct, reference to Prince is in *transition* (Summer, 1928), over five years after Joyce's conception of Issy's role in the novel had been formulated.[24] The earliest vision of Issy's role in the *Wake*, appearing in the first sketches from "Work in Progress," is included in the "Tristan and Isolde" material now at II,4. A letter to Harriet Shaw Weaver (March 7, 1924), forwarding the "Anna Livia" piece, makes Issy's role in this sketch clear: "The splitting up towards the end (seven dams) is the city abuilding. Izzy will be later Isolde (cf. Chapelizod)" (*Letters* I, 213). In this version of the story, the emphasis is upon Isolde of Ireland (a lady with a divided nature, "eysolt of the binnoculises" [394.30]) and her two lovers, Tristram and Mark. If we can single out a primary model for young Miss Issy, this "Isobel" seems to be it.

Two other temptresses who appear in Joyce's early versions—and on the opening page of *Finnegans Wake*—are Swift's Stella and Vanessa, the "sosie sesthers" (3.12). They become associated with Earwicker's sin ("bewilderblissed by their night effluvia with guns like drums and fondlers like forceps persequestellates his vanessas from flore to flore" [107.16–18]), and Earwicker plays Swift-as-"Bickerstaff" (and also Charles Dodgson) as he takes a "tompip peepestrella throug a three-draw eighteen hawkspower durdicky telescope" at his young stars (178.27–28). Earwicker as Swift is also the tutor ("My little love apprencisses, my dears, the estelles, van Nessies" [365.27–28]) to his two young Esthers, whom Swift gave the names Stella and Vanessa, as well as to a third, "Varina fay" (101.8), Swift's name for Jane Waring, an earlier love. His *Journal to Stella* records at least one of these complex relationships, and the secret language of this document translates into the *Wake* as the "pepette" letters (presumably written by Issy and addressed to her young lover).

The Swift materials provide Joyce another analogue for the old lover/young girl theme, but this source offers a comprehensive collation, bringing together elements found in the other models for Earwicker and Issy. Swift is a tutor (as Joyce portrayed Dante) to young girls (Pepette, Beatrice, or Alice) on whom he has sexual designs (akin to those already examined in King Mark, Lewis Carroll, Daddy Browning, and possibly Earwicker), and his relationship with these women is recorded in letters (like those between Sally and Dr. Prince). Perhaps the most important aspect of the Swift paradigm displays itself in his "split" personality: Dean Swift is both "Wise Nathan and Chaste Joseph," the "nathandjoe" of the *Wake* (3.12)—a hint at the biblical underpinnings of his character portrayal, but also an intimation of the "wise" and "chaste" public image. More interested in the private persona, Joyce casts Swift as another Lewis Carroll/Charles Dodgson (and Earwicker/Porter), a man with ambivalent attitudes toward pubescent females. That such a divided nature, possibly an aspect of Swift's madness, should take its form in writing love letters to himself [25] fits the last chink in this Joycean puzzle: less interested in the ingénue in the triangle than in the "doubled" male lead, Joyce directs his light into the dark corners of the male consciousness, questioning the motives of Swift, Dante, Dodgson, and Morton Prince—another male who may have been a "tompip" under the guise of medical practitioner. All of these participants in the *Wake* mystery, with their accompanying paraphernalia, including the letters that trouble Earwicker's dream as well as the "pee" and "peep" aspects of the park incident comprised in the descriptive "pepette," are present in the Swiftian model.

The Letters

If the solution to the puzzle of Issy's personality lies in her father's ambivalence toward her, as the guilty dream seems to suggest, then the letters which record various versions of the park incident and Earwicker's culpability offer important evidence about this "relationship." While there seem to be two basic letters, one dug up on the midden heap by Biddy the hen, the letter from Boston, Mass., and one being written by ALP, dictated to Shem to be "posted" by Shaun and addressed to the "Reverend" (615.12), the letters become fused in Earwicker's dream. Like the Swift letters, these seem to be written in some kind of "secret" language, which, if decoded, Earwicker fears will provide damaging evidence of his guilt in the park incident. The Christmas letter from Boston, Mass., is most often associated with Issy because it mentions a girl named "Maggy," leading to speculation that one of the "Maggies" writes the letter and that the "other" Maggy receives the letter. Much the worse for wear after months on the midden heap (it is now March or April and the letter was apparently written at the end of January), it contains bits of what appear to be absolutely innocuous gossip from a family relative in Boston. A second document (not produced until the end of the novel) is a letter being written by ALP about HCE, a letter that Earwicker hopes will vindicate him; fulfilling his hopes, this letter is a paean to his respectability and heroism. In terms of their contents, these two letters have little in common except that Anna Livia works into her final version all the "bits" that Biddy has pecked up on the midden heap and stuffed into her nabsack; therefore, certain items from the first letter become woven into the fabric of the second, just as bits and pieces of the previous day's events weave themselves—in exaggerated and distorted dimensions—throughout Earwicker's dream.

The dredging up of evidence from this first letter is really an attempt to make something out of nothing. Earwicker's central fear is that public knowledge of the letter's contents will result in a piecing together of that "something." The first attempt at this, and the one from which all others derive, is done by the "bird in the case . . . Belinda of the Dorans" (111.5). As a gossipy old hen, poking holes in the evidence, she "creates" two versions of the letter that we read (111, 113). The first version results from her pecking away at a "goodish-sized sheet of letterpaper originating by tranship from Boston (Mass.)" (111.8–10). But the letter itself is a "grotesquely distorted macromass of all sorts" (111.29), and the warping of the page (combined with Biddy's shortsightedness) causes "some features palpably nearer your pecker to be swollen up most grossly while the farther back we manage to wiggle the more we need the loan of a lens to see as much as the hen saw" (111.35–112.2). This version of the letter consists of what is left of the original document after Biddy has pecked away at it. What has been dredged up and stuffed into her nabsack appears two pages later (113). Biddy has turned the letter into "literature" (112.27) by piecing together the evidence she has dug up and, like a good critic, has come up with a "reading" of the letter (or some bits of it) that bears little—if any—resemblance to the original document. This second version contains incriminating evidence against both Earwicker and Issy: "He had to see life foully the plak and the smut, (schwrites). There were three men in him (schwrites). Dancings (schwrites) was his only ttoo feebles. With apple harlottes. And a little mollvogels. Spissially (schwrites) when they peaches. Honeys wore camelia paints. Yours very truthful. Add dapple inn" (113.13–18). The fictions that Biddy weaves from the "facts" she has exhumed are part of Earwicker's own guilt and his fear that a local gossip like Biddy will make his secret desires public information—which she does. Moreover, it speculates on the division of Earwicker's personality ("there were three men in him") which maintains the image of the daughter as double ("his only ttoo feebles").

The next variation on the Boston letter comes from Issy herself, the young student at her lessons, as she writes a practice letter for her teacher ("You sh'undn't write you can't if you w'udn't pass for undevelopmented" [279.n.14–15]). She admits that she "learned all the runes of the gamest game ever from my old nourse Asa. A most adventuring trot is her and she vicking well knowed them all heartswise and fourwords" (279.n.28–30). Issy is learning all about domesticity, preparing for "impending marriage," and she's learning it from her mother. This practice letter is intended for the relative in Boston named "Maggy," and the entire writing process is recorded, including comments on Issy's mannerisms as she composes the missive:

> Dear (name of desired subject, A.N.), well, and I go on to. Shlicksher. I and we (tender condolences for happy funeral, one if) so sorry to (mention person suppressed for the moment, F.M.). Well (enquiries after allhealths) how are you (question maggy). A lovely (introduce to domestic circles) pershan of cates. Shrubsher. Those pothooks mostly she hawks from Poppa Vere Foster but these curly mequeues are of Mippa's moulding. Shrubsheruthr. (Wave gently in the ere turning ptover.) Well, mabby (consolation of shopes) to soon air. With best from cinder Christinette if prints chumming, can be when desires Soldi, for asamples, backfronted or, if all, peethrolio or Get my Prize, using her flower or perfume or, if veryveryvery chumming, in otherwards, who she supposed adeal, kissists my exits. Shlicksheruthr. From Auburn chenlemagne [280.9–28].

As her mother's successor, Issy must learn to write letters—chatty, friendly notes to relatives far away, offering greetings or condolences or extending thanks for gifts sent; since *Finnegans Wake* is the epistle being written by ALP, dictated to her son Shem (Joyce), it seems reasonable that Issy should be receiving education in the writing of such an epistolary record. The subject of this letter is A.N., a designation that seems to point obliquely and begrudgingly to Anna Livia, but it also suggests "nourse Asa," presumably a female nanny, but in Norse mythology, the chief of the gods—i.e., Issy is addressing her father in a parallel salutation to Anna Livia's "Reverend. May we add majesty?" (615.12–13) in her letter. As we shall see, the intrusion of the father into Issy's letter is an important signal of her role in the novel. The letter provides a view of Issy's future role, offering tender condolences upon a death (Father Michael's), inquiries about cousin Maggy's health, the mention of recent wedding presents—including the "pershan of cates" and the pothooks which will introduce her to "domestic circles." Interspersed with the letter's commentary are descriptions of her actions: "Schlicksher . . . Shrubsher . . . Shrubsheruthr" as Issy rubs her eyes and licks her fingers in concentration. This letter demonstrates Issy's ability to be "veryveryvery chumming" when in pursuit of her "supposed adeal," in this case a Prince Charming like the one who rescued the real Cinderella from kitchen drudgery and made her a princess. She is learning the art of using "her flower or perfume" as "asamples" of her femininity in hopes of winning her prize—a rich "prince."

This letter, like the Christmas missive, seems to be perfectly innocent and domestic. But, of course, Earwicker's guilt leads him to suspect otherwise. The long footnote on the preceding page (like many of the footnotes in this chapter) has indicated that Issy may have designs on him ("He gives me pulpititions with his Castlecowards never in these twowsers and ever in those twawsers and then babeteasing us out of our hoydenname" [276.n.28–29]). And "Shlicksher . . . Shrubsher" as well as the signature "kissists my exits" take on double meanings. Once again it may be Earwicker's fears, rather than anything offered by the letter itself, which place suspicion on his young daughter's motives. The letter from Boston and Issy's practice letter to Maggy seem to offer neither accusation nor exoneration of Earwicker and his daughter. Biddy's version of the park incident probably represents Earwicker's fears as to what the local gossips may be saying about him while Issy's letter, with its erotic *double entendres*, is perhaps the product of Earwicker's own guilt. Since HCE's consciousness controls the dream, it is difficult to separate public suspicion and the compounding evidence from Earwicker's apprehensions.

Apart from this "practice" letter written by Issy for her tutor as part of her lessons, there are two other letters which seem to bear her stamp, these written to her "pepette" lover. Marked by Issy's gushy-gooey style, the preponderance of the diminutive form ("you perfect little pigaleen" [143.35]) coupled with babytalk and the lisping "s" signaling Issy's voice, these letters attest to her consistent interest in matters of love and sex. She seems to be experiencing a crush on a first love (the double *p* in "pepette" offers two possibilities as to the identity of her lover, including both Father Michael, her "pettest parriage priest" [458.4] and Brother Shaun [457.29]), and she is desperately jealous of any competition. Duplicating Swift's "little language," the letters appear to be an exchange between two females (Iseult of the Fair Hair and Iseult of the White Hands, for instance) even though they formally address themselves to a male ("sweet sir" [145.17] and "Jaunick" [457.36]). The possibilities multiply to include all members of the Earwicker family, with both brothers and father playing the role of lover, and mother and daughter included in the female dialogue. At the level closest to the narrative surface, these letters may well be a conversation between Issy and her mirror image as she sits at her writing table penning letters to her lover and looking at her own reflection. The tensions explored are between two females (patently jealous of the "other" Iseult, Issy derides her mirror image: "that her blanches mainges may rot leprous off her whatever winking maggis" [145.1–2]). There is a wicked streak in Issy, as her threats to that "other" woman who may steal away her lover make clear: "I'll bet by your cut you go fleurting after with all the glass on her and the jumps in her stomewhere! Haha! I suspected she was! Sink her! May they fire her for a barren ewe!" (145.2–5). But the subject of the letters is a man (a "male corrispondee" [457.28]). There lurks too the suspicion that Issy like Swift may well be playing both the male and female parts,[26] a hint at sex reversal as well as narcissism ("I will give your lovely face of mine away, my boyish bob" [459.33–34]). Still, Issy seems more interested in her own reflection than in anything else, and as a witness later admits, she was "near drowned in pondest coldstreams of admiration forherself" (526.28–29).

The letters are typically those of a young girl in love, offering promises to be faithful ("true in my own way" [459.19–20]), pleading with the lover to remember her ("please kindly think galways again or again, never forget, of one absendee not sester Maggy" [458.9–10]), and practicing seductive ploys ("I will pack my comb and mirror to praxis oval owes and artless awes" [458.35–36]). The tone fluctuates between flirtation ("Tell me till my thrillme comes!" [148.2]) and irritation ("you want to be slap well slapped for that" [148.6]). Issy is a thoroughly knowledgeable young temptress, and she admits that her lover "fell for my lips, for my lisp, for my lewd speaker. I felt for his strength, his manhood, his do you mind?" (459.28–29). She confesses, "Pipette. I can almost feed their sweetness at my lisplips" (276.n.38), underscoring the vampire in her ("Yes, the buttercups told me, hug me, damn it all, and I'll kiss you back to life, my peachest. I mean to make you suffer, meddlar, and I don't care this fig for contempt of courting. . . . Bite my laughters, drink my tears" [145.14–16, 18–19]).

Although Issy's letters to her lover demonstrate the sexy prattle used to beguile and bewitch the loved one, they do not show her to be the "triumph of feminine imbecility" that Glasheen has suggested,[27] nor does her response to the interrogation by the Four Old Men in III,3 represent a "mindless monologue" as Begnal has assumed.[28] Issy is at the very heart of the *Wake* mystery, just as she is at the center of Earwicker's dream; in this capacity she offers some very damaging evidence to the Elders (but fortunately they do not comprehend her meaning). She knows of the park "incident": "Of course I know you are a viry vikid girl to go in the dreemplace and at that time of the draym and it was a very wrong thing to do, even under the dark flush of night, dare all grandpassia!" (527.5–8). And she has recognized the man she saw there: "Of course it was downright verry wickred of him, reely meeting me disguised, Bortolo mio, peerfectly appealling, D.V., with my lovebirds, my colombinas" (527.24–27). The old men are confused, unable to pierce her message ("How is this at all? Is dads the thing in such or are tits the that?" [528.15–16]). But they come close to dissecting her evidence as they try to sort out the number of "maidens" in the case: "Think of a maiden, Presentacion. Double her, Annupciacion. Take your first thoughts away from her, Immacolacion. Knock and it shall appall unto you! Who shone yet shimmers will be e'er scheining" (528.19–22). The explication unravels the dream fabric: the "presentacion" virgin is Issy, who will be married like her mother, "Ann," in a nuptial, but by subtracting your "first thoughts" of her (presumably lascivious thoughts), she becomes again "immaculate." The shimmering Issy will be shining as Anna Livia, and both father and daughter seem to be absolved of any guilt: Issy is yet a virgin; Earwicker's lust for her is really desire for the mother. Just when we think the four have solved the mystery, they become confused again: "This young barlady, what, euphemiasly? Is she having an ambidual act herself in apparition with herself as Consuelas to Sonias may?" (528.23–25). They give up in defeat: "Dang!"

Clearly Issy is no mindless female, however much she babbles. And her father's guilt over the park incident and his fear that Issy may have knowledge of his sin are directly linked to Issy's sexual awareness. She does have "evidence" against him, and her knowledge can be a threat. On another night the parents were awakened by Jerry's crying and, as they prepared to engage in love-making, they were seen by their daughter: "The dame dowager's duffgerent to present wappon, blade drawn to the full and about wheel without to be seen of them. The infant Isabella from her coign to do obeisance toward the duffgerent, as first futherer with drawn brand" (566.21–24).[29] Earwicker is warned about the consequences of such a "show": "—*Vidu, porkego! Ili vi rigardas. Returnu, porkego! Maldelikato!*" (566.26–27). A similar sight of sexual prowess probably caused Miss Beauchamp to disintegrate and fragment, producing multiple personalities, but Issy's early knowledge results in her sexual precocity and engenders the lingering fear in her father that she knows—or perhaps remembers—too much.

As Joyce depicts it, Issy's "knowledge" exists as part of her feminine, intuitive, and primordial role as woman, directing her in the path that has already been made by her mother. And it seems consistent with Joyce's emphasis on the "reality of experience" as an essential contributor toward human sensibility that sexual precocity evidenced in daughters like Issy (or Milly Bloom) and learned from their mothers becomes a healthy manifestation of the survival process. In Joyce's universe, sexual survival is linked with the broader concern of affirming the legitimacy of basic human needs, making sexual motivation a measure of psychological equilibrium. In this sense Earwicker's fears and guilts are unnecessary. Similarly, Bloom's masturbation marks his sexual survival, and Molly's dalliance with Boylan affirms hers. Milly and Issy give promise to yet another generation by demonstrating their enthusiastic acceptance of that which is "human" through an equally enthusiastic response in matters sexual.

Anna Livia's Version

It is left to Anna Livia, who has the final "word" in the novel, to confirm the future for her daughter: "Yes, you're changing, sonhusband, and you're turning, I can feel you, for a daughterwife from the hills again. Imlamaya. And she is coming. Swimming in my hindmoist. Diveltaking on me tail. Just a whisk brisk sly spry spink spank sprint of a thing theresomere, saultering. Saltarella come to her own. I pity your oldself I was used to. Now a younger's there" (627.1–6). Anna Livia, growing old and flowing out to sea, is being replaced in the cosmic (and at the human) level by her daughter, just as Earwicker is being replaced by his sons, who have warred with him for the affections of his daughter. But the gossips of chapter 8, washing the Earwickers' dirty linen in public, have confirmed that Anna Livia too was a "gadabout in her day, so she must, more than most" (202.4–5), and that she too was a young temptress who led Earwicker to his first sexual fall. As a young girl she was busy "making mush mullet's eyes at her boys dobelon" and spent hours gazing at her mirror image ("I recknitz wharfore the darling murrayed her mirror" [208.32–33, 35]). The description of her as a "young thin pale soft shy slim slip of a thing then" (202.27) echoes her description of her daughter, whose present "spankiness" counters the mother's earlier shyness. And Anna Livia had a previous love too, another Michael (203.18), about whom the town gossiped: "O, wasn't he the bold priest? And wasn't she the naughty Livvy? Nautic Naama's now her navn" (204.4–5). In many ways the mother and daughter are mirror images of each other, as Issy has told the four Elders: "Narcississies are as the coaters of inversion. Secilas through their laughing classes becoming poolermates in laker life" (526.35–36). Issy is currently the inversion of her mother, and she dotes on her father as he is foolishly fond of her. But ALP's hints seem to suggest that diverse and flighty Issy will grow into the calm and unified mother/wife that Anna Livia now is: "For she'll be sweet for you as I was sweet when I came down out of me mother. . . . And let her rain now if she likes. Gently or strongly as she likes. Anyway let her rain for my time is come" (627.7–9, 11–13).

Anna Livia is present in the *Wake* primarily in her role as wife, her thoughts constantly circling around her husband, her letter constituting his exoneration. Rarely does she speak of her children, and when she does, it is to place them in contexts subordinate to their father. Whereas ALP fixes her attention specifically on Earwicker, as husband and lover, her daughter is shown to be at an age at which she finds all men equally interesting. But this diffusion will eventually develop a specific focus: the diverse rain will be gathered into the river that runs past Eve and Adam's, and Anna Livia's letter, practiced by Issy and written in defense of her lover, is a "Tobecontinued's tale" (626.18). Nuvoletta is a lass who, *Finnegans Wake* records, "made up all her myriads of drifting minds in one" (159.7) and produced a "singult" tear (159.13). Although she demonstrates more than any other character in the novel a capacity for multiple and often contradictory motivations within a single psyche, Issy is also the single embodiment of her father's desire and fears (sin-guilt), which manifest themselves in his mirror images of her. The father may have doubts about his own motivations, but the mother seems to be convinced that her daughter will continue in her wake. To Issy she gives the keys: "Lps. The keys to. Given! A way a lone a last a loved a long the . . ."

NOTES

1. Clive Hart, *Structure and Motif in "Finnegans Wake"* (Evanston: Northwestern University Press, 1962), p. 153.

2. Adaline Glasheen, "*Finnegans Wake* and the Girls from Boston, Mass.," *Hudson Review* 7 (Spring, 1954), 90. In *A Third Census of "Finnegans Wake"* (Berkeley: University of California Press, 1977), p. 138, Glasheen states that Issy "is mad, is a personality split into two (q.v.) temptresses, or seven (q.v.) rainbow girls, or twentynine (q.v.) leap-year girls."

3. Morton Prince, *The Dissociation of a Personality: A Biographical Study in Abnormal Psychology*, 2nd ed. (1905; rpt. New York: Greenwood Press, 1969).

4. The relationship here is undoubtedly complex, made more so (from the critic's point of view) by Joyce's profound silence on the subject of his daughter's illness. Morton Prince and Adaline Glasheen notwithstanding, *Finnegans Wake* seems to demonstrate Joyce's attempt at holding together the uneasy and unstable components of Issy's personality, perhaps demonstrating in this fictional daughter a psychological salubrity denied to Lucia. Despite the overwhelming evidence of her illness, Joyce persisted in his belief that Lucia's behavior was merely "girlish," something she would grow out of in time. In 1932, when Lucia was twenty-five years old and desperately ill, Joyce could still write Harriet Weaver, "she is only a child" (*JJ* 663). Indeed, Joyce was partially correct, since the hebephrenia from which Lucia was suffering manifested itself—in part—by an inability to reconcile childish behavior in the adult personality. But the events of 1932 proved irrefutable, and Joyce wrote Miss Weaver expressing concern that Lucia's letters were now incoherent and disjunctive: "Each phrase could bear a rational meaning and some of the phrases are fine. It is the lack of even casual connections" (August 6, 1932: *Letters* III, 254). While some critics might see an analogous personality in Issy, it seems inconceivable that Joyce—facing the inevitability of his daughter's madness during the years he was writing *Finnegans Wake*—would purposely transfer his fearful suspicions to so blatant a public scrutiny. It seems more likely that his unwillingness to accept the truth of his daughter's condition forms the

basis of Issy's complex character, one that dissolves toward multiplicity as a function of the dream structure rather than because of any innate personality dysfunction.

5. Clive Hart offers a comprehensive review of the varying positions regarding the identity of the dreamer and the consistency of the dream structure (*Structure and Motif*, pp. 80–81). Hart maintains a kind of middle ground against speculation by some critics that the dreamer of *Finnegans Wake* is someone other than Earwicker: "it does seem, nevertheless, that Joyce thought of *Finnegans Wake* as a *single* integrated dream rather than as the series of dream-episodes that Miss Weaver's letter [to James Atherton, *The Books at the Wake*, p.17] might imply" (p. 81). James Atherton offers a theory of multiple dreamers at the *Wake*, the reader himself a participant in the dream, in "The Identity of the Sleeper," *A Wake Newslitter*, NS, 7, no. 4 (October, 1967), 84. Ruth von Phul investigates the possibility that son Jerry is the dreamer in "Who Sleeps at *Finnegans Wake*?" *The James Joyce Review* 1 (June, 1957), 27–38. A more recent examination of the dream structure is offered by Michael Begnal in Michael H. Begnal and Grace Eckley, *Narrator and Character in "Finnegans Wake"* (Lewisburg, Penn.: Bucknell University Press, 1975), pp.19–121. Begnal posits a theory of multiple dreamers carefully isolated from one another by their distinct, although often intermingled, voices. I tend to agree with Clive Hart, however, that *Finnegans Wake* is a "dream-whole centred on a single mind" (Hart, p. 83). Hart also argues that the specific night of the dream is a Friday, even though the *Wake* posits a larger structure for the dream cycle with all of history spinning through Earwicker's mind (Hart, p. 70).

6. Glasheen, "Boston, Mass.," p. 90.

7. Prince, pp.20–51. See also Morris Beja, "Dividual Chaoses: Case Histories of Multiple Personality and *Finnegans Wake*," *James Joyce Quarterly* 14 (Spring, 1977), 241–50.

8. Prince, p. 47.

9. Ibid., p. 50.

10. Certainly there are some apparent similarities in the kinds of voices in which Issy speaks in *Finnegans Wake* (and also room for speculation on the kind and quality of her handwriting in the various letterwriting scenes) and the case of Christine Beauchamp. But these distinctions do not amount to a psychopathology. Chapter 10 of the *Wake* (the "lessons" chapter to which Issy adds the footnotes) supplies good evidence of Issy's separate—and calculated—use of voices to distinguish the tone of her commentary. Although it has long been assumed that her comments and the brothers' marginalia bear little import for the text proper (that no consistent link between text and commentary can be established—cf. Jennifer Shiffer Levine, "Originality and Repetition in *Finnegans Wake* and *Ulysses*," PMLA 94, no. 1 [January, 1979], 111–12), I believe that Issy's notes function in direct relation to the text and that the "voice" in which her comments are registered offers clues as to the relationship between text and notes.

Generally, Issy's comments are cast in three differing voices that might be glossed as "sugary," "cynical" (nasty/erotic), and "expository." Her change of voices suits the purposes of her role-playing in this scene; the examples here offer less subtle instances of such occurrences than many other of the footnotes to this chapter. For instance, "My globe goes gaddy at geography giggle pending which time I was looking for my shoe all through Arabia" (275.29–30) corresponds to "way back home in Pacata Auburnia" in the text proper. (The question of which text—the narrative or the commentary on it—assumes priority at any given time in this chapter is one worth examination.) In the geography lesson a place-name ("Pacata Auburnia") has been mentioned; not recognizing it as Ireland, Issy tries to find it on her globe, but instead of seeing countries she sees objects: "I was looking for my shoe all through Arabia." The tone and mannerism are typical of her reaction to a situation in which the male intelligence of her older brothers dominates: she plays the childish, frivolous female whose quality of mind is characteristically vague and easily led astray. This silly young female is the one most critics recognize as Issy.

But the cynical and intellectually astute Issy exists as well. She responds to the comment "At maturing daily gloraims!" with "Lawdy Dawdy Simpers" (282.34). The former is the Jesuit heading for written texts (*Ad Majorem Dei Gloriam*) and her comment plays on the bottomnote to such texts (*Laus Deo Semper*) by cutting God the Father down to size. "Lawdy Dawdy Simpers" betrays her consistent attitude toward the pomp and circumstance associated with males who represent sovereign power: she finds it simpering. But her intelligence stands in distinction to that of Shem and Shuan, whose commentary fences in the narrative while hers adds its subscripts. She possesses an innate and intuitive sense of the reality of things: recognizing the Dolph who asks, "Can you nei do her, numb?" to be "the trouveller" (286.33), her explanation includes all of Shem/Dolph's attributes as traveler, troubador, finder, and troubler. Challenged to "concoct an equoangular trillitter," she responds in a complexity of geometrical configurations: "As Rhombulas and Rhebus went building rhomes one day" (286.32). Her answer implies a knowledge of history as well as of geometry equal to that of her brothers and belies her usual appearance as a silly prattler unable to fathom the hierarchical and mathematical mysteries of the male world. I am currently preparing a fuller discussion of the relationship between Issy's notes and this text.

11. The appearance of the mirror and its duplicating image is central to the portrayal of Issy, remaining a consistent image throughout the development of her portrait in the *Wake*. In Jacques Lacan's ordering of experience, the "mirror stage" of development corresponds to the *imaginaire*, while the stage of language acquisition corresponds to a symbolic or discursive development. The mirror stage refers to the period between six and eighteen months, when the child is involved with its own image. That this "involvement" implies an alienation from self is central to Lacan's thesis, intriguing in light of Wakean evidence. The child's ability to pass from the mirror stage of language acquisition involves the resolution of the Oedipal conflict, one that is not resolved in Issy's character but is made (by her father's image of her) a dominant characteristic of her arrested development. Her language, like her image, is separated from her, allowing her to speak in distinct "voices" and to separate her actions

from her commentary on them. But what in Christine occurred as a result of psychic trauma, and enforced a dual thought and linguistic pattern, is not present in Issy as a simultaneity of experience and knowledge but rather as the persistence of a developmental stage in which the child discovers himself again and again in his own image. See Jacques Lacan, *Ecrits: A Selection*, trans. Alan Sheridan (New York: W. W. Norton, 1977). (I am grateful to Dr. Lacan for discussions with me on the subject of language dysfunction in psychotic disorders and, in particular, on the subject of Lucia Joyce's illness.)

12. Glasheen, "Boston, Mass.," p.89.

13. According to Dr. Prince, Miss Beauchamp "regarded herself as one 'possessed' in much the same sense as it is said in the Bible that a person is 'possessed.' She was well aware that she went into trances and in those trances did extraordinary things, and behaved in a way that shocked her sense of propriety. . . . But the psychological nature of these attacks was unknown to her, and in fact was carefully concealed, so that her knowledge was indefinite. She was ignorant of the phenomena of multiple personality" (Prince, p. 119). In earlier times Miss Beauchamp would have been suspect as a witch, in league with the Devil, someone who must be expelled from the society of god-fearing souls.

14. See Bernard Benstock, "Every Telling Has a Taling: A Reading of the Narrative of *Finnegans Wake*," *Modern Fiction Studies* 15, no. 1 (Spring, 1969), 3–25.

15. Glasheen, *A Third Census*, p. 137 (under "Ish").

16. Lilith, a character in her own right in the novel, appears as Lilly Kinsella, whose dirty drawers are being washed by the washerwomen in chapter 8. In her two aspects, Issy is both Lilith, the demon-goddess precursor to Eve, and Eve herself.

17. Glasheen, *A Third Census*, p. 227 (under "Peaches"). See also 556.6.

18. James S. Atherton, *The Books at the Wake* (New York: Viking Press, 1960), pp. 129–30.

19. *Ibid.*, p. 130.

20. *Ibid.*, p. 127.

21. There are a handful of other quotations which, once the Morton Prince/ Christine Beauchamp connection is established, seem perhaps tangentially connected (*FW* 280, 460). None of them alone would give the Prince/ Beauchamp allusion and many of them are tendentious at best. These two seem to be the only clearcut allusions to the Prince book, and the second is more obvious than the first.

22. David Hayman, *A First-Draft Version of "Finnegans Wake"* (Austin: University of Texas Press, 1963), pp.32–33, 36–37.

23. *Ibid.*, p.36.

24. James Joyce, "Work in Progress," in *transition*, ed. Eugene Jolas, 13 (Summer, 1928), 24.

25. See Atherton, p. 116, n. 4.

26. *Ibid.*, p. 116. See also Harold Williams, ed., *Journal to Stella* (Oxford: Clarendon Press, 1948), p. 183.

27. Glasheen, *A Third Census*, p. 138 (under "Issy").
28. Begnal, p.161.
29. Hart, p. 70.

MARGOT NORRIS

Anna Livia Plurabelle: The Dream Woman

> O
> tell me all about
> Anna Livia! I want to hear all
> about Anna Livia. Well, you know Anna Livia?

I

Like the babbling washerwomen, we too are curious to learn about
Anna Livia's looks, her sex life, marriage, and motherhood, so I will
tell you about Anna Livia, what she looks like, what she wears, how
she moves, what she sounds like, and what she does. You can see her
yourself if you go to Dublin and look at the Liffey—tidal, dirty, swift,
graced with handsome swans—for Joyce as surely rivermorphized the
woman as he anthropomorphized the river. The "portrait" that
emerges is paradoxical and incoherent and makes sense only when we
take into account the formal and technical problems of point of view
and language.

If we consider Anna Livia Plurabelle as the fantasy projection of a
male figure dreaming, not as an "empirical" woman or an archetype,
then her contradictions begin to make sense as expressions of the
dreamer's highly ambivalent, guilty feelings about his wife, daughter,
mother, and sister. Anna Livia assumes all of these functions in relation to a single dreamer. The intermingling of these figures not only
would explain the shifting and merging identities of women in the
Wake, the doubling and splitting that results in composite roles (Isolde
as both desired daughter and betraying bride), but it would also
account for the monstrous feelings that manifest themselves in a
nightmarish world of sexual violence in which the woman is raped,
beaten, and enslaved, and in which her only transcendence takes the

form of humble service to husband and children. Males are also subjected to humiliating assault and sexual abuse in the *Wake*, for to Joyce
all actions in dream are expressions of wishes and fears below the
waking level of repression. The antisocial and criminal acts in the *Wake*
represent such unleashed impulses. We can therefore study the trans-
formations of the female's form and functions in the work as symptoms of the dreamer's disturbances concerning psychological issues
that are generated within family life: erotic desires, aggressive impulses, conflicts over authority and dependence, repression and rebellion.

The same key that unlocks the encoded language of Freudian dream
unlocks the distorted dream world of *Finnegans Wake*: verbal associations, puns, metaphors, and klang associations. Anna Livia is a figure
of many—sometimes contradictory—functions, and by tracing the
linguistic path of her distortions, the reader may discover the rationale
of the dreamer. For example, although ALP as hen, or seaside bird, is
probably an older, humbler, more domestic version of the bird-girl in
Portrait, this transformation undoubtedly derives also from the mildly
derisive slang names of "old hen" or "biddie" for an old woman,
particularly a curious, prying old woman who pokes into everybody's
business, like the hen scratching the letter from the dump.

While Stephen's bird-girl stands in the stream as stately as a crane,
ALP as the little gnarlybird scurries quickly about the beach with a
merry, pecking rhythm, "a runalittle, doalittle, preealittle, pouralittle,
wipealittle, kicksalittle, severalittle, eatalittle, whinealittle, kenalittle,
helfalittle, pelfalittle gnarlybird" (10.32). The little bird also gathers all
manner of goods into her "nabsack," like Leopold Bloom, whose
pockets bulge with all sorts of accumulations—soap, potato, flower,
and even a letter.

Joyce's *tour de force* of dream technique is the sustained and elaborate
analogy of river and woman that prevails throughout the work. Joyce,
who loved a woman named Barnacle, cast many of the female figures
in his fiction as "seaside girls"—Eveline, Gerty, Milly, Molly. But
unlike the bird-girl standing in the stream, who merely *looks* like a bird,
Anna Livia both *looks* and *acts* like the river Liffey. Even her human
activities are made to coincide with river functions: bathing, launder-
ing, baptizing, running errands, bringing things, carrying refuse,
tempting, giving life and pleasure, wrecking and destroying. Joyce's
reasons for linking Anna Livia and the river so steadfastly are probably

also multiple. For one thing, the association allowed him to treat time and space as versions of each other—an antinomy that he wanted to reconcile in the manner of Nolan opposites and that he therefore invested in Shem (time) and Shaun (space). Merging Isabel and Kate with Anna Livia as her young and old versions, Joyce makes the chronological development of the female from young girl to old woman correspond to the topological course of the river from spring to delta. The river is an element in the mighty oppositions Joyce invests in ALP and HCE: river/land, midget/giant, female/male.

River and land, however, do not have archetypal connections in Joyce's mind with female and male, respectively. Anna Livia is the river, HCE is the land. But in *Ulysses* the roles of Molly and Bloom are in some ways reversed. Bloom is Ulysses, the seafarer, the voyager, Sinbad the Sailor, and Molly is the landlocked earth goddess, the waiting Penelope. Bloom bustles in the morning and runs around Dublin all day, visiting and running errands (including some for Molly), while Molly lies in bed at home. The *Wake*, on the other hand, begins with "riverrun," Anna Livia Plurabelle's tempo of quick, nervous, tripping movement, as, like a river, she runs swiftly throughout the work, "ducking under bridges, bellhopping the weirs, dodging by a bit of bog, rapidshooting round the bends" (194.33), while HCE, the fallen giant, lies recumbent on the earth. "Woman formed mobile or man made static" (309.21) describes the motor functions of ALP and HCE in *Finnegans Wake*. In short, it would be a mistake, I think, to interpret bird and river as symbols with traditional or archetypal meanings (soul, flux, woman) rather than as Freudian dream figures that take their significance from the associations in the dreamer's mind.

We must understand the dreaming male figure in order to understand the female figure. Yet Joyce, paradoxically, sets up a hermeneutical spiral in *Finnegans Wake* through which the best insights into the condition of HCE (presumably the male dreamer) are given by Anna Livia in her final monologue. This interpretive doubling is a bit like Lewis Carroll's *Through the Looking Glass,* where we are momentarily in doubt whether Alice dreams the Red Knight or the Red Knight dreams Alice.

The inferences we draw about HCE from ALP's monologue are very sad indeed. He appears to be an elderly invalid, a convalescent, probably a stroke victim. The famous "wake" is just a domestic morning call to rise: "Rise up, man of the hooths, you have slept so long!" (619.25). Anna Livia gives him his freshly laundered shirt and cleaned clothes to wear, admires his appearance, and invites him for a stroll: "Come and let us! We always said we'd. And go abroad" (620.10). She takes his hand (621.20) and talks to him about many things, including his fall, which has disfigured him (with chemicals, as though he were injured when "shot" by a photographer rather than by a soldier), and deformed him: "Maybe that's why you hold your hodd as if. And people thinks you missed the scaffold. Of fell design" (621.27). Her husband, led by the hand, holding his head strangely, answers only with nods and grimaces: "But you understood, nodst? I always know by your brights and shades" (621.22). He takes big strides because he is much taller than ALP (they are midget and giant throughout the work), but he seems ill-coordinated and treads on her new shoes, the "goodiest shoeshoes" (622.10). She speaks to him hopefully, telling him the stroll is good for his health and will cure him—"It seems so long, since, ages since. As if you had been long far away" (622.13)— and takes him to familiar places to jog his memory: "You know where I am bringing you? You remember?" (622.16). She speaks to him as if he were a child, reminding him to take off his hat and say "how do you do, his majesty" when greeting the Earl of Howth, but his speech is impaired, as we hear when she imitates it, "hoothoothoo, ithmuthis-thy!" (623.10). Unlike her earlier great accomplishments in raising her fallen husband, putting Humpty Dumpty back together again, reconstructing him like Isis gathering the fragments of the dismembered Osiris, the act of raising her fallen husband now takes the form of the simple, loving injunction, "And stand up tall! Straight. I want to see you looking fine for me" (620.1).

What follows is mainly descriptive: Anna Livia's paradoxical "portrait," romantic and vulgar, flattering and unflattering, filtered through the imagination of a dying old man who dreams of virile conquests and senile passions, domestic life, humiliating dependencies, and of the river and the woman he has known in beauty, ugliness, youth, and age.

II

I will begin with Anna Livia's appearance, for Joyce's description of the woman virtually reflects a naturalist's observation of the river. When

Anna Livia is romanticized, her muddy waters become auburn waves, "deepdark and ample like this red bog at sundown" (203.25). The flotsam and jetsam of the river become lovely ornaments ("arnoment" [208.8]) when seen in this rosy glow: garlands of meadowgrass, bulrushes, and waterweed (207.3), twinkling "stone hairpins" (312.21)—like the Siren's treacherous rocks—and sparkling fireflies ("virevlies" [199.36]), that are construed as jewels rather than vermin in her hair. The washerwomen, in their catty way, wonder if the lovely *waves* of the river woman are *permanent* waves, and if they are real, "was she marcellewaved or was it weirdly a wig she wore" (204.23). But when they depict Anna Livia letting down her hair, they describe the tresses falling like a waterfall and undulating like a stream: "she let her hair fal and down it flussed to her feet its teviots winding coils" (206.29) (*Fluss* is German for stream; coils suggests curls).

When its red color becomes truly fiery, the waves of river and woman are described like the burning lava of a volcano, "the bergs of Iceland melt in waves of fire" (139.20), flowing in "auburnt streams" (139.23). This paradoxical description of Anna Livia as an erupting volcano in Iceland has all the oxymoronic charm of Puccini's Turandot: "What is the ice that gives you fire?"[1] But less flattering descriptions of Anna Livia fuming or foaming at the mouth—"smugpipe, his Mistress Mereshame" (241.14) (*Meerschaum* is German for sea foam as well as for a soft clay pipe)—suggest the cigarette factory that employs Bizet's Carmen, "factory fresh and fiuming at the mouth" (243.2). From Jaun's jaundiced point of view, smoking is unseemly for a woman. "Tobbaccos tabu," he warns Issy, "Don't on any account acquire a paunchon for that alltoocommon fagbutt habit" (435.30). ALP, "puffing her old dudheen" (200.18), is therefore a polluted, industrial Liffey feeding the smokestacks on her bank, or a reeking old Nighttown hag of the sort Shaun describes to Issy: "By the stench of her fizzle and the glib of her gab know the drunken draggletail Dublin drab" (436.25).

Joyce's ambivalent, complex portrait of Anna Livia Plurabelle requires simultaneous characterization on a number of levels. Like Chaucer's "loathly lady" in "The Wife of Bath's Tale," Anna Livia is depicted by Joyce as untrustworthy and adulterous if young and fair, but loyal and long-suffering if old and foul. Anna Livia is sometimes a beautiful, desirable woman who runs away with her lover—a Russian Anna Karenina ("Annona, gebroren arroostokrat Nivia" [199.34]) dressed "in a period gown of changeable jade" (200.1) or an Irish princess, Isolde, wearing "her ensemble of maidenna blue" (384.30). But at other times she is a "queer old skeowsha" (215.12), a frumpy, witch-like, little hag, a nagging and ugly little Judy of the puppet show, abused and beaten by her Hunchbacked Punch. But she is nonetheless loyal and turns procuress, or "proxenete" (198.17), to recruit young whores to revive her impotent old husband.

Joyce depends on odd, double meanings of words to produce both the simultaneous beautiful/ugly and the simultaneous river/woman effect. For example, Anna Liva's complexion is modulated between fair and dark. The four old codgers remember it as "solid ivory" (396.10), although with their faulty memories they may be confusing her complexion with her teeth, since they think of her as both woman and horse. Shem calls her "turfbrown" (194.22), but most often she appears to be in-between or "frickled" (204.23), like a river dappled in light and shade. Like Molly, who orders a special lotion from the druggist, ALP is vain of her complexion. Joyce finds in the paradoxical powers of mud a perfect treatment for both river and woman—a "mudfacepacket" (492.20)—which renders her beautiful, or filthy, depending on the point of view. In another nice detail, Joyce has the freckled ALP protect her face with a "fishnetzeveil for the sun not to spoil the wrinklings of her hydeaspects" (208.10). The fishnet is a versatile article, and Joyce uses it again as "an overdress of net" (384.31)—the functional net of the fishermen now becomes a delicate mesh of tulle. Anna Livia's ambiguous odor, fair or foul, perfume or "the rrreke of the fluve of the tail" (208.24) that trails fifty miles behind her, may be explained by the fact that *eau de cologne* is also called toilet water. Anna's smell may therefore be either perfume or sewage. "And you won't urbjunk to me parafume, oiled of kolooney" (624.23) she tells her husband, but admits, "I'm in everywince nasturtls" (624.25).

Anna Livia is much more servile to HCE than Molly Bloom is to Poldy. This might readily be explained as dream wish-fulfillment, if we suppose that *Finnegans Wake* is dreamt by a male dreamer. In a sense, the *Wake* takes up where *Ulysses* leaves off. We learn in Molly's monologue that Bloom has requested breakfast in bed, and in *Finnegans Wake* we indeed find ALP building a fire and cooking breakfast: "There'll be iggs for the brekkers come to mournhim sunny side up with care" (12.14). The egg, however, is not served *to* HCE. The egg *is* HCE, the fallen Humpty Dumpty himself, about to be eaten for breakfast—as though Molly had her revenge on the suddenly imperious Bloom.

Molly thinks unenthusiastically about nursing Bloom "pretending to be laid up with a sick voice" (U 738), but ALP dutifully nurses the ailing, "hungerstriking" (199.4) HCE, who, like an ingrate, dashes down his breakfast tray and proceeds to threaten and abuse her. Molly complains about her woman's work, "what between clothes and cooking and children" (U 768). But Anna Livia, cooking and slaving for HCE, almost literally works her fingers (or knees) to the bone, like a river eroding and leveling a mountain: "Her pyrraknees shrunk to nutmeg graters while her togglejoints shuck with goyt" (199.21).

Joyce derives Anna Livia's sexual experiences from the things— animals, boats, people—that touch the water of the river. Their touch is an erotic touch, a dog lapping the water or licking her, boy scouts wading through her, boats riding her, or the hermit Michael Arklow washing his hands and wetting his lips in the stream. But ALP is not a passive or heartless medium. Her feelings are much like Molly's for they stem from loneliness and a pride that is comforted only by being sexually desired by a man. As Boylan's lovemaking puts some heart back into the neglected Molly (U 758), so the young monk's touch manages to raise ALP's self-esteem and water-level: "She ruz two feet hire in her aisne aestumation" (204.2). Like Molly, ALP needs her voluptuous figure to keep herself attractive to men, "kindling curves you simply can't stop feeling" (203.22), and worries about occasional bloating and running to fat. As a tidal river, Anna Livia swells with the tide, like Molly at the onset of her period. ALP also gets "a little width wider" (376.2), and a little heavier, like the river filling with stones, "getting hoovier . . . fullends a twelve stone hoovier" (376.14). Like Molly, who wants "one of those kidfitting corsets . . . with elastic gores on the hips" (U 750), Anna Livia, as woman and river, tries to control her shape with girdles and banksides, "stout stays" (208.14), or a "brandnew bankside . . . and a plumper at that" (201.5). Before ALP acquires her heft, a giant swan descends on the rivulet "too frail to flirt with a cygnet's plume" (204.11), or on the girl, "leada, laida, all unraidy" (204.10), to impregnate her, "Leda, Lada, aflutter-afraida, so does your girdle grow!" (272.2). This rape by the bird has its sublime version, "bearing down on me now under whitespread wings like he'd come from Arkangels" (628.9), and its ludicrous version, "he raped her home, Sabrine asthore, in a parakeet's cage" (197.21). A swan descends on the lake, a swan descends on the woman, and the twin sons and daughter are engendered to constitute the Earwicker family.

Besides the references to Leda and the Sabine women, there are other mentions of sexual violence and rape in the work. In Joyce's earlier novels, such scenes occur only at the level of fantasy, as when Molly's fantasy about picking up a sailor turns menacing: "That black-guardlooking fellow with the fine eyes peeling a switch attack me in the dark and ride me up against the wall without a word or a murderer anybody" (U 777). In the *Wake*, as in *Ulysses* when Boylan is described as "a Stallion driving it up into you" (U 742), sexual activity takes the form of frenzied horserace images. ALP/Isolde is described as a filly "so and so hands high, such and such paddock weight" (396.8) ridden hard by the amorous athlete, "Amoricas Champius" who "with one aragan thrust druve the massive of virilvigtoury flshpst the both lines of forwards . . . rightjingbangshot into the goal of her gullet" (395.35). Jaun threatens to whip Issy like a horse: "I'll just draw my prancer and give you one splitpuck in the crupper, you understand, that will bring the poppy blush of shame to your peony hindmost" (445.14). Jaun is also under the illusion that women enjoy sexual violence: "Rip ripper rippest and jac jac jac. . . . That's the side that appeals to em, the wring wrong way to wright woman. Shuck her! Let him! . . . All she wants!" (466.13). Although the four old men describe the rough sport in II.4 as "a pretty thing . . . of pure diversion" (395.26), it is not clear whether ALP/Isolde responds with joyous cries, "joysis crisis" (395.32), or a curse, "Jesus Christ!" But old ALP, in her farewell speech to HCE, seems able to forgive violent fellatio and beatings as though they were only a cruel wind whipping over the river: "Wrhps, that wind as if out of norewere! . . . Jumpst shootst throbbst into me mouth like a bogue and arrohs! Ludegude of the Lashlanns, how he whips me cheeks!" (626.4)

Perhaps Anna Livia is described as a horse because as ALP (*Alpen-traum* in German) she is the night*mare*, "the galleonman jovial on his bucky brown nightmare. Bigrob dignagging his lylyputtana" (583.8). Horses, especially *swift* horses, recall Swift's houyhnhnms, although the race here is hardly fair, with HCE, the giant Brobdingnagian, spurring his miniature or lilliputian nag. The four old codgers, reminiscing about sports, college days, and fast women, remember ALP as both racehorse and racecar (396.28). Conveniently, the Curragh race-track in Dublin is located on the Liffey, as Joyce animates the word "race" to refer to both the competition of speed and the swift current of the stream.

We receive very different versions of the marriage of ALP and HCE in different parts of the book. Like Joyce's early cynicism in *Dubliners*, these are negative visions of marriage as a power play, governed either by female manipulation, as in "The Boarding House," or by male brutality, as in "Counterparts." In II.3, Anna Livia, with the pluck of her nautical analogue, the female pirate Grace O'Malley, captures the seafaring Norwegian captain, a veritable "blowbierd" (332.22), and cures him of his wanderlust, "her youngfree yoke stilling his wander-cursus. . . . The Annexandreian captive conquest" (318.9). It is a thoroughly nautical wedding, ending, presumably, with the two ships—his lord*ship* and her lady*ship*—"captain spliced" (197.13). Like the prankquean, who baptizes and converts what she kidnaps, ALP manages to have her sailor baptized ("popetithes") in her own female way, "let this douche for you as a wholly apuzzler's (326.10)—like Clothilde ("clothildies" [325.28]) converting Clovis. But the sailor eventually resents being caught, "Cawcaught. Coocaged" (329.13), and the wedding is now described as a victory celebration, but with threatening martial overtones, "cannons' roar and rifles' peal" (330.8), as though this were really a "shotgun wedding." (Joyce is no doubt playing with the klang-association of "martial" and "marital" and "maritime" here, as he earlier plays with the klang association of "sailor" and "tailor"—"Sinbad the Sailor and Tinbad the Tailor" [*U* 737].) Other clichés for oppressive weddings, such as "tying the knot," are used to describe the groom's feelings of entrapment: "Slip on your ropen collar and draw the noosebag on your head" (377.8). The shotgun wedding is presumably the result of the bride's having gotten "knocked up," a predicament jauntily described as a "knock-knock" joke: "Knock knock. War's where! Which war? The Twwinns" (330.29). But the sailor should have known they were "poles a port and zones asunder," and remembered the maxim, "tie up in hates and repeat at luxure" (328.8).

While this version of the marriage stresses ALP's capture of HCE, the last of the Shaun "watches" reverses these roles. Here HCE "waged love" on his "Fulvia Fluvia" (547.7), and conquered her like a Caesar—"He came, he kished, he conquered" (512.8)—but only after first "squeezing the life out of the liffey" (512.6). He treats ALP like the spoils of battle, and with wed*lock* makes her his Roman slave: "I pudd a name and wedlock boltoned round her the which to carry till her grave, my durdin dearly, Appia Lippia Pluviabilla" (548.4). Joyce's use of a Roman conqueror of ALP may have been prompted by the Roman genius for controlling bodies of water with sophisticated hydro-engineering technology. If in this chapter (III.3) Joyce celebrates Roman military and engineering achievements, then in the next chapter he pays tribute to the Roman contribution to jurisprudence by presenting the story of Honophrius and Anita (Humphrey and Anna) as a domestic case at law. This section is a generic cross between pornography and soap opera. Because it relates social promiscuity among family members, business associates, and friends, it has the tortured and recursive syntax of soap opera plots, with their tangles of illicit love relationships. Anita, as usual, gets the worst of it, as the menfolk solicit, molest, and debauch her until she is faced with the soap opera question: "Has he hegemony and shall she submit?" (573.32). Her lot in domestic life doesn't improve much over her fate in the military setting; she is still HCE's "ambling limfy peepingpartner, the slave of the ring" (580.25), like a character in one of the Blooms' pornographic novels.

In III.4, Joyce describes the couple's bodies as a park or game preserve, a conceit he might have taken either from Shakespeare's *Venus and Adonis* or from Lawrence's *Lady Chatterley's Lover*—a reference that would be ironic in either case. Unlike Shakespeare's lyrical description of Venus's delicate front, Joyce gives us a prosaic description of HCE's indelicate back. ALP also fares worse than the flower-bedecked Connie Chatterley, for since her body *is* the park, copulation takes the form of her gamekeeper planting an olive tree (cf. *Oliver* Mellors) in her side (564.21). ALP is both park and game: "Woman's the prey!" (582.31). Besides game parks, the couple's bodies become cricket parks in this chapter—because Joyce simultaneously animates wildlife, sport (hunting, cricket, horseracing) and play (chess, backgammon) connotations of the word *game* in his dream work. ALP laughs during the cricket match, seemingly either in derision, watching "her old stick-in-the-block . . . slogging his paunch about" (583.26); or to cheer him on "to scorch her faster, faster" (584.4). But HCE has to be told to "goeasyosey . . . for fear he'd tyre and burst his dunlops" (584.11). ALP's laugh in the end bursts into a symphony of barnyard noises, "yeigh, yeigh, neigh, neigh," topped with a triumphant hen's crowing like a cock, "in a kikkery key to laugh it off" (584.21)—implying that she achieves an orgasm, notwithstanding her aging ("long past conquering cock of the morgans" [584.24]) husband.

However turbulent their marriage, ALP and HCE appear mellow in their old age, nostalgically "eskipping the clockback . . . sweet-heartedly" (579.5) for "their diamond wedding tour" (578.32) or their "goolden wending" (619.24). Time provides a perspective on many things, and ALP's final letter and monologue explain many violent events and bizarre personae as fantasies, musings, and dream distortions. The great military battles, Balaklava and Waterloo, as well as HCE's piratical appearance as the Norwegian captain, are explained as her own musings about how grand HCE looks in his suit: "When you're in the buckly shuit. . . . You make me think of a wonderdecker I once. Or somebalt thet sailder, the man megallant, with the bangled ears. Or an earl was he, at Lucan? Or, no, it's the Iren duke's I mean. Or somebrey erse from the Dark Countries" (620.3). Joyce might have patterned the figure of HCE as sailor/pirate not only on Bloom/Ulysses, but on his own appearance when he wore a black eye-patch after his various eye operations. Pirates fit the image of ALP as river and HCE as boat—nomadic, roving folk; the earring, "bangled ears," suggests Earwicker's name, Persse O'Reilly, Pierce Oreille, pierced ear. Molly, in her monologue, remembers "the tall old chap with the earrings I dont like a man you have to climb up to go get at" (U 765), a curious fantasy about a tall man and a small woman, like "Grossguy and Littleylady" (598.33) of Finnegans Wake.

ALP admonishes HCE about his infidelities: "Only don't start your stunts of Donachie's yeards agoad again. I could guessp to her name who tuckt you that one, tufnut! . . . One of these fine days, lewdy culler, you must redoform again" (624.16). But she quickly decides that an offensive action is better than a defensive one: "I am so exquisitely pleased about the loveleavest dress I have. You will always call me Leafiest, won't you, dowling?" (624.21).

Anna Livia not only forgives past transgressions but assumes the heroic mission of saving her husband from slander and raising him from his fallen state. In dream, her mission takes many forms, gallant and grotesque. Looking a bit like a serpentine monster herself with her snake-like "little bolero boa" (102.11) and wearing forty curlers, like small snakes, in her hair, "curlicornies for her headdress" (102.11), she goes off, like St. George to the dragon, Perseus to the Medusa ("burnz-burn the gorggony old danworld" [102.7]), and Mary to the serpent of Eden—"to crush the slander's head" (102.17). She also goes before judges to explain her husband's actions, unfortunately giving such highly personal and irrelevant information (about her urinalysis, his laxatives, and the like [492–3]) as can only embarrass him further. In her last letter she denies outright that he mistreated her—"Item, we never were chained to a chair" (618.24), an accusation made earlier on 243.10—and suggests that rough love-play was part of youthful frolic: "You remember? When I ran berrying after hucks and haws. With you drawing out great aims to hazel me from the hummock with your sling. Our cries" (622.17). HCE as the brutal Punch becomes only a figure of speech, "You were pleased as Punch" (620.23), describing a man who likes to tell war stories and appear tough to the ladies. Molly, surprisingly, serves as a model for Anna Livia in her heroic function too. Bloom sends her to intercede with Mr. Cuffe after he loses his job, "sending me to try and patch it up I could have got him promoted there to be the manager" (U 752). Molly also contemplates saving Bloom from his drinking buddies who make a fool of him, like the authors of the ballad who taunt HCE: "Well theyre not going to get my husband again into their clutches if I can help it making fun of him then behind his back" (U 773).

Anna Livia uses music also, the water music made by the bubbling Liffey, to soothe and encourage the fallen HCE, reviving him, like the unconscious Lear, with melody. Playing the fiddle in her "windaug," she produces a "reedy derg" (198.25), like the sound of wind among the bulrushes. "Sure she can't fiddan a dee," say the washerwomen, hard critics, "Sure, she can't" (198.26). She tries whistling tunes like *The Heart Bowed Down* when her cooking fails to cheer HCE. "Sucho fuffing a fifeing 'twould cut you in two!" (199.29), the washerwomen remark. Like Molly, who gave up a promising operatic career—"I could have been a prima donna only I married him" (U 763)—Anna Livia also says, "I wrote me hopes and buried the page" (624.4) when she married HCE. But perhaps ALP's music is so awful because she is "deaf as a yawn . . . Poor deef old deary!" (200.15). Hers is the song of the captive Israelites "by the waters of babalong" (103.10), or an old Irish air sung by the faithful wife to her imprisoned husband—a song sung at twilight, a Celtic twilight, "Annie Delittle, his daintree diva, in deltic dwilights, singing him henpecked rusish through the bars" (492.8).

Anna Livia marries under the powerful influence of the thunder voice, like the thunder in Vico's marriage myth, that is interpreted as the voice of God bidding the promiscuous couples into caves and marriage: "I heard Thy voice, ruddery dunner . . . we'll cohabit re-spectable" (624.5). Molly is also awakened by thunder the day she has sex with Boylan, and it also puts the fear of God into her, "till that thunder woke me up as if the world was coming to an end God be merciful to us I thought the heavens were coming down about us to punish" (*U* 741). As river, Anna Livia has particular reason to be afraid of the thunder, for she would be a more likely target of lightning—"the dart of desire has gored the heart of secret waters" (599.25)—than the rest of "pacnincstricken humanity" (599.28).

Thunder threatens the children also in *Finnegans Wake*, like the father's voice which spoils the children's games and frightens them into running home. On such occasions the mother becomes the com-forter, the protector of the children against the father, as in the story "A Little Cloud," where the wife, also named Annie, soothes the infant frightened by the father: "My little mannie! Was 'ou frightened, love?" (*D* 85). "Opop opop capollo, muy malinchily malchick!" ALP croons to little Jerry when he is awakened by the thunder: "No bad bold faathern, dear one" (565.20).

Joyce's treatment of motherhood in *Finnegans Wake* is as idealized as Stephen's ("*Amor matris*, subjective and objective genitive, may be the only true thing in life"[*U* 207]), as guilt-ridden as Cranly's ("Your mother must have gone through a great deal of suffering"[*P* 241]), and as irreverent as Mulligan's ("Fertiliser and Incubator"[*U* 402]). Anna Livia is portrayed as the nurturing, bountiful mother, a "fiery goose-mother" (242.25) or "Santa Claus . . . with a Christmas box apiece for aisch and iveryone of her childer" (209.23). This is the comforting mother Stephen remembers as a little boy. The prankquean, who washes and converts the boys after she kidnaps them ("she washed the blessings of the lovespots off the jiminy with soap sulliver suddles . . . and she converted him to the onesure allgood"[21.27]), resembles May Dedalus, who bathes her grown son at the basin, scrubs his ears, picks the lice off his body, and tells him to make his Easter duty. Anna Livia is often described as a mother of many children, with as many heirs as she has hairs—and even more, "superflowvius heirs" (526.25), like the many children born to May Dedalus or Mina Purefoy. In II.3, Kate announces to HCE that Anna is having a painful delivery, like Mina Purefoy, "her birthright pang that would split an atam" (333.24). Throughout the children's homework chapter, which is much con-cerned with the mother and motherhood, the emphasis is placed on "head, back and heart aches of waxedup womanage" (270.9), and female martyrs and saints are noted, such as "blistered Mary Achinhead" (262.n.6) and "Mater Mary Mercerycordial of the Dripping Nipples" (260.n.2). Anna Livia refers to her own suffering and bereavement in her final monologue: "Why I'm all these years within years in soffran, allbeleaved. To hide away the tear, the parted" (625.29).

The Mulligan puckishness is in the twins, however, for as Mulligan presents his obscene fertilization plan ostensibly in the interest of objective science, so the boys proceed to use their mathematical expertise to explore the "whome" of their "eternal geomater" (296.36). The boys' voyeurism is a form of surveying the river and surrounding landscape—hence their instruments and calculations. The journey back to the womb is not only spatial and geometrical, however, but also temporal, a return to the delta in which earth and water first united to form the primal mud, the origin of life, "your muddy old triangonal delta" (297.23). The boys express the curiosity of children hiding behind or under the mother's skirts for protection, like ALP's hiding the "lipoleums" under her hoops to "sheltershock" them (8.30). The father, like Noah, suffers an analogous sexual inspection by the sons, in the form of the voyeurism of the soldiers in the park.

Interestingly, the mother in Joyce's work is rarely punitive—a fact the more surprising since Joyce's masochistic fantasies, like those of Bloom's namesake, Leopold von Sacher-Masoch, include the figure of the terrible woman, Venus in Furs, Circe, Bella Cohen. Even Molly, pampered and bossy, is an undeveloped version of this type, and Joyce, in his letters, attempted to project the image of the severe mother onto Nora herself. But the punitive function in Joyce's fiction is most often foisted onto the male clergy—Father Dolan with his pandybat and Father Arnall with his hellfire and brimstone sermon—so that it is not surprising to find Shaun, in the guise of the priest in III.2, as the sadistic figure, now erotically elaborated to direct his cruelty toward the woman. Yet Anna Livia, generally passive except in the service of husband and children, is given powerful functions through her river and water attributes, as the Siren capable of wrecking and dashing boats to pieces, bringing about "the wreak of Wormans' Noe" (387.20), and as the Deluge, drowning "Pharoah and all his pedestrians" in the Red Sea, as well as Martin Cunningham, "Merkin Cornyngwham . . . completely drowned off Erin Isles" (387.28). Anna Livia as the prankquean punishes van Hoother, not like a mother but like an offended deity, in the form of the Deluge, the great flood, as "she rain, rain, rain" (21.22) on "her forty years' walk" (21.26)

III

How then do we account for these diverse forms and functions of Anna Livia Plurabelle—old, young, ugly, beautiful, faithful, treacherous, brutalized, manipulative, rejected, desired, redeeming, tempting? "Dreams go by contraries" (*U* 571), we learn in *Ulysses*, and as the dreamer's wishes turn into their opposite in dream, so the woman is transformed again and again into her opposite. If the dreamer is fallen (or dying), then his contradictory fantasies of the woman make sense as symptoms of a generalized anxiety over lost or diminishing potency.

Fighting age and decrepitude, the dreamer desires the young woman, or young women, since he wants not a relationship but, like Daddy Browning and his peaches, reassurance about his imperiled prowess. However, this desire—like its opposite, the little boy's desire for the older woman—becomes a violation of the incest taboo. The young woman recalls to the dreamer both his daughter and his wife when she was young, and Isabel and ALP are therefore frequently merged into the same figure—a "daughterwife" (627.2). To defend himself against the guilt aroused by his incestuous longing, the dreamer projects the guilt onto the young woman, pretending that the desire is all on her side and that she is the temptress enticing him. Surrender to the temptress brings punishment and destruction, like the Sirens' shipwreck and drowning of sailors, or a prosaic and confining marriage, or, at its most extreme, public exposure and criminal prosecution of the hapless dreamer. The fears of sexual inadequacy cause the dreamer's desire for the beautiful young woman to boomerang as a fantasy of betrayal, a fear that she will reject the old man to elope with a young, virile male, like Tristan or Dermot. Fantasies of rape may function as a defense against fears of both impotence and rejection. The most violent scenes are those reported by the four impotent old men, the "four dear old heladies" (386.14), who also remember vividly the great flood and scenes of catastrophic retribution for the sins of their youth. The woman's function as temptress, adulteress, and victim of male brutality is therefore the result of a complicated dialectic of the dreamer's fears, desires, and guilts.

The young woman ostensibly ruins the man, but is desired, while the old woman tries to save the man, but is rejected. Her redemptive function is understandable enough since this is the maternal role, the healing of wounds and righting of wrongs, and Anna Livia performs this service both for her husband and for her children. But why the rejection? Why is the loving mother appreciated and the loving wife abused? Perhaps it is because the old woman's ministrations and aid make the old man feel the humiliation of his dependence and disability, as in old age he is reduced to a child again, a helpless "overgrown babeling" (6.31), a huge, babbling infant led about by the hand or lying beached like a whale or the fallen tower of Babel. One is reminded of Father Flynn in "The Sisters"—also a stroke victim, paralyzed, deranged, slobbering— left to the mercy of his efficient, gossiping sisters, who take care of his physical needs but can do little to ease the mental torment of his degraded condition. HCE's dashing down his breakfast tray may be motivated less by mean spite toward ALP than by a last flicker of rebellious pride.

When not dreaming of the fevered courtship of youth and the dotage of age, the protagonist dreams of a marriage in which his feelings toward the wife are complicated by the presence of the children. While the dreamer is also engaged in psychological power struggles with his children—particularly the sons—the children are at the same time pawns in a conflict with the wife. When he dreams of Anna Livia using pregnancy to trap him into marriage, threatening to take his children away (the domestic thrust behind the tale of the prankquean), and interrupting coitus to attend a weeping child in the night, the husband appears to recognize that the children are a threat to his freedom and his satisfactions. This apparent cynicism toward marriage and parenthood must be placed in the perspective of dream psychology, for in dream it is the negative feelings about family life that find expression. We see in the Earwicker marriage little of that fundamental domestic contentment that sustains the Blooms throughout their marital crises.

Yet for all of his ambivalence toward the woman, the dreamer endows Anna Livia with an incomparable strength and grace. The wish to anchor the woman, who is mediated by the fantasies of the male, to a status ultimately beyond the dreamer's fear or desire may be Joyce's most important reason for the elaborate and enduring river/woman analogy. By making her the river as well as the woman, Joyce makes Anna Livia inhuman as well as human, beyond judgment, pity, or admiration, and subject only to wonderment. This is how he leaves her with us at the end of the work, as one of the powerful and unearthly seahags, dancing their wild dances to the roar of the sea: "I can seen meself among them, allaniuvia pulchrabelled. How she was handsome, the wild Amazia, when she would seize to my other breast! And what is she weird, haughty Niluna, that she will snatch from my ownest hair! For 'tis they are the stormies. Ho hang! Hang ho! And the clash of our cries till we spring to be free" (627.27).

NOTE

1. M. J. C. Hodgart, "Music and the Mime of Mick, Nick, and the Maggies," in *A Conceptual Guide to "Finnegans Wake"*, ed. Michael H. Begnal and Fritz Senn (University Park: Pennsylvania State University Press, 1974), p. 88.

CAROLYN G. HEILBRUN

Afterword

The claims of James Joyce upon immortality are unique and multiple. Chief among these is our consciousness of his effort and achievement. No critic, however industrious (and no writer has had more industrious students of his work), has been able to discover in Joyce's writings anything which Joyce did not, with deliberation, put there. In anticipating the ideal insomniac as his reader, Joyce must have delighted in the knowledge that, however complicated the processes to be uncovered in his work, no one would reveal anything which exceeded or betrayed his intention. There are no more accidents in *Ulysses* than in the Parthenon: all is planned. Unconscious ambiguity is as unknown to Joyce as it is palpable in all his great contemporaries.

Inevitably this means that Joyce's great achievements are balanced by the exclusion from his work of what his consciousness refused him: knowledge of women. Alone of the great modern masters, Joyce could not imagine a woman whom convention did not offer him. Those other Irishmen, Yeats, Shaw, and Wilde, demonstrate that the question is not one of nationality alone, but rather of vision. Joyce's is uniquely a vision of male possibility and frustration.

Does that mean that Joyce is a "male chauvinist"? Only if one defines that phrase with care. Joyce admired Ibsen and ignored his most profound contribution. Joyce perceived, as these essays so clearly show, the harsh realities of women's limited lives in Dublin, yet he never questioned them. He imagined the great and isolated Leopold Bloom and yet remained what James Van Dyck Card has called a monk and an Irishman: that is, a man who hates women.[1] Ought one rather to call him a misogynist, a man who hates women for becoming what he has determined they should be?

Yet to have said this is to have said little about Joyce. His greatness, like Dickens's greatness, surpasses the diminishing of the female sex, the refusal to imagine it beyond what "reality" offered. Supremely accurate in his portrayal of reality, Joyce failed only one test of the imagination: to create not only a man with "feminine" characteristics, but also a woman with "masculine" ones. (Who but Shakespeare has not somewhere failed?) That particular failure may go some way to explain why Joyce, like Freud, has appealed to American male intellectuals more profoundly than to the intellectuals of any other country. These two men share with American culture generally a view of heroism as beyond the range of women.

The essays in this volume exist to celebrate, rather than to undermine, the greatness of Joyce's achievement. At the same time, however, they demonstrate not only how thoroughly Joyce knew the paralysis of Dublin that affected men and women alike, but also how determinedly he averted his gaze from what he himself called the greatest revolution of our time: "the revolt of women against the idea that they are the mere instruments of men." [2] Apparently that great consciousness, observing everything, failed to imagine a woman beyond the experience of a monk and an Irishman. He never imagined woman as a paradigm of humanity because, in his own life, woman had never thus presented herself to him.

NOTES

1. James Van Dyck Card, "Joyce's Women: A General Comment," paper delivered at the Conference of the Modern Language Association, December, 1975.
2. Arthur Power, *Conversations with James Joyce*, ed. Clive Hart (New York: Barnes and Noble, 1974), p. 35.

Notes on Contributors

RUTH BAUERLE is editor of the recent *A Word List to James Joyce's "Exiles"* and of the forthcoming *James Joyce Songbook*. She teaches at Ohio Wesleyan University.

SHARI BENSTOCK is an administrator in Schools of Basic Medical Sciences and Clinical Medicine at the University of Illinois, Urbana-Champaign. She is currently at work on two books: *Post-Impressionism and the Modern Imagination*, a study of modernist painters and writers, and *Women of the Left Bank: Paris, 1910–1940*, a study of the contributions to modernism made by women of the Paris expatriate community. Research on both these books will be done in France during 1981–82. Most recent publications include *Who's He When He's at Home: A James Joyce Directory*, co-authored with Bernard Benstock (University of Illinois Press, 1980).

ROBERT BOYLE, S.J., is professor of English at Marquette University. He received his B.A. from the University of Illinois in 1939 and his Ph.D. from Yale. In addition, he holds degrees in Sacred Theology and Philosophy. He has published numerous articles on Joyce and on other writers, and his books include *Metaphor in Hopkins* (1961) and *James Joyce's Pauline Vision: A Catholic Exposition* (1978).

CAROLYN G. HEILBRUN is professor of English at Columbia University and is the author of *The Garnett Family, Christopher Isherwood, Toward a Recognition of Androgyny, Reinventing Womanhood*, and other works.

SUZETTE HENKE is associate professor of English at the State University of New York at Binghamton. She received her doctorate from Stanford University in 1972. She is author of *Joyce's Moraculous Sindbook: A Study of "Ulysses"* and has published articles on modern literature in such journals as the *James Joyce Quarterly*, the *Journal of Women's Studies in Literature*, the *Virginia Woolf Quarterly*, *Modern British Literature*, and the *American Imago*.

MARGOT NORRIS is associate professor of English at the University of Michigan. Her publications include *The Decentered Universe of "Finnegans Wake,"* published by Johns Hopkins University Press in 1976, as well as essays on Ibsen, Kafka, and the Surrealist painter Max Ernst. She is currently at work on a study of the deconstruction of anthropocentrism in modern thought, a study which will be entitled "The Beasts of the Modern Imagination."

BONNIE KIME SCOTT is associate professor of English at the University of Delaware, where she also served as acting coordinator of women's studies for 1980–81. She has published articles on James Joyce, Irish studies, and women writers in collections and in journals including *The James Joyce Quarterly*, *The Irish University Review*, *Eire-Ireland*, and *The Journal of Irish Literature*.

ELAINE UNKELESS has taught English at Brooklyn College, Boston University, and Columbia University. She received her doctorate from Columbia in 1974 and a J.D. from New York University School of Law in 1981. She has published articles on modern literature in the *James Joyce Quarterly*, *Modernist Studies: Literature and Culture 1920–1940*, and *The Virginia Woolf Miscellany*.

FLORENCE L. WALZL is professor emeritus of English at the University of Wisconsin-Milwaukee. She has written widely on *Dubliners* and has had articles on Joyce published in *Publications of the Modern Language Association*, the *James Joyce Quarterly*, *College English*, *Texas Studies in Language and Literature*, and various other periodicals. She has also had essays published in *Twentieth Century Interpretations of "A Portrait of the Artist as a Young Man*," ed. William M. Schutte, and *"Dubliners": Text, Criticism, and Notes*, ed. Robert Scholes and A. Walton Litz.